The Master Musicians

New Series Edited by Eric Blom

HANDEL

The Master Musicians

HANDEL

by

C. F. ABDY WILLIAMS

Illustrated

London   J. M. Dent and Sons Ltd.
New York   E. P. Dutton and Co. Inc.

BOOK
PRODUCTION
WAR ECONOMY
STANDARD

R 252/5m

NOTE TO THE REVISED EDITION

THIS book was written when biographers of Handel were still in the habit of turning too confidently to the Rev. John Mainwaring's *Memoirs of the Life of the late George Frederic Handel.* Because that book was written in the year after the composer's death, and its author had his information from John Christopher Smith, Handel's amanuensis, it was too readily taken for granted that all the facts it contained were authentic. Even Chrysander, the author of the most exhaustive, though incomplete, work on Handel, took too many of Mainwaring's statements on trust. No independent study based on a direct investigation of such sources as are still available had appeared before the present work, whose author was thus obliged, failing such a study of his own, to draw upon the books already existing, which, to do him justice, were at that time (1901) thought to be thoroughly reliable. Chrysander as well as Victor Schoelcher certainly gave a great deal of useful information; but they were in some respects misleading. R. A. Streatfeild's useful work did not appear until 1909.

Research into Handelian biography has been greatly facilitated recently by the appearance of two extremely valuable works: Mr. Newman Flower's *George Frideric Handel,* which clears up many old errors and contains several new facts of importance, established by the author's discovery of various valuable documents, and Professor Edward J. Dent's *Handel,* a concise work, but packed with information and matter for speculation of the utmost interest. To both these authors I wish to express my indebtedness for a great number of facts which enabled me, thanks to their researches and penetration, to bring the late C. F. Abdy Williams's book into line with modern biography and criticism. Since it was possible to set right some errors for which it would be unjust to blame an author who could not well have been cognizant of them, it seemed worth retaining a contribution to the 'Master Musicians' series that was found to be still very valuable in many other respects. Editorial interpolations are distinguished by square brackets.

As in the companion volumes of the series, the appendices have been added to and recast: the Calendar (Appendix A) is a wholly new feature, and so, it may be claimed, is the much more detailed list of Handel's works; Appendix C, giving details of those of Handel's contemporaries who are not universally known, was designed mainly in order to reduce the number of footnotes; the Bibliography has, needless to say, been brought up to date.

In conclusion I should like to tender my thanks to an enthusiastic and well-versed Handelian, Mr. C. F. Crowder, who was kind enough to look through the proofs of this book and to offer valuable suggestions.

E. B.

1935.

P.S. (1944) Several corrections kindly suggested by Professor Otto Erich Deutsch have been added to the present reprint.

PREFACE

THE following account is an endeavour to give a popular narrative of the chief events of Handel's life without entering much into technicalities which, though interesting to the musician, are not perhaps so necessary for the general reader. The exhaustive treatises of Chrysander, Victor Schoelcher and Rockstro are full of details and discussions of the greatest interest and value to the student who wishes to go deeply into the works of the great composer.

I have avoided the irritating attempts of Hawkins and others to represent Handel's pronunciation of the English language by a spelling which makes many words almost unintelligible: it is sufficient that the reader should know that Handel's pronunciation of English, like that of many foreigners, was imperfect, and that its imperfections chiefly consisted of using *d* in place of *t*; *g* in place of hard *c*; *p* in place of *b*, etc.

In order to interrupt the course of the narrative as little as possible, I have dealt with the compositions in a couple of short chapters at the end, and in Appendix C appear brief notes on some of the chief characters who came into connection with Handel.

I take this opportunity of thanking those gentlemen who have been kind enough to assist me; especially the Town Authorities of Halle, who caused two excellent photographs to be taken for this work; Mr. F. J. H. Jenkinson, librarian of the Cambridge University Library, who gave me special facilities, without which the publication of my book would have been much delayed; also to Messrs. C. Scribner & Sons for permission to reproduce some pictures from their *Cyclopaedia of Music*.

C. F. A. W.

BRADFIELD,
    February 1901.

CONTENTS

ILLUSTRATIONS

The half-tone plates will be found between pages 20 and 21

CHAPTER I

ANTECEDENTS, BIRTH AND YOUTH

IN the year 1685, which saw the birth of Bach and Handel, the art of music was in a flourishing condition in Italy, and the influence of Italian music and Italian singers had spread over the whole of Europe. Instrumental music pure and simple was in its infancy: opera and church music reigned supreme. Voices were cultivated to a high point of perfection, and many musicians were singers as well as composers.

In France Lulli (1632–87) had introduced accompanied recitative and made other improvements, paying special attention to correct declamation and settling the form of the overture.

Italian music had reached Germany and was much cultivated at the various courts; but native German cantors were also busy, founding the school of church and organ music which culminated in Johann Sebastian Bach.

The *Singspiel*, a theatrical representation in which spoken dialogue was interspersed with songs, had been much cultivated, especially at Hamburg, where, however, it was soon to give way before German opera under Keiser.[1]

In England a great composer had arisen in Henry Purcell, 1658–95, one of a family of native musicians. Purcell confessedly 'endeavoured a just imitation of the most famed Italian Masters.' He was prolific in every department of music then known, and established a form of English opera which was used for a century and a half. Italian opera had not reached England when he died. Except Purcell, no English composers of this time can be said to have established a European

---

[1] The *Singspiel* eventually developed in the operetta.

reputation. Their compositions are mostly adapted for performance in English cathedrals only, and the tendency to import foreign musicians for all other than church music was becoming apparent.

Singers were beginning to be of supreme importance. Both opera and church music were under their influence. The dramatic element in the former was subservient to the necessity for providing proper opportunities of display for the *prima donna, seconda donna, primo uomo, secondo uomo,* etc., each of whom must have his or her allotted arias, whether in opera or oratorio, which did not differ from each other from a musical point of view. Much of the music was written for artificial sopranos, some of whom became famous in departments other than music; thus Farinelli, a male soprano of noble birth, after making a reputation on most of the stages of Europe, became a political adviser of the King of Spain.

Church music was represented in both the Roman and Lutheran churches by the Mass, the oratorio and the motet. The latter also cultivated the cantata. Passion music performed during Lent was a feature of the Lutheran Church, and was often called oratorio; [1] and the chorale, a form peculiar to this church, was very widely cultivated.

In the early days of opera and oratorio, counterpoint had been to a certain extent in abeyance, having given way to the newly discovered charms of harmony; but in the latter decades of the seventeenth century the best composers had reverted to the use of counterpoint, in combination with the two modern scales and the wider harmonic horizon which had thus been opened up. The old modes had almost disappeared, though

[1] Carissimi's oratorio, *Jephtha,* follows the plan of the Passion music: a 'Historicus' narrates the events in recitative, while the various persons and the chorus enter at appropriate places. The work is in Latin, and the only instrument used to accompany is the organ.

2

they continued for some time to come to influence composers, especially those who wrote for the church.

Much instrumental music was composed, but it had not the important position that it afterwards attained in the quartet and symphony. The high school of violin solo playing was being founded by Corelli, Vivaldi, Geminiani and others; and the famous Italian school of violin makers had culminated in Antonio Stradivari. Organ music was being developed in Germany by Pachelbel, Buxtehude, Böhm, Reinken and many others, among whom the various members of the Bach family were prominent. The orchestra was gradually being improved, as an accompaniment to the voices in drama and church music; and it was also used for dance music, the dances being composed in 'suites' of pieces. Of these old dances the minuet long survived as one of the movements in the sonata and symphony. In Italy every town had at least one opera house; in Venice there were six. In Germany each town sustained a band of 'town musicians' whose duties were to play the accompaniments to the church cantatas and to provide whatever instrumental music was required for public occasions. They, like the choirs, were paid partly by the town and partly by the money collected in the streets for outdoor performances.

The position of musicians was not attractive from a modern point of view. Their best chance of success was, as a rule, to obtain permanent employment in the establishment of royal or ducal houses, in which they held the position of servants; they could not leave without permission, which was frequently refused. But music was just beginning to take rank among the learned professions, and we meet instances about this time of troubles arising because musicians resented the inferior position to which custom relegated them. This feeling was, however, not confined to musicians: most learned men were obliged to be subservient to some rich patron, on whom they depended for their living, nor could they have their works published without the support of an influential personage. There was not as yet a public to appeal to. The arts and sciences were looked upon merely as amusements or recreations for the upper classes of society. In England the practice of music was regarded as a trade. One Green, a blind organist of St. Giles's, Cripplegate, was, as late as 1724, fined £5 for exercising the trade of teaching music within the City of London without being a member of the Company of Musicians, and his means of living was thus ruthlessly taken from him.

In 1609 there settled at Halle in Saxony a coppersmith from Breslau, named Valentin Hendel.[1] He became a master of his craft and a burgher of the city, married Anna, the daughter of a coppersmith named Samuel Beichling of Eisleben, and was succeeded in his business by his two elder sons, Valentin and Christoph, in 1636. His third son, Georg, born in 1622, became a surgeon and barber.[2] At the age of twenty he married Anna Oettinger, the widow of a barber to whom he had been apprenticed, and became thereby a burgher of Halle.[3] A few years after his marriage he was advanced to the dignity of surgeon and valet de chambre

---

[1] The name is variously spelt Handel, Hendel, Haendel (the modern German form), Hendeler, Händeler, Hendtler, Hendall, Handell, Handle, Hondel. In Italy Handel retained the original spelling of Hendel; his parents used Händel to distinguish their particular branch of the Hendel family. After settling in England, he always used the spelling familiar to us. In this work, which is for English readers, the spelling Handel will be used throughout.

[2] The profession of surgery was in those days nearly always combined with that of a barber. The striped pole, still seen outside some barbers' shops, is supposed to represent the bandages used in surgery.

[3] The widow was eleven years his senior, and Chrysander supposes Georg Handel to have been an apprentice of her former husband.

to Prince Augustus of Saxony and later to the court of Brandenburg. By this marriage he had three sons and three
daughters, only two of whom lived to grow up. When he
was sixty-two years old his wife died, and he married a woman
some thirty years his junior, Dorothea Taust, daughter of the
pastor of Giebichenstein, a village on the Saale a short distance
from Halle, to which he had been appointed district surgeon
in 1652. The offspring of the second marriage consisted of
two sons and two daughters. The elder son died at his
birth, and the younger, born on 23rd February 1685, was
named Georg Friedrich.

It is interesting to notice the conditions under which this
child, who was destined to become known to the whole
civilized world, entered it. His father was sixty-three years
old: a very respectable tradesman, who had pushed himself
by his own energy and ability to the highest point in his
profession. He was ambitious of leaving a good name
behind him; seems not to have amassed a fortune, but to have
lived comfortably as a citizen of Halle. The neighbourhood
in which he lived at this time was no mean one, as can be
seen by the photograph of the house [which has so long been
cherished at Halle as the birthplace, though that is now
known to have been an adjoining building of which no trace
is left to-day [1]], and he had purchased a family vault in the
churchyard for himself and his heirs.

The mother, we are told, was 'clear-minded, of strong piety,
with a great knowledge of the Bible; deeply attached to her
parents; with little wish for marriage, even in the bloom
of her youth; a capable manager, earnest and of pleasant
manners.' [2] We shall see that the child inherited the qualities

[1] See Newman Flower's *George Frideric Handel,* book I, chap. i.
—E. B.

[2] Funeral sermon on Dorothea Handel, quoted by Chrysander,
vol. i, p. 7, etc.

of both parents: from his father his ambition to distinguish himself by making use of the enormous genius with which he was endowed; from his mother that piety and filial devotion and charity which were characteristic of him.

George Frederic was baptized at the Liebfrauenkirche at Halle on 24th February, the sponsors being the Steward of Langendorf, Anna Taust, an unmarried daughter of the pastor, and Zacharias Kleinhempel, a barber of Halle.

Music began to attract the child's attention from his earliest years. In the nursery his toys were trumpets, drums, flutes and anything that produced musical sounds. For a time this caused amusement, but it soon began to be serious. In the opinion of old Georg Handel, music was 'an elegant art and a fine amusement; yet, if considered as an occupation, it had little dignity as having for its subject nothing better than mere pleasure and entertainment,'[1] and in this he undoubtedly expressed the general opinion.

No doubt old Handel was not far wrong in thus condemning music from the point of view of a man living in a small German town, and knowing nothing of the great side of the art. At that time the town musicians were often of a low class, who subsisted largely by piping before the doors of the inhabitants. Organists and cantors were, with few exceptions, poorly paid, and therefore thought little of, for the efforts of the Bach family to raise the position of their art would scarcely have had effect as yet in a town so far from Thuringia as Halle. German opera was not yet invented, and in Italian opera old Handel would only see the fashionable amusements of the wealthy, carried out by foreign hirelings. The father, wishing to raise his son in the social scale, did all in his power to quench this terrible trait in his character.[2]

[1] Mainwaring, *Memoirs of Handel.* 1760.

[2] The following passage, in the earlier editions of this book, was based on Mainwaring, who knew Handel only from hearsay and

But, though prevented from learning instruments, the boy was bound at any rate to hear music. Chorales were played every evening on the tower of the Liebfrauenkirche; the chorale and cantata would be heard by him when attending divine worship; and the father could not stop the music which at Halle, as in every other German town, was weekly per-formed in the streets by the choirs and town musicians.[1] The street music of those days was not the blatant noise produced at the present time; it was more or less artistically performed by persons regularly employed by the church or town. Hence the boy could not entirely be deprived of the satisfaction of the strongest desire of his nature. Moreover he had from childhood a naturally obstinate character; and, just as in after-life he surmounted obstacles which would have crushed most men, so in early childhood the opposition he encountered seems to have had the effect of making him more determined than ever. A story is usually accepted as true, that by some means he managed to convey to a garret a small clavichord before he was seven years of age, and there he taught himself

obviously exaggerated the reports he heard: 'Since music was taught in the grammar schools, the boy was not allowed to attend them: he was prevented going to any place where music was performed: all instruments were banished from the house, and the boy was forbidden ever to touch them, or to enter any house where "such kind of furniture" was in use. The case appeared so desperate that some suggested cutting off his fingers.' It is now regarded as highly probable that Handel did go to the Lutheran grammar school.—E. B.

[1] This custom is still preserved in small towns in Thuringia. The writer in 1899 heard good performances of some partsongs of Mendelssohn and others by the choirs at Arnstadt and Ohrdruf. Burney, in his *State of Music in Germany*, p. 73, mentions the singing of young students in three or four parts in the streets of Frankfort; and after dinner he heard several symphonies reasonably well played by a street band. Military music was, and is still, regularly performed in German towns.

7

to play while the household was asleep, or too occupied to notice what he was doing. The story is not impossible. The clavichord was of various sizes, and the smaller kinds were extremely portable. Praetorius gives a picture of an 'octave clavichord' which must have been very small indeed, and Mersenne speaks of one two and a half feet in length by only one-third of a foot in breadth. These small instruments were used by nuns when practising in their cells, their very weak tone not penetrating the walls. It does not seem impossible that a determined boy of six should be able to smuggle such a clavichord into the house and to use it without being found out. Schoelcher suggests that his mother or nurse may possibly have helped him, and Chrysander suggests his Aunt Anna, a maiden sister of his mother, who after her father's death came to live in the Handel household. But whether the story is true or not, there is no doubt that by the age of seven Handel was able to astonish men by his extraordinary musical powers.[1]

A cousin of George Frederic, Georg Christian Handel, was at this time valet de chambre to the Duke of Saxe-Weissenfels, whose court was known for its good music, and old Georg, who seems to have been professionally attached to that court, proposed to go and visit him. The child begged hard to be taken, but was refused permission. The journey of some forty English miles from Halle was made by post-chaise, and young Handel, determined to go, ran after the carriage till it was well away from Halle. His father discovered him and severely scolded him. The boy answered with tears and passionate entreaty to be taken into the chaise; and, as it was too far to send him back alone, he was taken in, while his father found

[1] It is not improbable that in so unmusical a household a clavichord had already been banished to the garret earlier and that the boy went up there unobserved to play on it. Even without special precaution its weak tone would not be heard downstairs.—E. B.

some means of informing the mother of the escapade, in order to relieve her anxiety.[1]

Arrived at Weissenfels, the boy managed to get into the chapel, where the organist became so interested in him that he allowed him to play the voluntary at the conclusion of a service. The duke heard him, inquired who he was, and had the boy and his father brought before him. Then he turned to the old surgeon, talked seriously to him about the importance of the art of music, and went on to say that, though every parent had naturally a right to choose the profession he thought his son would do well in, yet in his opinion it would be no less than a sin to deprive the world of so much genius by preventing the boy from following a profession for which nature had so evidently marked him out.

He was far from urging that the musical studies of any one should be followed to the detriment of other things, but that it was possible to combine them with other studies; his wish was only that, in the choice of a profession, no violence should be done to the natural bent of the character. He then filled the boy's pocket with money and promised him a reward if he minded his studies. The duke urged that music should at least be tolerated, and that the boy should be given a competent teacher.

The poor father, not knowing what to answer, said nothing for or against the proposal. He half desired that nature should follow her course; but his chief wish always lay in the direction of the law. It is not without interest that at this very time a lively discussion was going on at Hanover

---

[1] This is no doubt one of Mainwaring's legends, though, like most stories of the kind, it may well contain a grain of truth. If Georg Handel merely wished to visit a relative, there is no reason why he should not have taken his son. That the latter ran after the carriage is scarcely credible; but he may have been discovered hanging on behind when it was too late to send him back.—E. B.

as to the proper position of music among the arts and sciences. It was asserted that it could not rank among them at all. Steffani published several pamphlets in which he boldly contended that not only was it both an art and a science, but that it had its foundations deep down in human nature, and as such must rank equally with all other human learning.

On his return to Halle, Georg placed his son under the charge of Friedrich Wilhelm Zachau (or Zachow), organist of the Liebfrauenkirche. Zachau, who was only just over thirty, was a learned and very industrious musician, and his new pupil 'pleased him so much that he never thought he could do enough for him.' He taught him the organ, counterpoint and composition. The master and pupil analysed together a very large collection of every kind of music of the best German and Italian composers which Zachau possessed. Zachau explained the differences of style, the excellences and defects of the various masters, and made his pupil copy many scores that he might more thoroughly assimilate the different methods of composition. He became to Handel an oracle, and the feeling of love and respect for him never ceased throughout Handel's life. The instruction lasted three years, and, as soon as the pupil was sufficiently advanced, he was made to compose a motet or cantata every week,[1] besides fugues on given subjects. In the Buckingham Palace collection there are six sonatas for two oboes and a bassoon, composed at the age of eleven. The style is very similar to that of Bach's organ trios, the two oboes being usually in free imitation, while the bassoon or cembalo performs an independent bass.

Composition came very rapidly to him, and Chrysander considers that he developed in this direction earlier than J. S. Bach. In after years these trios, which had been discovered in Germany by Lord Polworth, were shown by

[1] None of these early vocal works is known to be in existence.

Weideman, a flute player, and member of the orchestra in London, to the composer, who laughed and said: 'I used to compose like the devil in those days, chiefly for the oboe, which was my favourite instrument.'

But these studies did not occupy the whole of his time. From early youth Handel was, like his great contemporary Sebastian Bach, an indefatigable worker, and he learned the harpsichord, violin and oboe in addition to his work with Zachau, while he also deputized for his master at the organ. Moreover, his father, still secretly hoping to wean him from his dreadful predilection for music, made him go through the regular course of schooling, apparently at the Lutheran Gymnasium.

Zachau, who had a considerable reputation as a teacher, acknowledged in 1696 that he could teach him no more, and recommended that he should be sent to Berlin, where the Elector of Brandenburg had established a good opera house, in which the best Italian singers performed. Music was very much cultivated there by the Electress Sophia Charlotte, Princess of Hanover. A pupil of Steffani, she was a first-rate musician, and studied philosophy under Leibnitz. She was in the habit of personally directing operas at the harpsichord; the singers and dancers were princes and princesses, while the orchestra consisted of the best artists from all countries, who were received with open arms at the court. He was accordingly taken there by a friend of his father's, and soon astonished all who heard him.[1]

Handel does not seem to have had regular instruction in Berlin, but to have picked up all the knowledge he could from hearing music and mixing with musicians. After a little while his father became alarmed by a proposal on the

[1] In the original edition the author repeated the story of Handel's meeting with Ariosti and Bononcini in Berlin; but it is now known that they did not arrive there until 1697 and 1702 respectively.—E. B.

part of the elector to send him to Italy to complete his musical education, and afterwards to attach him to his court. This was no uncommon proceeding in those days: a clever child would be educated at the expense of some great man and would afterwards be, though nominally free, attached to the court, without much chance of leaving it for the rest of his life. A case of this kind occurred later with Bach's son Carl Philipp Emanuel, who had the greatest difficulty in escaping the 'species of slavery,' as Fétis called it, in which he was involved as cembalist to Frederick the Great in Berlin. Whenever he demanded his release, his pay was simply augmented under pretence of additional work; his wife and her children, being Prussian by birth, could not legally leave Prussian territory without permission, which was withheld. Having once escaped to Hamburg, no inducements would persuade him ever to take employment under a German prince again. Another case in point was that of Dr. Pepusch, who escaped to England as a country where liberty was better understood than in Germany.

Handel's father therefore had good grounds for dreading that his son might become attached to the court of Berlin, and Handel himself had an independence of character which in later years cost him his health, his fortune, and nearly his life. He could not bear to be dependent on a wealthy patron, as most artists and men of letters were in those days. Chrysander also points out another motive for declining the offer. The father still hoped his son might become a lawyer. He was hastily brought back to Halle, and resumed his studies under Zachau, analysing, copying and composing large quantities of music, and working hard in every way that could tend towards acquiring skill and knowledge. In a part of Thuringia, not so very remote from Halle, there was at this time another boy, who was ruining his sight by copying forbidden music by moonlight, and was eking out a scanty living by singing at weddings, funerals and in the street, while working hard to perfect himself as a composer and performer.

While Handel was thus occupied, his father died on 11th February 1697; but as there could be no question for a boy of twelve in fairly comfortable circumstances to work for his living, he continued his studies, began to compose church cantatas and organ pieces, and attended school. [The Latin School at Halle was opened in 1698,[1] and he seems to have passed into that from the Lutheran Gymnasium.]

In order to carry out his father's wishes, if it were possible, he entered the university of Halle as a law student in February 1702. For some time he had been deputizing for Johann Christoph Leporin, organist of the castle and the cathedral; and when Leporin was dismissed for neglect of duty and general bad conduct, Handel succeeded him on 13th March 1702 as organist, being engaged for a year on probation. Nature now conquered: [although he seems to have pursued legal studies until the summer of 1703, there is no doubt that he must have decided then and there that] music was to be the work of his life.

On his accepting the post, the usual exhortations and admonitions were administered: he was to fulfil the duties entrusted to him in a way becoming a competent organist, with faithful and diligent care; to be present on Sundays and festivals, and as any extra occasions required; to play the organ properly, to play over the psalm or hymn tune with fine harmony; to come in good time to the church; to look after the organ; to give advice as to any necessary repairs; to give due respect to priests and elders of the church; to be obedient to them, and to live peaceably with the church attendants; and to lead a Christian and exemplary life.

[1] According to Newman Flower, who conjectured that Handel must have gone to the Gymnasium, but does not suggest his changing for the Latin School, which seems likely.—E. B.

For all this he was to receive free lodging and a salary of £7 10s. a year. [Having his own home at his mother's house, half of which she had let since the death of her husband, whose business she had sold, Handel earned some extra money by letting his lodging.] Before Leporin's time the salary had been £3, and the holder of the post died 'probably from hunger,' says Chrysander.

The organ, built in 1667, was a good one, well decorated, with twenty-eight sounding stops and two keyboards. It had a remarkable set of bellows, three in number, which contained so much wind that one depression of the three levers [1] was sufficient for 180 bars of music, or the whole of the Creed.

In this, his first appointment, Handel found much to occupy and interest him. It was the rule in Halle, as in all other German towns of any pretensions, for a cantata to be performed by the choir and town musicians every Sunday. At Leipzig the cantata was performed on alternate Sundays at the Thomas and Nicholas churches; but at Halle the choir and orchestra served no less than seven different churches in turn. The cantata takes much the same place in the Lutheran Church as the anthem in the English cathedral service, and Handel had now ample opportunity of acquiring skill in composition in a very practical manner. [2] But he did more than this; he caused his former schoolfellows to meet together for music on half-holidays at his mother's house, and his fame soon began to spread beyond his native town.

At this time there was in Magdeburg another youth, four years Handel's senior, who was giving his relations much concern by his musical tendencies. This was Georg Philipp

[1] The bellows were, of course, worked by the feet, as in all German organs. The blower was called *Bälgetreter,* i.e. 'bellows-treader.'

[2] Halle Cathedral, however, was Calvinist, not Lutheran. A good deal of controversy arose over Handel's appointment, in fact, because he was a Lutheran.—E. B.

Telemann, who, like Handel, had been destined for the law, but who became so famous in his own time that Hawkins describes him as 'the greatest church musician of Germany.' Later on he was chosen to succeed Kuhnau at the Thomas church at Leipzig, but for some reason declined the post, which was then given to Bach. In 1701 he passed through Halle on his way to Leipzig to study law, and there meeting the 'already important' G. F. Handel, he was almost persuaded to give up law for music. He struggled on, however, heard lectures and worked hard at law, until his musical abilities were discovered by the Leipzig authorities, who engaged him to compose cantatas for the Thomas church and made him organist of the New Church. Law was given up: he studied music and was in constant intercourse with Handel, and the two young enthusiasts, whose early experiences had so much in common, greatly encouraged each other.

Handel served his probation year, composed several hundred cantatas, which he did not think worth keeping, and then, finding that he could learn no more at Halle, left for Hamburg in the summer of 1703. How he made the journey we are not told, but it was probably not done on foot, for he seems always to have been better off than J. S. Bach.

CHAPTER II

THE *Singspiel* had been attempted, but without success, by Heinrich Schütz in 1628. It gave way before the Italian operas of the wealthy. Fifty years afterwards, in 1678, a regular theatre was established at Hamburg by some private persons, in spite of great difficulties. Preachers stormed at it from the pulpit and scattered pamphlets through the city; religious and civil feuds divided the town into parties, too occupied to go to the theatre; yet the *Singspiel* gradually won its way. It must be observed that Hamburg, being a free town, was a paradise for artists, who here had to do with the public, and the public only; they themselves were free and not under the will of a royal or ducal employer, as in a *Residenzstadt* or court. Moreover, the theatre itself was not dominated by Italian singers as were the court theatres. None but Germans composed for it, or performed at it, and what they produced was for the benefit of burghers like themselves. The first *Singspiele* were exclusively occupied with scriptural events, and seem to have been the successors of the old miracle plays. Religious subjects were given up for ever in 1692, their place being taken by secular subjects, which were considered far more suitable for the stage than the former; and scriptural subjects were now confined to the oratorio and the church cantatas.

At the time of Handel's visit, Hamburg was at the zenith of its musical fame, and both musicians and poets of the first rank were working there. Among these were Postel and

Menantes, who wrote the dramas which Reinhard Keiser set to music. Keiser directed the theatre for forty years, and raised it to a degree of excellence surpassing that of the famous Berlin theatre. He composed no less than one hundred and twenty operas and *Singspiele,* which became known and popular throughout northern Germany, and even reached Paris. The subjects of the operas, like those of Handel in England in later years, were all taken from classical mythology and history and were treated as mere plots on which to put together eighteenth-century ideas of love stories. The performers were students, apprentices and flower-girls who happened to have good voices, chief among them being Conradi, the daughter of a Dresden barber, whose musical education was so poor that she had to be taught everything by ear.

Among Handel's first Hamburg acquaintances was Johann Mattheson, who was four years his senior and, being gifted and vain, patronized him. But he introduced him to others and obtained for him access to the various organs and concerts. He also introduced him to Sir Cyril Wyche, the English ambassador, in whose family music was assiduously cultivated. Here Handel obtained pupils and engagements.

Mattheson tells us that Handel played a *ripieno* second violin in the opera house orchestra, and pretended, for a joke, that he did not know how to count five; but on one occasion the harpsichordist (who was at that time also the conductor) being absent, and Handel taking his place, he proved himself to be a great master. Handel seemed fond of a joke, though he laughed little. Mattheson speaks of several things that occurred to himself and Handel which seem to have caused them amusement, but of which the context is lost.

On 17th August 1703 Handel and Mattheson journeyed by post, in company with a pigeon-fancier, to Lübeck, forty miles to the north-east of Hamburg. Here Dietrich Buxtehude, then advanced in years, was organist of the Marienkirche, and was seeking a successor, who was bound to marry the daughter of the retiring organist as a condition of holding the post.[1] Mattheson, who had been invited to become a candidate, says:

I took Handel with me; we played on all the organs and clavi-cymbals there, and finally agreed that he should only play on the organ and I only on the clavicymbal. We listened with much attention to good artists in the Marienkirche. But, as a matrimonial alliance was proposed in the business, for which neither of us had the slightest inclination, we departed, after receiving many tokens of esteem, and having had much enjoyment.

[Buxtehude's daughter, Anna Margreta, was ten years older than Handel and six years older than Mattheson. A bride-groom for her, and organist for the church, was eventually found in the person of Johann Christian Schiefferdecker, who had been cembalist at the Hamburg opera, but not before Bach had also turned down the appointment on account of Buxtehude's daughter in 1705.]

Handel was not a brilliant violin player, but his skill on the organ was by this time very great.

He was greater on the organ than Kuhnau [says Mattheson], especially in extempore fugues and counterpoints; but he knew little of melody till he came to the Hamburg opera. . . . In the last century scarcely any one thought of melody, but everything was influenced by harmony only. He had, most of the time, free board at my father's table, and in return he showed me several contrapuntal effects, while I did him no small services in the dramatic style; and we helped one another.

Mattheson also tells us that he composed at that time 'very

---

[1] It was not uncommon in those days for an organist, cantor or clergyman to be obliged to marry the daughter or widow of his predecessor.—Chrysander, p. 86. [Buxtehude himself had married the daughter of his predecessor, Tunder.—E. B.]

long, long arias and endless cantatas, which, though they had a full harmony, had not proper taste or skill in treatment; but in course of time they became much more polished, through the School of Opera, with which Handel was connected.'

Mattheson was at this time tutor to the son of the English envoy. He soon afterwards became secretary of the English Legation at Hamburg and married the daughter of an English clergyman. He had a most remarkable career. At the age of nine he played the organ in several churches, sang songs of his own composition, playing the accompaniment on the harp, learned the double bass, violin, flute and oboe. A little later he began the study of the law, learned the English, Italian and French languages, thoroughbass, counterpoint, fugue and singing. At the age of fifteen he was singing the chief soprano parts in the opera at Kiel; at eighteen he produced an opera of his own, *Die Pleyaden,* at Hamburg, and became attached to that theatre as one of the principal tenor singers, which post he held in addition to his connection with the British Embassy. He wrote many operas and masses, twenty-eight oratorios, many sonatas and other music. But he is chiefly known by his literary work on every conceivable subject connected with music, such as the works of Aristoxenus, Bacon, thoroughbass, biography, science, criticism, acoustics, etc. His best-known work is the *Grundlage einer Ehrenpforte,* a collection of biographies of contemporary musicians. His ambition was to publish a work for every year that he lived, and he accomplished more than this, for when he died at the age of eighty-three he had published eighty-eight books. In addition to his extraordinary musical erudition and capacity, he was an accomplished fencer and dancer and courtier. Such was the man with whom Handel was now on the most intimate terms.

On 5th December 1704 Mattheson's opera, *Cleopatra,* produced on 20th October of the same year, was performed.

Mattheson was in the habit of conducting at the harpsichord when he was not singing the part of Antonius, and returning to the harpsichord after the death of this character, which took place about half an hour before the end. But on this occasion Handel refused to leave the instrument, and a quarrel ensued. Mattheson gave Handel a box on the ear as they left the theatre, and they fought with swords in the market-place before a crowd of people. Fortunately Mattheson's sword broke on a large metal button on Handel's coat, and no great harm was done. Through the mediation of a councillor and a director of the theatre they became better friends than before. Handel dined with Mattheson on 30th December, and they went together to the rehearsal of Handel's first opera, *Almira, Queen of Castile,* a *Singspiel* produced in the large theatre of Hamburg on 8th January 1705. The text of this opera, like that of Mattheson's *Cleopatra,* was written by Friedrich Feustking, a theological student, from an Italian original.

The original manuscript is lost, and the existing copy in the State Library at Berlin is incomplete. The characters are three sopranos, two basses and three tenors, with chorus of Castilian grandees, courtiers and guards. The first act opens with a scene in the amphitheatre of Valladolid, in which Almira is about to be crowned by Consalvo, Prince of Segovia, to whom is allotted a bass part. Trumpeters and drummers are arranged on balconies on each side of the stage. Consalvo addresses the queen in German recitative followed by an aria:

> 'Almire
> Regiere
> Und führe
> Beglücket den Scepter, grossmüthig die Krohn.' [1]

[1] Chrysander tells us that Feustking's words for Mattheson's *Cleopatra* were so improper that several pages of his libretto had to be suppressed. Feustking thereupon attacked Hunold Menantes,

George Frideric Handel

(Portrait by F. Kyte)

HOUSE MARKED AS THE BIRTHPLACE AT HALLE

HANDEL'S HARPSICHORD
(*Victoria and Albert Museum*)

PORTRAIT BY T. HUDSON
(*National Portrait Gallery*)

FACSIMILE OF FIRST PAGE OF 'MESSIAH'

GEORGE FREDERICK HANDEL Esqr
born February. XXIII. MDCLXXXIV.
died April XIV. MDCCLIX. L.F.Roubiliac inv^t et sc^t

MONUMENT BY ROUBILIAC IN WESTMINSTER ABBEY

STATUE AT HALLE

FACSIMILE OF LAST PAGE OF 'JEPHTHA'

('May Almira reign, and bear the sceptre with happiness, and the crown with magnanimity.') The crowning takes place, and the chorus sing eleven bars in Italian: 'Viva, viva Almira.'

Then follows a chaconne, to which the court dances, and then a saraband, afterwards used in *Rinaldo* for the well-known song, 'Lascia ch'io pianga.'[1] Almira, in a German recitative, appoints Osman (tenor), son of Consalvo, her field-marshal and Fernando her secretary. The latter sings his thanks to the queen in German recitative, followed by an Italian aria. A letter is brought to Almira from her father; Consalvo urges her to read it in a *presto* aria, 'Leset, ihr funkelnden Augen mit Fleiss.' Almira, in a German recitative and Italian aria, confesses her love for Fernando. This aria is in the well-known *da capo* form.

We are now introduced to a royal garden, in which Edilia, a princess, sings of her love for Osman, accompanied (during

who was the author of *Nebuchadnezzar*. Menantes replied by parodying the above rhymes in *Almira,* as follows:

> 'Mein Käthgen
> Im Städgen
> Hats Lädgen
> Geöfnet, beglücket grossmüthig im Schrank.'

('My Kittie has opened a little shop in the town, and is fortunate and generous in business.') This hit Feustking hard, for he had a mistress called Catherine. The matter was taken up by others; hundreds of pamphlets appeared in course of time; Feustking was accused of atheism, and the burghers being in a state of ferment over certain ecclesiastical matters, the affair eventually led to disturbances which had to be put down by military forces in 1708. One of the pamphlets written by Feustking is interesting as containing the first printed reference to Handel, in which he speaks of the 'excellent music of Herr Hendel.'

[1] It was also used in the oratorio, *Il Trionfo del tempo.*

part of the time) by two solo violins, two flutes and a bass.
Osman appears, refuses Edilia's proffered love, whereupon
Edilia invokes thunderbolts and other disagreeable things on
his head in Italian, while he answers in German. The
jealousy of Almira now introduces complications. She dis-
turbs Fernando in the act of carving *Ich liebe di(ch)* on a tree,
and takes it for granted that the words should read *Ich lieb
Edi(lia)*. A fine aria in E minor follows, 'Geloso tormento
mi va rodendo il cor' ('The torment of jealousy gnaws at
my heart'). The scene now discloses a ballroom in the
palace, with a band of oboes in the gallery. Edilia chooses
Fernando for her partner; Osman becomes jealous, Edilia tries
to revenge herself through Osman's jealousy. A suite of
dances now follows, in which all the performers take part.
The queen discovers Fernando dancing with Edilia; a quarrel
ensues, the queen sings 'Ingrato, spietato' (the music of which
is unfortunately lost) and the first act ends.

The second act begins in the queen's audience chamber, to
which Raymondo (bass), King of the Moors, is brought; all
the other characters stand round the throne. Some by-play
in Italian and German fills the first three scenes. In scene iv
Fernando is discovered writing a letter in his room, and orders
his servant Tabarco to keep the door shut. Someone outside
knocks, and Tabarco sings a kind of patter song:

Hab-bia-te pa-	zien-za

accompanied by violas and basses only.

Osman is eventually admitted and asks Fernando to assist
him in making love to Almira. Almira, however, is expected
by Fernando, so Osman, in a German aria accompanied by
two flutes, *viola da braccia* solo and bass, hides himself, and

sings 'Sprich vor mich ein süsses Wort; rede, flehe,' etc. ('Speak for me a kindly word; urge and pray her,' etc.). Almira arrives and becomes again jealous on seeing the letter written by Fernando, which is intended for her, but which she takes for granted is intended for Edilia. More misunderstandings take place, in Italian and German, which are finally settled before the end of the act.

In scene vii Osman is still hiding. Consalvo now appears, and with considerable diplomacy offers his son Osman to Almira in a German aria. Osman now comes out of hiding and renounces Almira in favour of Edilia.

Scene viii takes place in another part of the court. Raymondo now makes love to Almira, who answers in a very beautiful accompanied recitative: 'Ich kann nicht mehr verschweigen' ('I can no more keep silence'), followed by an aria: 'Movei passi a le ruine.' Almira, seeing Osman coming, hides. Osman challenges Fernando: Almira snatches Osman's sword away. Fernando laughs at Osman to the accompaniment of two oboes and bassoon.

More quarrels take place. Fernando, supposed to be a foundling, is discovered to be a prince; a comic scene takes place, in which Tabarco gets hold of a mail-bag and reads all the love-letters in it, making sarcastic remarks thereon.

Act III opens with one of the favourite devices of those days, in which the actors, becoming the audience, have a play acted before them. Such a scene is here enacted in honour of Raymondo, King of the Moors.

Fernando, dressed as Europa, enters on a chariot, preceded by a band of oboes, followed by a crowd of Europeans who dance. Osman, representing a Moor, is brought in under a splendid canopy, carried by twelve Moors, preceded by a band of trumpets, and followed by African people, who dance a rigadoon. Consalvo follows as Asia, surrounded by lions, preceded by a band of cymbals, drums and fifes, and followed by Asiatics, who dance the saraband which had previously been heard in the first act ('Lascia ch' io pianga').

Tabarco represents Foolishness, with harlequins and charlatans, while his band consists of a hurdy-gurdy and bagpipe. He sings, with two oboes as accompaniment (in German): 'Come and celebrate my fame; for the greater part of earth is subject to my sway.' The charlatans then dance a jig.

More quarrelling, daggers are drawn, and Fernando finds himself in prison through the duplicity of Consalvo, who tries to get Almira to sentence him to death, and nearly succeeds. Tabarco brings a pretended death-warrant to Fernando, in prison, but is followed by Almira, who, overhearing him sing of her and not Edilia, releases him. General understanding all round now takes place—a short chorus occurs, of which the music is lost, and the opera concludes with the usual trio, in which all the principal voices take part.

We have given a fairly full account of Handel's first opera, as it shows the kind of material with which he had to work. If we eliminate the short choruses and imagine the language to be Italian throughout, we have the pattern on which all the later operas were composed: a succession of recitatives and arias connected together by a slight and very obvious plot. Handel made the most of his opportunities, and many of the arias even in this early work are exceedingly fine. That he was not insensible to the orchestral possibilities is shown by the use of the two oboes and a bassoon in the mocking-song, and the veiled sound of the violas in the song 'Have patience.'

This opera, produced on 8th January 1705, had so great a success that it was performed without intermission until 25th February, when Handel's second opera, *The Success of Love through Blood and Murder, or Nero,* represented as a *Singspiel,* was performed with great applause. Mattheson took the chief part in both these operas.

From the account of *Almira* given above we see that it was put on the stage with all the magnificence available at that time, and in all Handel's later operas the same luxury of scenery and action is found. He never did things by halves. He supplied the finest music and required the finest singers, orchestra and stage effects procurable.

The words of *Nero* were by Feustking, and, out of three hundred Hamburg opera texts read by Chrysander, he finds 'none in which stupidity reaches a higher degree.' Handel sighed, and said: 'How can a musician make fine music when he has no good words? There is no soul in the poetry, and it is painful to have to set such stuff to music.' [1]

The score of *Nero* is lost, but the libretto, which is extant, contains seventy-five airs in German. It was only performed three times, the theatre being closed after its third representation. Handel, who had for some time given up playing second violin, now occupied himself with teaching and occasionally playing the harpsichord at the theatre. He lived a quiet life, worked hard and, refusing all temptations to indulge in pleasure, saved his money, and began those economical habits which lasted through his life, and by which he was able in after years to do so much for charitable objects. He was now independent of his mother's help. By teaching all day he not only supported himself, but was able to return the money she sent him, and to add something of his own to it. [2]

Keiser's envy was excited by Handel's success. He is said to have rearranged the words of *Nero*, and produced it on 5th August 1705 under the title of *The Roman Embarrassment, or the Noble-minded Octavia*, and in 1706 he produced *Almira*

[1] Chrysander, vol. i, p. 127.
[2] It is not known how much Handel was able to charge for lessons. Mattheson received from three to six thaler (nine to eighteen shillings) a month for his pupils.

under the title of *His Serene Highness the Secretary, or Almira, Queen of Castilia*. Both of these operas were openly directed against Handel, who, however, had already withdrawn from the theatre. Keiser's compositions were distinguished for justness and depth of expression and originality of form. His harmonies were strong and penetrating. Like Bach he had an instinct for instrumentation and was never tied by conventional customs. Handel was much influenced by him and never denied the obligations he was under to his genius.[1] In 1706 Keiser and his colleague Drüsicke were forced to give up the management of the theatre, owing to the debts they had contracted, and were succeeded by Saurbrey, who persuaded Handel to compose an opera (text by Hinsch, a poet not much better than Feustking). It was divided into two portions, *Florindo* and *Daphne,* on account of its length. It was not produced until 1708 and the score is lost.

Handel's compositions at Hamburg were not confined to opera. A *Passion according to St. John* by him was performed during Holy Week, 1704. The text was made by Wilhelm Postel from the nineteenth chapter of St. John's Gospel. Mattheson was at this time in Holland and could not take part in it. Some years later he mentions it in condemnatory terms. Mainwaring mentions two chests full of cantatas, sonatas and other music as having been left at Hamburg when Handel went to Italy, but Mattheson knew nothing of these. Perhaps the cantatas belonged to the Halle period, but Handel unquestionably wrote harpsichord and chamber music for his pupils at Hamburg.

All the Hamburg operas were in the German language, with Italian arias. This mixing of languages seems to have been a regular custom in those days; we shall meet with it again in England. Pieces other than opera were performed

[1] Fétis.

in Italian, French, High German and Low German. The reason is not far to seek. The recitative, which told the story, was in the language understood by the audience; while the arias were put into Italian, as a language more suitable for musical treatment.

CHAPTER III

ITALY

HANDEL had wished, even before he left Halle, to complete his studies in Italy. But he had not yet the means for so long and costly a journey. An offer was made in the winter of 1703-4 by Prince Gian Gastone de' Medici, son of the Grand Duke Cosmo III of Tuscany, to take him to Florence, but his sturdy independence of character refused to allow him to go as the servant of a prince; if he went, it must be as his own master.

The prince, with whom he was on very friendly terms, showed him a large collection of Italian music. Handel said he could see nothing in the music which answered the high character his highness had given it; he thought it so indifferent that the singers must be angels to recommend it. When the prince pressed him to come to a country of so great a culture, Handel said he was at a loss to conceive how such great culture should be followed by so little fruit.[1]

He remained at Hamburg till 1706, by which time he had saved two hundred ducats (about £96) besides having sent remittances to his mother from time to time. He must have worked hard and lived simply to have saved so large a sum in three years.

Few details are known as to the dates and other circumstances of the Italian tour. Schoelcher thinks that Handel arrived at Florence about the month of July 1706. Mainwaring says that he reached Florence soon after the return of

[1] Mainwaring, *Memoirs.*

28

Prince Gastone de' Medici, who introduced him at the court of his brother, Prince Ferdinand of Tuscany, who lived in the palace of Pratolino in the hills near the city; but it is not known when this was. Chrysander considers that he paid a short visit to Florence and then went on to Rome, and that about a dozen or more of solo cantatas were produced by him during this visit, one of which, called *Lucrezia,* became very popular; also he re-wrote the overture to *Almira,* adding some dances.

We have definite information that he was at Rome in January 1707,[1] and a psalm for five-part chorus, *Dixit Dominus* (110), is dated at the end 'S. D. G. (Soli Deo Gloria) G. F. Hendel, 1707, 11 d'Aprile, Romæ.' In this psalm he began the practice, which he continued to the end of his life, of dating his compositions. Chrysander says that the double fugue 'Tu es sacerdos in aeternum' is scarcely possible to perform, and that the part-writing in a long fugue on 'Et in saecula saeculorum, amen,' is restless; in fact the whole composition shows that he was not yet completely master of the contrapuntal art. Another psalm, *Nisi Dominus* (127), which he took with him to Italy, seems to date from the Halle period, since it is in the form of a German cantata; and a third, *Laudate pueri Dominum* (113), subscribed 'S. D. G.: G. F. H.: 1707 d. 8 July, Roma,' is a rearrangement for five voices of the same psalm written in Germany for a single voice.

Handel returned to Florence in July 1707. Florence was the original home of opera, for it was here that the little society of savants and musicians, meeting at the house of Bardi (on which an inscription records the fact), in their endeavours to revive the ancient glories of the Greek drama, were led to the invention of recitative and the aria. These first inventors and composers of opera, Peri, Caccini, Corsi and Galilei, who

[1] According to one of Mr. Newman Flower's numerous discoveries.—E. B.

flourished about 1600, were now to find a worthy successor in the Saxon, Handel, a century after they had originated the form of art which had flourished so well in Italy. His first effort in Italian opera on Italian soil was *Roderigo,* or *Rodrigo,* the text of which was provided by a poet whose name is now lost. The singers were four sopranos, one alto and one tenor. The overture is in the usual form, beginning with a slow movement followed by a fugue, but it ends with a suite of dances, consisting of a jig (so exactly like Corelli's music that it might be mistaken for his), a saraband, a *matelote* or sailor's dance, a minuet, two bourrées and finally a passacaglia with a brilliant violin solo in the style of Corelli, and very florid passages for all the violoncellos. Some of the music is taken from *Almira,* but a good deal altered. Like the latter, *Rodrigo* affords plenty of opportunity for scenic effect, and the work abounds in brilliant violin and violoncello solos.

To represent Esilena's constancy, she is made at the words 'La mia costanza' to sustain the note E through five and three-quarter bars of common time to an elaborate accompaniment. In scene iv Handel repeats the device already used in *Almira,* of accompanying a song with violins, flutes and viola, without any bass instrument; and in scene v Rodrigo is accompanied by violas and basses only. In scene vi he produces a mysterious ghostly effect by a modulation from the key of A flat to that of C flat, then A flat minor, which keys were not available on the harpsichord, owing to the system of tuning then in use. The cembalist is accordingly directed to cease playing, and the strings alone play the accompaniment at this point.

There seems to have been no trumpeter in Florence, for in a song containing the words 'Già grida la tromba' ('Now sounds the trumpet'), Handel's favourite instrument, the oboe, takes the place of the trumpet. That he could write for the trumpet at this time is proved by the score of *Almira,* and he is not likely to have willingly lost so good an opportunity of using this brilliant instrument, had one been available.

The work was awaited with some prejudice by the Italians. He had not yet given them any proof of his powers, and he himself seems to have confessed in later years to Mainwaring that he was not at that time fully master of the Italian style. But the audience received it exceedingly favourably, and Prince Ferdinand[1] gave him a hundred sequins (about £50) and a dinner-service of porcelain as a mark of his approval.[2]

Prince Gastone de' Medici, who had met Handel at Hamburg and had, as we have seen, proposed to take him to Florence in a dependent position, seems to have borne him no ill-will for his refusal of the offer, for we read that he entertained him at Florence. About October or November 1707 Handel paid a visit to Venice, where he met Steffani, Lotti, Gasparini and other musicians, and it is most probable that his great friendship with Domenico Scarlatti, who was of the same age as himself, began at this time. A story is told that Handel, at a masked ball, sat down at the harpsichord, and that as soon as Domenico heard him play, he exclaimed: 'This must be either the famous Saxon or the Devil!' It is said that after being thus discovered Handel was asked to compose an opera for Venice. But, as Chrysander points

---

[1] Not the Grand Duke (Cosmo III), as the original edition has it. Ferdinand was one of his sons.—E. B.

[2] The author here tells the following story, which is too well known to be entirely omitted, or indeed not to be explicitly denied: 'The principal part in *Rodrigo* was sung by Vittoria Tesi, who, according to Mainwaring, seems to have fallen in love with the young composer and to have obtained leave of absence in order to follow him to Venice, where she took part in his *Agrippina*.' It is now known that Vittoria Tesi-Tramontini, which was her full name, was born in 1700, and was therefore seven years of age at the time *Rodrigo* was produced.—E. B.

out, it is scarcely likely that a musician who was seeking reputation and profit would introduce himself in this way. His skill on the harpsichord caused much admiration and astonishment among the Italians, some of the more super-stitious of whom attributed it to magic, and it is not impossible that Handel, being present at a masked ball, may have been asked to play without discovering himself.

It must have been in October or November 1707 that Handel was introduced to Prince Ernest of Hanover, brother of the Elector Georg Ludwig (afterwards George I of England), who was in Venice at that time. He also met the English ambassador to Venice, the Earl of Manchester, who was a passionate lover of music. For the moment, however, Venice did not hold him for long, and if plans for an opera had been made at all at this time, they did not materialize immediately. In the early spring of 1708 Handel, probably accompanied by Domenico Scarlatti, went back to Rome.

We have seen how Italian opera arose in Florence through the efforts of a small society of enthusiasts to revive the ancient Greek drama in a modern form. These learned and artistic societies were not uncommon in Italy during the seventeenth and eighteenth centuries.

In 1690 an 'Academy' of poets, savants and musicians was founded at Rome for the cultivation of poetry and music, under the name of 'Arcadia,' the members being called Arcadian Shepherds and having names such as Olinto, Almiride, Egeria, etc., assigned to them. Among them were Marchese Ruspoli, afterwards Prince of Cervetere, and his wife Isabella, who was a 'shepherdess'; the priest Crescimbeni, who wrote the history of the Arcadians; Countess Capizucchi; the poet Stampiglia and Cardinal Paolucci.

Membership of the Academy was not confined to the inhabitants of Rome, but was spread throughout Italy, and at one time numbered fifteen hundred. It included several of the popes, all the cardinals, many foreign princes, the Queen of Poland, and other ladies of high position; the musicians Corelli, Alessandro Scarlatti, Pasquini, Marcello, the German poet Postel and an Englishman, Daniel Lock. Handel frequented the Arcadians, but the question of his being elected a member did not arise, apparently because musicians of his age were not eligible. He also came under the patronage of Cardinal Pietro Ottoboni, at whose palace numbers of people practising or interested in the arts met weekly for the cultivation of poetry and music. Corelli was attached to the Ottoboni household and directed the musical performances.

No opera was permitted at this time in Rome, but every other kind of music was cultivated. The performers were the best artists available, and Ottoboni, besides sustaining an orchestra, had command of the papal choir. He was a man of great wealth, which he spent in employing the best artists and in succouring the poor.

Another patron of the arts in Rome was Prince Ruspoli, whose wealth and magnificence almost equalled the cardinal's. He was a friend of Prince Ferdinand de' Medici, and it is no doubt for this reason that he invited Handel to stay with him for a month in March 1708. There the oratorio, *La Resurrezione,* dated 'Roma la Festa di Pasqua dal Marchese Ruspoli 11 [1] d'Aprile 1708,' was composed. The author of the words was Carlo Sigismondo Capece. It contains parts for two flutes, two German flutes, two bassoons, two trumpets, harpsichord, *viola da gamba,* theorbo, archlute and strings. A 'song of angels' is accompanied by four violins. It was first performed, as the inscription indicates, at Ruspoli's on Easter Sunday.[2]

[1] The actual date of performance was 8th April.

[2] Not at Ottoboni's, as biographers have stated again and again. —E. B.

In Rome attempts were made to convert Handel to the Roman religion—perhaps by Cardinal Benedetto Panfili, who wrote the poems for several cantatas set to music by the young Saxon, including *Il Trionfo del tempo e del disinganno, Apollo e Dafne* and *Fillide ed Aminta*. He was asked whether he had ever considered the origin and creed of the Lutheran religion, or of the one true church; for this was a matter of salvation, of more importance than our life and all our works. Handel frankly answered that he had neither the calling nor the ability to make independent researches into the differences of church teaching, but he assured his interlocutor that he was firmly resolved to continue all his life as a member of that church in whose bosom he had been born and brought up. It is satisfactory to note that these theological differences in no way disturbed the friendly relations that existed between Handel and the church authorities at Rome.

It was shortly after the production of *La Resurrezione* that *Il Trionfo del tempo e del disinganno* was composed. Nearly thirty years later Handel worked it up into the English oratorio, *The Triumph of Time and Truth.* The characters were Bellezza (Beauty), Piacere (Pleasure), Tempo (Time) and Disinganno (Undeceiving, i.e. Truth); the text treated of the temptations caused by the two former characters and their subordination by the two latter. It was called a 'serenata,' since the words were not taken from Scripture. It contains two quartets, an unusual combination of voices in those days.

The vigorous character of the music was new to the Italians, and Corelli complained of its difficulty, especially with regard to the overture. Handel, having tried in vain to get him to give the requisite fire and strength to the music, snatched the violin out of his hand and played the passages himself, to show the company how little Corelli understood them. Poor Corelli, of a shy and retiring disposition, confessed that he could not understand the matter and had not the requisite power. 'But, my dear Saxon,' said he, 'this music is in the French style, which I do not understand.' Thereupon Handel composed a 'symphony' in the Italian style, in place of the overture. Hawkins tells us that Handel was competent at any time to take a violin from the hands of a player and show him how he wished the passages performed.

[Among the cantata texts furnished by Cardinal Panfili was one extolling Handel himself in the character of Orpheus. Biographers, finding no trace of the music, concluded that the composer's modesty forbade him to set this to music. But the setting was recently discovered,[1] and it has to be concluded that in the eighteenth century it was no more reprehensible for a composer to sing his own praises than it was to draw upon other people's music in composition. Neither case was regarded as involving ethical questions.]

Il Trionfo, performed at Ottoboni's, was not a success, but it is not likely that this was enough to drive him from so much congenial society in Rome. His stay was more likely cut short by political circumstances. Trouble had for some time been brewing between the Pope, Clement XI, and the Emperor of Austria on account of the Spanish succession, and the Pope had walled up eight of the eighteen gates of Rome. As an army was now advancing against the city, Handel may well have departed in June 1708 to escape being besieged. He travelled to Naples, and found Austrian troops everywhere in Neapolitan territory. That he was sorry to leave, is shown by a manuscript, *Partenza di G. H. Cantata di G. F. Handel,* the words of which are a lamentation over the fate that drives him from the beautiful banks of the Tiber. Chrysander says that it is more than probable that the two Scarlattis and Corelli travelled with him to Naples.

A chamber trio, *Se tu non lasci amore,* signed 'G. F. Handel,

[1] At Münster in Westphalia by Professor Edward J. Dent, see his *Handel,* p. 34.—E. B.

li 12 Luglio 1708, Napoli,' shows that he was at Naples in July, and all authorities are agreed that here he wrote the Italian serenata, *Aci, Galatea e Polifemo*, which is really a cantata for three voices and orchestra, without chorus, overture or division into acts.

The introductory duet is accompanied by two violoncellos and a double bass. The part of Polyphemus was written for a bass singer of extraordinary compass, since the music comprises a range of two octaves and five notes; and even a greater compass is found in the solo cantata, *Nell' Africane selve*, where the singer has to leap

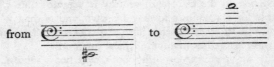

from   to

Chrysander thinks that the remarkable bass for whom these two works were written was Boschi, who afterwards sang in London. Burney says: 'Handel's genius and fire never shone finer than in the bass songs which he composed for Boschi, whose voice being sufficiently powerful to penetrate through a multiplicity of musical parts, Handel set every engine to work in the orchestra to enrich the harmony, and enliven the movement.' According to Mainwaring a palace, with free board, was placed at Handel's disposal, together with carriages and every convenience, by a wealthy lady, Donna Laura, and he was very much sought after by members of the best society, who considered themselves fortunate when they were able to entertain him. This Donna Laura seems to have been Spanish, for amongst the Italian cantatas is found one for voice and guitar in the Spanish language. [What is more certain is that at Naples he met Cardinal Vincenzo Grimani, a member of a wealthy Venetian family who owned the theatre of San Giovanni Crisostomo in Venice, for which he commissioned Handel to write an opera. Thus *Agrippina* was composed in three weeks during the stay in Naples.]

The dates and times of Handel's sojourns at the various Italian towns can only be guessed at by reference to such of his works as have come down to us in their original form, with the dates and places of their composition given on them. He seems to have left Naples in the autumn of 1709.

Amongst the works composed there are seven French canzonets with harpsichord accompaniment which were written more as studies in the French style of Lulli than for performance. They contain many corrections and improvements in pencil and ink.

Handel returned once more to Rome, where he must have remained until near Christmas, for he heard the Calabrian *pifferari*, who every year come to Rome to celebrate the birth of Christ by singing and playing an ancient melody in memory of their predecessors, the shepherds of Bethlehem. This melody was years afterwards employed by Handel in the *Messiah* under the name of the 'Pastoral Symphony,' over which he wrote 'Pifa,' i.e. *pifferari*.[1] He also performed *Aci* here. But he must have left the holy city before Christmas, for he was in Venice for the production of *Agrippina* on 26th December 1709. It marked the opening of the carnival season and was, according to Mainwaring, received with great favour, the audience shouting: 'Viva il caro Sassone' ('Long live the dear Saxon').

The characters in *Agrippina* are eight in number: Agrippina, wife of Claudius, soprano; Nero, soprano; Poppæa, soprano; Claudius, the emperor, bass; Otho, alto; two Freedmen, bass and alto; Juno, alto. There is no tenor.

The overture made a considerable sensation, thanks to its fullness and dignity, the Italian overtures being of a much lighter character. A chorus occurs in act II, accompanied

[1] Derived from *piffero,* It.: a fife or shepherd's pipe.

by trumpets, drums and the usual strings, and one of Otho's songs has a Bach-like accompaniment of flutes and muted violins, while the basses play *pizzicato* throughout. Two solo violoncellos are employed in the last act, which ends with a set of dances. Some of the music was afterwards used for *Jephtha, Triumph of Time and Truth* and *Judas Maccabaeus*. An aria, sung by Agrippina, previously used in *La Resurrezione*, accompanied by violins in unison with the voice, and without any bass, i.e. unison throughout, became enormously popular. It was brought to England, introduced without Handel's name into the opera *Pyrrhus* by Alessandro Scarlatti, and finally published in an English song collection to the words:

> In Kent so fam'd of old,
> Close by the famous knoll
> A swain a goddess told
> An am'rous story.

This air, which was the first piece of music by Handel to reach England, was attributed to Scarlatti.

The Venetian audience was so carried away by the force and beauty of the music that to an onlooker they would have appeared to have lost their senses. At every pause in the music the theatre resounded with cries of 'Viva il caro Sassone,' and other extravagant expressions. The grandeur and dignity of his style entirely astonished them. A number of important Hanoverian and English personages who happened to be in Venice at the time were likewise carried away by the music, and they pressed Handel to visit Hanover and England.

CHAPTER IV

FROM HANOVER TO LONDON

AMONG the Hanoverians present during the run of *Agrippina,* which went on for twenty-seven nights, were Prince Ernest, whom Handel had already met, and Baron Kielmansegge, a courtier with whom he was to come into touch again after the accession of George I to the English throne. There was also Steffani, that remarkable Italian composer and diplomat, at that time *Capellmeister* to the Hanoverian court. These, and perhaps others attached to the same court, strongly urged Handel to seek the patronage of, or at least pay a visit to, the Elector Georg Ludwig; but he seems to have been disposed to pay more attention to the attractions of England, no doubt painted to him in glowing colours by the Earl of Manchester. In the end Handel did go to Hanover, but with the idea of making it merely a stage on his journey to England. He accompanied Steffani. Not long after their arrival, Steffani, who was fifty-six and perhaps tired of his appointment, threw it up, ostensibly because of a quarrel with some of the singers, but quite possibly with the idea of making an opening for Handel. At any rate, the young man was appointed *Capellmeister* on 16th June 1710.

The following is his account of the transaction, quoted in his own words by Hawkins:

'When I first arrived at Hanover I was a young man, under twenty; [1] I was acquainted with the merits of Steffani, and he had

---

[1] An obvious mistake: he was twenty-five.

heard of me. I understood somewhat of music, and,' putting forth both his broad hands, and extending his fingers, 'could play pretty well on the organ. He received me with great kindness, and took an early opportunity to introduce me to the Princess Sophia and the elector's son, giving them to understand that I was what he pleased to call a virtuoso in music; he obliged me with instructions for my conduct and behaviour during my residence at Hanover, and being called from the city to attend to matters of a public concern, left me in possession of that favour and patronage which he himself had enjoyed for a series of years.'

Handel's salary at Hanover was fifteen hundred ducats—about £300. Bach's salary at this time was £15 13s. 3d.; such was the difference between the income of a rising church musician and that of a rising composer of operas. Handel at once obtained leave of absence in order to go to England, but he is said to have first paid a visit to his mother and Zachau at Halle. If so, he found then that his youngest sister, Johanna Christiana, had died in 1709, at the age of twenty; his elder sister, Dorothea Sophia, had married a lawyer, Dr. Michael Dietrich Michaelsen, who later became a member of the Prussian War Office. Mainwaring says that his mother had become blind, but this is an error, for she retained her sight for another twenty years.

What is certain is that he went to Düsseldorf, where he was the guest of the Elector Johann Wilhelm of the Palatinate, who presented him with a silver table service. From here he journeyed through Holland to London, arriving there in the late autumn of 1710.

Opera had grown out of the masque in England through the genius of Henry Purcell, whose recitative, 'no less rhetorically perfect than Lulli's, was infinitely more natural and frequently impassioned to the last degree: and his airs, despite his self-confessed admiration for the Italian style, show little trace of the forms then most in vogue, but breathing rather the spirit of unfettered national melody, stand forth as models of refinement and freedom.'[1]

Purcell wrote incidental music ('act tunes,' songs, etc.) to a large number of plays by Restoration dramatists such as Shadwell, d'Urfey, the youthful Congreve and others. He also composed one short but real opera, *Dido and Æneas,* a complete masterpiece, as well as two works which may well be regarded as forerunners of the modern pantomime: Dryden's *King Arthur* and *The Fairy Queen,* a debased and spectacular adaptation of *A Midsummer Night's Dream.* These two works are not unfairly described by Chrysander's epithet of 'half-operas.'

Purcell had no successor of his calibre to carry on, much less to develop, his work. He died in 1695, and music in London was for some years chiefly confined to 'consorts' of vocal and instrumental music, Italian "Intermezzi, or inter-ludes, and mimical entertainments of singing and dancing,' performed by Italian and English musicians. In 1704 a musical entertainment, 'after the manner of an opera,' called *Britain's Happiness,* was performed at Drury Lane Theatre,[2] the vocal part of which was composed by John Weldon, after-wards organist and composer of the Chapel Royal, the instrumental part by Charles Dieupart, a French violinist

[1] W. S. Rockstro, in Grove's *Dictionary of Music and Musicians,* first edition, vol. ii, p. 507.

[2] The theatres in London were (1) in Drury Lane; (2) in the Haymarket, called the Queen's, or King's, or the Great Theatre, or the Opera House; (3) in the Haymarket, called the Little Theatre; (4) a theatre in Lincoln's Inn Fields; and (5) in Covent Garden, a new house opened on 7th December 1732 by John Rich. Other places of public entertainment at which Handel's music was per-formed were Marylebone Gardens; Ranelagh Gardens, with a large rotunda, having a bandstand in the centre; and Vauxhall Gardens, originally known as Spring Garden.

and cembalist. This work was also performed at the same time at the Lincoln's Inn Fields theatre, with music by Leveridge, the famous bass singer. In the same year Matthew Locke's opera *Psyche* and John Banister's *Circe* were revived. These attempts were not in themselves very successful, but they prepared the British public for Italian opera, which was now 'stealing into England, but in as rude a disguise as possible, in a lame hobbling translation, with false quantities, sung by our own unskilful voices, with graces misapplied to almost every sentiment, and with action lifeless and unmeaning through every character.' [1]

In January 1706, *Arsinoe, Queen of Cyprus,* by Stanzani, which had first been performed at Bologna in 1677, was set to English words by Thomas Clayton and performed at Drury Lane by English singers 'after the Italian manner.' The music seems to have been merely adapted by Clayton. Burney says that 'not only the common rules of musical composition are violated in every song, but also the prosody and accents of our language. The translation is wretched; but it is rendered much more absurd by the manner in which it is set to music. Indeed, the English must have hungered and thirsted extremely after dramatic music at this time to be attracted and amused by such trash.' It had a run of twenty-four nights.

In 1706 Stampiglia's libretto of *Camilla* was adapted in the same manner by Owen MacSwiney and performed, with a run of nine nights, at Drury Lane, the singers being the same as in *Arsinoe*; and at the Haymarket Theatre, Sir John Vanbrugh and Congreve gave a translated opera, *The Temple of Love,* set to 'Italian music' by Greber, a German. It was worse than the previous attempts, and, being only performed twice, was succeeded by d'Urfey's comic opera, *The Wonders of the Sun.*

[1] Colley Cibber, as quoted by Burney, *History of Music,* vol. iv, p. 198.

In 1707 *Camilla* was revived at Drury Lane, and was sufficiently attractive to damage the fortunes of the ordinary English plays. In the same year Addison, who had been in Italy, employed Clayton to set his opera *Rosamond* to music, which was performed three times at Drury Lane, and the abject poverty of the music caused it never to be performed again. It was succeeded by *Thomyris, Queen of Scythia*, written by Motteux, and 'adjusted' to airs by G. B. Bononcini and Scarlatti by Dr. Pepusch. The English portions were sung by English performers, the Italian by an artificial soprano, Valentini (surnamed Urbani) and Margherita de l'Épine, whom Pepusch married some ten years later. Its music was the best that had yet been heard.

Italian singers were now beginning to pour into England, and the public, after having been regaled for so many years on the poorest of music, was ripe for something better. In January 1708 the *London Daily Post* announced that 'by agreement between Swiney and Rich, the Haymarket is to be appropriated to operas, and Drury Lane to plays.' *Love's Triumph*, by Ottoboni, the English words 'adjusted' to the airs of Carlo Giovanni by Motteux, and with choruses and dances after the French manner, was tried, to see if the English audience preferred French or Italian music. It had no success. Scarlatti's *Pyrrhus and Demetrius*, translated by MacSwiney and arranged by Nicola Haym, followed; it had a considerable success, perhaps owing to the appearance in it of an artificial soprano, Nicola Grimaldi, known as Nicolini, a great Neapolitan singer, but a still greater actor. The promoters of Italian opera may now be considered to have succeeded in firmly establishing it on English soil. The taste of the public was improving, and there was a growing demand for better music. As in Hamburg the operas were performed in a mixture of Italian and German, so in London these first performances were in Italian and English. Busby calls these polyglot operas 'gallimaufries.'

In January 1710 *Almahide,* an opera by an unknown composer, was performed entirely in Italian, and on 3rd May
Hydaspes, by Francesco Mancini, was performed in Italian
'with English singing between the acts.'

The advent of Italian opera was opposed by Steele, and
more strongly by Addison, who attacked it with all the power
of his sarcasm and wit. Steele, in the *Tatler,* having abused
the confusion of languages in the early operas, Addison began
to talk of the taste for performances in which not a word
could be understood. Amateurs, tired with only understanding half the piece, found it more convenient not to understand
any. 'It does not,' says he, 'want any measure of sense to see
the ridicule of this monstrous practice.'

The *Tatler* and afterwards the *Spectator* could not stem the
rising tide—it is possible that they even helped the movement
by calling attention to it; for many an undertaking is pushed
forward as much by the attacks of its enemies as by the exertions
of its promoters. Moreover, the English opera, *Rosamond,* by
Addison and Clayton, produced at Drury Lane in 1707, had
proved a failure; and Burney thinks that the hostility evinced
by the *Spectator* was a deliberate attempt to conceal the failure.

A composer who had made himself famous throughout
Italy was now visiting London, and his presence was at once
taken advantage of to provide something better than the
London public had yet experienced. The director of the
Haymarket Theatre, Aaron Hill, a literary young man of
Handel's own age, who could turn his hand to anything,
artistic or commercial, arranged a book in English from Tasso's
Jerusalem Delivered and engaged Giacomo Rossi to translate
it into Italian for Handel to set it to music. The latter went
to work with such enthusiasm that the poor poet could not
keep pace with him. The music was written in a fortnight,
and Rossi complains that 'Signor Hendel, the Orpheus of
our century, in setting it to music, has hardly given him time

to write it.' [Many earlier pieces, however, were used by the composer.] The success was enormous. An air, 'Cara sposa,' sung by Nicolini, was considered by the composer to be one of the best he ever made; and Walsh, the publisher, made £1500 by the publication of this opera, which was called *Rinaldo*.[1]

The first performance took place on 24th February 1711, and its success roused Addison to anger and ridicule. Unusual care and expense was lavished on the stage arrangements and machinery. The gardens of Armida were filled with live birds, which Addison contemptuously called sparrows. It was played fifteen nights in succession, a rare thing in those days. The part of Rinaldo was written for Nicolini, whose voice, formerly a soprano, had now become a contralto, and the great bass, Giuseppe Boschi, made his first London appearance in this work. Hill dedicated the work to Queen Anne, [to whom Handel had been presented, doubtless by one of the Hanoverian emissaries.] The air 'Cara sposa' was played on all the harpsichords in England. The march became the regimental march of the Life Guards for forty years, and seventeen years later was adapted by Pepusch to the highwaymen's chorus in *The Beggar's Opera*. A piece in the second act was sung in all merrymakings to the words, 'Let the waiter bring clean glasses'; and the air 'Lascia ch' io pianga' is still popular. With reference to the £1500 gained by Walsh, Handel is said to have proposed that Walsh should compose the next opera, and that he (Handel) should sell it, in order that they might be on a more equal footing. The work afterwards reached Italy (where it was performed at Naples by Leonardo Leo) and Hamburg, and was revived again and again in London.

Meanwhile the court and the public were most enthusiastic

[1] The 'publication' of an opera in those days usually meant only the publication of its favourite songs, with figured bass accompaniment.

over Handel's harpsichord and organ playing, and when the time drew near for his return to Hanover, Queen Anne made him promise to come again as soon as possible. He had astonished and delighted every one by his many-sided genius.

The first regular weekly concerts we hear of in London were those given by Thomas Britton, the small-coal man. This extraordinary character made his living by selling coal about the streets, at first carried in sacks on his back, later pushed from house to house on a barrow. When his daily round was finished he went home to his shop near Clerkenwell Green, changed his clothes, and was then ready to receive his company. He was a most enthusiastic collector of music and musical books. He converted the long, low loft over his shop into a regular concert room, in which were all kinds of instruments, including a small organ. For some thirty years this room, which could only be approached by a narrow outside staircase, and was 'so mean in every respect as to be only a fit habitation for a very poor man,' was the weekly resort of all musical amateurs of whatever wealth or rank, and of all professional musicians. Britton made no charge for his concerts; all who came were his guests. Dukes and duchesses, gentlemen and ladies, musicians and singers, all met on equal terms in the small-coal man's loft, to listen to and perform the best chamber music of the day. Handel was a welcome and frequent performer on the organ here, and here he met all the best musicians of London. Matthew Dubourg, who was afterwards associated with him in the performance of the *Messiah* at Dublin, and who became his chief violinist, made his first public appearance at Thomas Britton's rooms, as a child, standing on a stool and playing a solo by Corelli. Handel probably first met him here. Besides the organ Handel used to play the harpsichord at Britton's room. In this he had a rival later on in William Babell, organist to George I, who became his pupil and did much to spread a knowledge of his clavier music. Amongst it was published by Walsh a 'Harpsichord piece' played by Handel in one of the songs in *Rinaldo*, which made a great sensation; but he is supposed to have extemporized it, for in the score are found some blank bars marked 'cembalo.'

Handel had a very pleasant visit to London, which he seems to have left some time after the close of the opera season on 2nd June. [He did not return straight to Hanover, but first paid another visit to Düsseldorf, where the Elector Palatine wished to have his advice about various musical matters. The resumption of his duties at Hanover seems to have already been unduly delayed, for the temporary patron at Düsseldorf saw fit to write two letters to the Elector of Hanover, apologizing for having retained Handel and begging him not to lay the blame on his *Capellmeister*.[1]] Georg Ludwig does not seem to have been annoyed with Handel, for he soon granted him leave to pay a visit to his mother at Halle, where, according to a baptismal register, he stood godfather to his niece, Johanna Michaelsen, on 23rd June. The infant's second Christian name was Friederike, derived, no doubt, from her uncle and godfather. Handel never ceased to have a special affection for this child of his only living sister, and he made her the principal beneficiary in his will.

Attached to the Hanoverian court was the Abbé Hortensio Mauro, who was also employed as private secretary, master of the ceremonies and political agent. Handel composed for Princess Caroline of Anspach, stepdaughter of the elector and afterwards Queen of England, thirteen chamber duets and twelve cantatas; but he seems to have composed nothing else except his oboe concertos. Mainwaring says that the words of the twelve cantatas were written by Mauro. His chamber

[1] One of these letters, discovered by Dr. Alfred Einstein in the secret State Archives of Bavaria, is quoted in Newman Flower's *George Frideric Handel*.—E. B.

duets bear signs of the influence of his friend Steffani, whose works he studied diligently and who had considerable influence on his artistic development.

Handel was always seeking to perfect himself in his art. Wherever he found anything worth learning he set himself diligently to learn it. Except for the few years he studied under Zachau he was his own teacher, simply observing and assimilating all that he could learn from the works of his predecessors and contemporaries. He composed no opera at Hanover, where there was no opportunity of performing dramatic works, and he did not find sufficient scope at the small court to satisfy him for long. He had seen during his visit to London that this was the right place in which to exercise his talents, and, unable longer to resist the pressing invitations he received, he once more obtained leave of absence 'on condition that he engaged to return within a reasonable time.'[1] How he interpreted this condition will be seen in due course.

In the late autumn of 1712 he was again in London. The opera was now under the management of Owen MacSwiney, who obtained from Handel the opera of *Il Pastor fido*. It must have been brought from Hanover in an advanced state, for it was ready to go into rehearsal[2] on 4th November and was produced on the 26th of the same month. The author of the libretto was Rossi, who dedicated it to the 'Most illustrious Lady Anna Cartwright.' The prices of the seats were 'as usual'—boxes, 8s.; pit, 5s.; gallery, 2s. 6d. Nicolini had left England, and his place was taken by Cavaliere Valeriano Pellegrini, an artificial soprano, the other parts being sung by Valentini, Leveridge, Margherita de l'Épine, Mrs. Barbier, a contralto, and Signora Schiavonetti. The opera was sung entirely in Italian. It failed to please and was withdrawn in February after only six performances.

[1] Mainwaring.   [2] It is dated 'Londres, ce 24 Octobre.'

Handel, being only on a visit to London, and with no assured position, did not as yet settle down. He was the guest at this time of a Mr. Andrews, of Barn Elms, in Surrey, who also had a house in town. After living with Mr. Andrews for a year, he yielded to the pressing invitation of the Earl of Burlington, who was only seventeen years of age and lived with his mother in the recently built fine house in Piccadilly, now the home of the Royal Academy, and here he remained no less than three years. He had full liberty to make any disposal of his time that suited him, and we read that 'he was very regular and uniform in his habits. He worked in his study every morning till the dinner hour, when he sat down with men of the first eminence for genius and abilities of any in the kingdom,' who were, like himself, guests of Lord Burlington. He thus became acquainted with Pope, Gay and Arbuthnot, the last of whom afterwards befriended him with his pen when he was being severely handled by his enemies. In the afternoons he would frequently attend service at St. Paul's Cathedral, of which Brind was then organist. The organ, by 'Father Smith,' was comparatively new, and he was particularly pleased with its tone. Moreover, it had pedals, a very unusual feature at that time. On this organ Handel used to play the concluding voluntaries, and many persons were attracted by his performances. He would then often adjourn to the Queen's Arms tavern in St. Paul's Churchyard, with members of the choir. Here was a large room with a harpsichord, and he would sometimes remain there making music for the whole evening. On other evenings, if there was no opera in progress, he would assist at the concerts at Burlington House, in which his own music took a large place.[1] Such was his daily life during his second visit to London.

Maurice Greene, who afterwards became professor of music

[1] Hawkins, *History of Music.*

in the University of Cambridge and Master of the King's Musick, was at that time articled to Brind and became a great admirer of Handel, even going so far as to blow the organ in order to enjoy the pleasure of hearing him play. He constantly went to see him at Burlington House and afterwards at Canons, so that his visits became more frequent than welcome. Handel, however, bore with him until he found that Greene was paying the same attentions to Bononcini, whereupon he refused any longer to receive him. We shall meet with Greene later.[1]

Il Pastor fido was followed by a five-act opera, *Teseo,* on 10th January 1713, 'with raised prices.' The libretto was written by Nicola Haym, and it was dedicated to Lord Burlington. The work is on a far larger scale than its predecessor. It was finished on 19th December 1712, and was rehearsed and put on the stage in twenty-one days. All the dresses were new, as were the scenery and machinery. The house was well filled, and the first performances were very successful; but even at this early stage financial troubles began to afflict operatic enterprise. They seem, indeed, to have been inseparable from Italian opera throughout its history. Mac-

[1] There is a good anecdote relating to Maurice Greene and Handel which, if not complimentary to Greene, at least shows the ready wit of the 'Saxon giant.' One day Greene took coffee with Handel, having previously left the manuscript of an anthem for the great German's approval. A variety of subjects were discussed, but not a word said by Handel concerning the composition. At length Greene, whose patience was exhausted, said, with eagerness and anxiety which he could no longer conceal: 'Well, sir, but my anthem—what do you think of it?' 'Oh! your antum. Ah! I did tink dat it vanted air.' 'Air?' said Greene. 'Yes, air; and so I did hang it out of de vindow,' replied Handel.—Crowest, *Musical Anecdotes,* v. 1. This story, which is told by Busby, is discredited by the best authorities (Schoelcher, Chrysander, Rockstro) on the ground that not only does it contain a foolish pun, but the gratuitous insult is entirely contrary to what is known of Handel's kindly nature.

Swiney, the director of the theatre, had to fly from his creditors, and the singers had to take their chance of making what they could by further performances on their own account, dividing the proceeds amongst themselves. Handel went without his fee, but was to some extent indemnified by a performance on 16th May 'for the benefit of Mr. Hendel, with an entertainment for the harpsichord.' The 'entertainment for the harpsichord' seems afterwards to have become a regular feature between the acts of both opera and oratorio, and several of Handel's concertos were written for this purpose.

One of the chief arias in *Teseo* contains the following theme:

Nè vuò che de' miei   dan - ni e   de' sofferti af-   fan - ni e de'

J. S. Bach has, in a church cantata, composed 1714:

Soprano. Ich hat-te viel Be - küm-mer-nis, ich hat-te viel Be - küm-mer-

Tenor.   Ich hat - te viel Be-küm-mer-nis ich hat - te

Handel, in *Acis and Galatea* (1720), has:

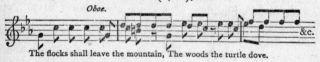

The flocks shall leave the mountain, The woods the turtle dove.

Bach, in an organ fugue, composed in 1724 or 1725, has the theme:

Handel has frequently been accused of appropriating the musical ideas of others to his own use—of stealing them, in fact. Did Bach in this case steal from Handel? We shall refer to this subject in a later chapter.

Two important works, with English words, next claim our attention: an *Ode for the Birthday of Queen Anne* and a *Te Deum and Jubilate*. The first was performed on 6th February 1713, probably at St. James's Palace, on the forty-ninth birthday of the queen. The author of the words is unknown. It praises Queen Anne for bringing about the Peace of Utrecht, [the *Te Deum* for which Handel had finished on 14th January on the chance of its being required for an official performance.] The birthday ode consists of short choruses, solos and duets. Some of the music was afterwards used in *Deborah*, and one of the movements is taken almost note for note from an oboe concerto. The sixth chorus contains the germ of part of the Hallelujah Chorus in *Messiah*.

Handel composed a *Te Deum* on the model of that of Purcell which was performed every year at the Festival of the Sons of the Clergy at St. Paul's. At that time the English statute required that the chief musician of the court should be a native. The holder of the post was John Eccles, part of whose duty it was to supply any music that was required for state functions. He had, in fact, an ode of his own performed on the queen's birthday. But Anne overrode the law. She commissioned Handel to prepare his *Te Deum* for the celebration of the Peace of Utrecht and to add a *Jubilate*. This peace was signed on 31st March 1713, and in July the queen went from Windsor to St. James's Palace to return thanks to God for the blessings of peace. The Utrecht *Te Deum and Jubilate* were performed at St. Paul's Cathedral on the day of thanksgiving (7th July). [By this time the queen was too ill to attend, but she heard the music privately later.] She did not love the Hanoverian court, and it was perhaps for this reason rather than because of any great appreciation of art that she rewarded the Hanoverian *Capellmeister* with a salary of £200 for life. It was a means of keeping him away from his German patron. As he was already in receipt of £300 a year from the court of Hanover, and was at no expense for board and lodging, he must have been in very comfortable circumstances for a bachelor. To what uses he put the money he was able to earn will appear in the course of this narrative.

Finding life very pleasant and profitable in London, Handel outstayed his leave of absence, and indeed seems to have made up his mind never to return to Hanover.

He was living and working practically in the country, where the first Earl of Burlington's love of solitude had caused him, in the middle of the seventeenth century, to build a house 'in the middle of the fields, where no one would come and build beside him.' Gay refers to 'Burlington's fair palace' in *Trivia*:

> There Hendel strikes the strings, the melting strain
> Transports the soul and thrills through every vein;
> There oft I enter.

All that was expected of Handel in return for the hospitality given him was that he should direct the earl's concerts, and this comfortable arrangement might have gone on for some time but for the death of Queen Anne on 1st August 1714. She was succeeded by Handel's employer, the Elector of Hanover, who was about to be crowned at Westminster with the title of George the First of England. Handel carefully avoided him. Not only had he broken his engagement, but in composing the Utrecht *Te Deum* he had given further offence, because the Treaty of Utrecht was not liked in Germany.

CHAPTER V

THE elector landed at Greenwich on 18th September 1714 and was crowned at Westminster Abbey on 20th October. Handel must have looked on with some fear for his future prospects. For a servant to absent himself without leave from a court was, in those days, an unpardonable offence. A *Capellmeister* was, as we have seen, in the position of a servant who, once having accepted office, could not resign without permission from his employer. Handel had now been some two years in London. He had long overstepped the 'reasonable time' for which he was given leave of absence. He had accepted a pension from Queen Anne, who was bitterly opposed to the Hanoverian succession and had taken no pains to conceal her aversion; he had provided a splendid piece of music for a Tory celebration, which was entirely distasteful to the Whigs, the supporters of the Hanoverian dynasty. He therefore carefully abstained from presenting himself at court and continued his quiet retired life at Burlington House. He composed a small opera called *Silla*, which was never performed in public; Chrysander suggests that it may have been performed privately at Burlington House, but there is no record of the matter. Schoelcher thinks it was written at Rome; but there was no opera house there in those days, and Handel was not the man to waste time in composing anything that had not a reasonable chance of being performed. A copy of *Silla* in the British Museum (Add. MSS. 5334) is superscribed 'an opera by Gio. Bononcini.' Handel's original manuscript is at Buckingham Palace. Its small scope and the little significance of the songs are suggestive of its having been written for amateurs of no great skill.

The theatre was carried on by Heidegger, a remarkable man, something of a poet, a capable manager and the ugliest man in London. On this account his portrait was frequently engraved. He was of German descent, but born at Zürich, which, together with his overbearing manners, earned him the nickname of the 'Swiss Count.' Lord Chesterfield made a bet that no one so ugly could be found in London, but after a search an old woman was discovered and Heidegger was declared to be the handsomer of the two. But Lord Chesterfield won his bet by insisting on Heidegger's putting on the old woman's bonnet, when he appeared uglier than ever.

Heidegger gave ten performances of *Rinaldo* this season which were attended by the Prince and Princess of Wales, and arranged or wrote the libretto for a new opera by Handel, to be called *Amadigi*. The libretto is dedicated to the Earl of Burlington because the music was composed in his house. Much of the music of *Silla* is used in it, but in a more developed form.

The plot of the opera turns on the love of Melissa, a sorceress, for Amadis, who, finding that in spite of her machinations, her rival Oriana is preferred by her lover, kills herself. A rival of Amadis, Dardanus, also dies, and reappears as a ghost. The opera ends with a chorus in gavotte form, which is afterwards repeated by the instruments alone, during a dance on the stage. The new opera was produced at the King's Theatre, Haymarket, on 25th May 1715, with great splendour. The parts were sung by Nicolini, who had returned to England, Signore Vico and Schiavonetti, and Anastasia Robinson, a young English singer of great reputation, who afterwards became the wife of the Earl of Peterborough. We learn that in consequence of the unusual amount of machinery and scenes employed no persons, even the subscribers, were allowed to go behind the scenes on account of the danger they might incur. Amongst the novelties was a fountain with real water. An orchestral effect which Handel had previously used in *La Resurrezione* at Rome, but which was new to the English public, was that of the violins playing in octaves. The popularity of *Amadigi* is attested by the fact that a burlesque called *Amadis,* 'with all the sinkings, flyings, and usual decorations,' was produced at the theatre in Lincoln's Inn Fields.

[Handel was neither asked to write music for the coronation of George I, nor did he offer to do so. The breach was not yet healed, and although the king went secretly to *Amadigi* and to the revival of *Rinaldo,* he showed no signs of wishing to see his truant *Capellmeister* at his new court. Eventually a reconciliation was effected, however. Unfortunately the accounts of the occurrence are extremely confusing and seem to become further complicated rather than elucidated by research.

One story is that Geminiani, the famous violinist-composer, being anxious to secure the best possible accompanist for a performance before the king, pressed for permission to introduce Handel. It is far from certain that this request was granted, though it has been said that it was this appearance of Handel's at court which led to the confirmation of his salary of £200 by the king, who added another £200 of his own, and to Handel's appointment as music master to the daughters of the Prince of Wales at a further annual fee of the same amount.

According to other accounts it was the performance of the *Water Music* which restored Handel to the king's favour. This tale had now better be told, failing absolute certainty, as it is known by tradition, and then followed by such comments on some divergent views of it as may tend to modify the reader's own judgment.

Baron Kielmansegge, who was now in England and Master of the Horse to the king, arranged, it seems, a picnic party on the Thames for the king, the Prince and Princess of Wales and a number of courtiers. The date given is 22nd August 1715. They proceeded in barges from Whitehall to Lime-house. The baron persuaded Handel to supply some music to be played in a barge following that occupied by the king in close proximity, and the pieces written for the occasion after-wards became known as the *Water Music*. They were scored for four violins, one viol, one violoncello, one double bass, two oboes, two bassoons, two horns, two flageolets, one flute and one trumpet. The king, much struck by the charm and skill, the melodiousness and variety of the music, asked who had composed it, and Handel was ushered into his presence. He praised the work, forgave the culprit and may on this occasion, rather than on that already mentioned, have bestowed his extra salary of £200 on him.

The first comment to be made is that it is curious, if this is really what happened, that Handel did not re-enter the service of his patron. He continued to reside at Burlington House and had no connection with the court beyond the lessons he gave to the children of the Prince of Wales. No official title was bestowed on him.]

Then the *Daily Courant* of 19th July 1717 gives the following account:

On Wednesday evening at about 8, the King took water at Whitehall in an open barge, wherein were also the dutchess of Bolton, the dutchess of Newcastle, the Countess of Godolphin, Madam Kilmanseck, and the Earl of Orkney, and went up the river towards Chelsea. Many other barges with persons of quality attended, and so great a number of boats, that the whole river in a manner was covered: a city company's barge was employed for the musick, wherein were fifty instruments of all sorts, who play'd all the way from Lambeth (while the barges drove with the tide, without rowing, as far as Chelsea), the finest symphonies, composed express for this occasion, by Mr. Hendel: which His Majesty liked so well, that he caused it to be played over three times in going and returning. At eleven, His Majesty went ashoar at Chelsea, where a supper was prepared, and then there was another very fine consort of musick which lasted till 2: after which His Majesty came again into his barge, and returned the same way, the musick continuing to play till he landed.

[Mr. Newman Flower takes this as conclusive proof that the *Water Music* incident cannot have taken place in 1715, and it is certainly tempting to follow him in this, as the earlier story may quite possibly be a fabrication, although a definite date is assigned to it, while the later one cannot but be true. The fact that Handel is definitely known to have enjoyed the favour of George I again before 1717 cannot be held against Mr. Flower, since he may have regained it through his introduction at court by Geminiani. Still, it is extremely likely that music by Handel was played on the river more than once, and not necessarily the same music. Probably the solution suggested by Professor Edward J. Dent, who follows Streatfeild, is the right one: it certainly seems plausible that Handel wrote at least two different sets of pieces for these aquatic performances, and that when he published the *Water Music,* which was not till 1740, it may have been the whole of, or a selection from, the two sets.

No new opera was written by Handel for the season of 1716, which was given over to the revival of various older works, both by himself and by other composers, the reason being, no doubt, that they were new to the king.] In July George went to Hanover and Handel accompanied him. During this visit he set to music the poem of the famous Passion Oratorio by Brockes, *Der für die Sünder der Welt gemarterte und sterbende Jesus,* which had been set by Keiser in 1712 and was used later by Telemann and Mattheson. Handel's

version was performed in Hamburg in 1717. Bach copied
the score, calling it, in an odd mixture of Latin and Italian,
Oratorium Passionale : Poesia di Brocks et Musica di Handel. His
copy has in one place different words from the other copies.
The work is in the usual form of recitatives, arias and choruses,
with a portion of the chorale *Schmücke dich, o liebe Seele* to be
sung by the congregation. Handel's inveterate habit of
utilizing old work for new compositions led him to incorporate
the music of the prayer in Gethsemane, 'Mein Vater, ist's
möglich, so lass den Kelch vorübergehen,' into Haman's
prayer to the queen for pity in *Esther*, a proceeding for which, as
Chrysander says, 'no one can praise him.' Much of the music
is taken from his previous works, and most of what is new was
used for later works: *Esther, Deborah* and the opera *Giulio Cesare*.

His old friend Mattheson took the opportunity of his being
in Germany to write several letters to him on the subject of
his book, *Das neu eröffnete Orchester.* Handel afterwards wrote the
following letter in French to him, which is not without interest:

SIR,—The letter I have just received from you obliges me to
answer you more fully than I have previously done on the two
points in question. I do not hesitate to assert that my opinion is in
general conformity with that which you have so well expounded
and proved in your book on solmization and the Greek modes. The
question, it seems to me, reduces itself to this: whether one ought to
prefer a method which is easy and one of the most perfect, or one
which is full of great difficulties, capable not only of disgusting music
students, but also causing them to waste valuable time, which could
be far better used in exploring art and cultivating the natural gifts.
Not that I would say that one can find absolutely no use in solmization; but since one can acquire the same knowledge in far less time
by the method which is so successfully used at present, I do not see
why one should not choose the road which leads us more easily
and in less time to the object desired.

As to the Greek modes, I find, sir, that you have said all that
can be said on them. A knowledge of them is doubtless necessary

to those who wish to practise and perform ancient music composed in these modes; but since we are now freed from the narrow limits of ancient music, I do not see of what use the Greek modes can be in modern music. These, sir, are my sentiments, and I should be glad if you would let me know whether they respond to what you expect from me.

With regard to the second point, you can judge for yourself that it requires a good deal of research, which I am unable to give owing to my many pressing engagements. When I am a little less occupied, I will think over the more important epochs in the course of my profession, in order that you may see the esteem with which I have the honour to be, sir,

Your very Humble and Obedient Servant,

G. F. HANDEL.

LONDON, 24*th Feb.* 1719.

Handel's views will probably be subscribed to by most practical, active musicians. The study of solmization and the Greek modes is interesting to those who have leisure for antiquarian pursuits, but it is of no value to the composer.

The second question, as to personal details of his life, Handel had no time to discuss. The interviewer was not yet in existence, and Handel would certainly have resented his presence if he had been.

In 1716 he visited Anspach, a small town near Homburg, though in what capacity, or how long he stayed there, is not known. Here, we are told, he met Johann Christoph Schmidt, whom he had known as a fellow-student at the university of Halle, and who was 'so captivated with his powers, that he accompanied him to England, where he became known as John Christopher Smith and regulated the expenses of Handel's public performances, filling the office of treasurer with great fidelity.' He also acted as secretary and copyist.[1]

Handel, as usual, took an opportunity of visiting Halle. Zachau was dead, his widow in very poor circumstances and

[1] Anecdotes of Handel and Smith, quoted by Schoelcher, p. 44.

60

her son a ne'er-do-well. He made a point of sending her remittances from time to time in repayment for the kindness he had received from her husband, and he would have done the same for a more worthy son.

It is not known exactly when he returned to England; Chrysander says about Christmas 1716, by which time his *Concerto grosso* in F major (Op. 3, No. 4)[1] was composed for the benefit of the Opera orchestra. In 1717 *Rinaldo* and *Amadigi* were given, but no new work appeared, and at the end of June the opera season closed without any prospect of renewal. It suffered from lack of support and the theatre was given over to French dancers. Handel had to seek other employment. This he found at Canons,[2] a great palace in the Italian style near Edgware, which has now disappeared. The Earl of Carnarvon,[3] in his capacity of paymaster to Queen Anne's army, had amassed an enormous fortune, and had built this mansion at a cost of £230,000. The greatest luxury and magnificence was maintained here, and the earl, who was strongly suspected of having made his huge fortune by peculation, but 'who loved ever to worship the Lord with the best of everything,' had, amongst other things, a private chapel in the style of the churches of Italy. This chapel, however, was not the still existing church of Whitchurch or Little Stanmore,[4] but actually part of Canons itself. But the earl had the interior of Whitchurch decorated with frescoes by Verrio and Laguerre, two French artists who were sent for specially to paint them, and he also presented it with an organ case by Grinling Gibbons, not to mention a valuable set of communion plate.

[1] Opus numbers were used only for instrumental works in those days, and in Handel's case they were not chronological even so.

[2] Called Cannons in contemporary accounts.

[3] He was not created Duke of Chandos until April 1719.—E. B.

[4] As the author in the first edition says, following an old tradition only too solidly established by other writers.—E. B.

In the Canons chapel itself a full orchestra was maintained under the direction of a resident chapel-master, as in foreign courts. The first holder of the post was Dr. Pepusch, who was dismissed in Handel's favour in 1718, but never seems to have borne him any ill-will afterwards.

Handel set to work in his new post with great enthusiasm. Like Haydn in later times at Esterház, he now had good singers, a chorus and orchestra entirely at his disposal, as well as a cultured audience to listen to his productions, for many of the nobility and gentry came to hear the services. He remained at Canons some three years,[1] during which time he wrote the twelve Chandos Anthems for solos and chorus of three, four and five voices, on the model of the motet or cantata of the Lutheran Church, and preceded by an overture, the words being selected from the Psalms. Some of these anthems were afterwards rearranged by him for use in the chapel of George I.

At Canons also he wrote the masque of *Haman and Mordecai,* later named *Esther,*[2] whether by command of the duke or of his own free will is not known. The text was arranged by Pope, from Racine's *Esther,* and the music was largely borrowed from the Brockes Passion. It was performed on the stage at Canons, 29th August 1720, but was in reality Handel's first English oratorio, designed to introduce to the English people a form of music which they had not yet heard. But it was not performed in public till twelve years later. Its overture was thereafter played every year for more than half a century, together

[1] He was not continually in residence there, his patron having a town house in Albemarle Street.—E. B.

[2] The Whitchurch organ bears an inscription recording that 'Handel was organist of this church from 1718 to 1721 and composed the oratorio of *Esther* upon this organ,' a twofold mistake, Handel being attached to the private chapel at Canons, not to the parish church, and being, needless to say, at no time in his life given to composing at the organ.—E. B.

with the Utrecht *Te Deum,* at the Festival of the Sons of the Clergy at St. Paul's Cathedral.

At Canons was also composed the serenata of *Acis and Galatea,* to words by John Gay. In Randall's edition it is called a 'mask' and in a text-book printed at Dublin 'the celebrated masque.' In a copy made by Smith in 1720 it is called a 'pastoral.' It is quite different from the *Aci, Galatea e Polifemo* composed at Naples in 1708. A concerto was played on the organ by Handel between the acts when the work was performed in public, but at Canons it seems to have been originally performed with scenery but without action; there was no break in the music.

Handel's first instrumental publication, *Suites de Pièces pour le Clavecin,* said to have been composed for Princess Anne, appeared on 14th November 1720. It was announced in the *Daily Courant,* under the title of *Lessons for the Harpsichord.* The publisher was Cluer. The preface ran:

I have been obliged to publish Some of the following Lessons, because Surrepticious and incorrect Copies of them had got Abroad. I have added several new ones to make the Work more usefull, which if it meets with favourable Reception; I will Still proceed to publish more, reckoning it my duty, with my Small Talent, to serve a Nation from which I have receiv'd so Generous a Protection.–G. F. HANDEL.

• These pieces soon became universally popular and were reprinted in France, Switzerland, Holland and Germany; but the promised further supply was not published till 1733. It contains a chaconne with sixty-two variations on the same succession of chords as the Goldberg air to which Bach wrote thirty variations, but the treatment of the subject by the two composers is entirely different.

Handel's work is simply a popular air with variations, comparatively easy to play and perfectly plain to the ordinary listener. Bach embellishes the simple harmonic groundwork with every conceivable device of imitation, canon, augmentation, diminution, change of time signature and rhythm, and he demands the highest possible technical and intellectual skill from the performer. This difference, which is found more or less throughout the works of the two composers, is quite sufficient to explain why Handel was always popular, while Bach's music but slowly won its way to favour.

HANDEL.

BACH.

The set of variations known as the *Harmonious Blacksmith* occurs amongst the *Suites de Pièces* written at Canons. How the name arose is not known: perhaps some fanciful editor gave it, as was the case with Beethoven's so-called 'Moonlight' Sonata. It is quite certain that Handel never used it. Crotch stated that he had seen a book at Cambridge containing the melody of this piece attributed to Wagenseil.[1] But various traditions and stories have arisen, which, although well known, must be referred to here. The first is that Handel took shelter from the rain in the shop of a blacksmith named Powell in the village of Edgware, and that the blacksmith sang an old song in time to the hammer as it struck the anvil, the sound of which seems to have harmonized with some of the melody. On returning home the composer worked the blacksmith's song up in the way that is so familiar to all. Another tradition is that the tune was suggested by a combination of the note produced by the church bell which happened to be tolling and that of the anvil. Richard Clark, in *Reminiscences of Handel,* claims to have discovered Powell's anvil, and Schoelcher says that a square shed was pointed out to him in the middle of the village street at Edgware as Powell's forge. Rockstro traces the history of Powell's anvil and hammer, which, after passing through various hands, were sold to Mr. Maskelyne of the Egyptian Hall in 1879. The anvil, when struck, sounds the note B and immediately afterwards E.

[The versions of this legend are suspiciously numerous and varied, but they may be said to have been finally disposed of by Newman Flower, whose elaborate and convincing account is unfortunately too long to quote here. Professor Dent's succinct summary in his small book on Handel [2] may, how-

---

[1] Who was five years of age when the Suites were published! —E. B.

[2] Duckworth's 'Great Lives' series.

ever, usefully be given. The air of the *Harmonious Blacksmith,* he says,

was never called by this name before 1820; about that time a young music-seller at Bath, who had previously been a blacksmith's apprentice, earned the nickname of 'the harmonious blacksmith' because he was always singing that particular tune. Somehow the name got transferred from the singer to the song, and in 1835 the story of Handel's having been inspired to compose the tune after hearing a blacksmith at Edgware produce musical notes from his anvil was first put into print in a letter to *The Times*. Not long afterwards an imaginary blacksmith of Edgware was invented, and his alleged anvil sold by auction.]

Handel must have frequently had occasion to traverse the nine miles of road between Canons and London, which was infested with highwaymen, so that it was not safe for any one to go without a retinue. On two successive days in February 1720 the Duke of Chandos was himself attacked by highwaymen, some of whom were killed and others captured by his servants.

The chief events of Handel's connection with Canons having been told consecutively, it will now be necessary to turn back to others which happened during that time. On 8th August 1718 Handel's sister, Dorothea Sophia, the wife of Michaelsen, died at Halle. He thereupon wrote to his brother-in-law:

SIR, MY VERY HONOURED BROTHER,—Do not judge, I pray you, of my wish to see you by my delay in starting: it is to my great regret that I find myself kept here by affairs which are unavoidable, and on which I may say my fortune depends, and which have dragged on longer than I expected. If you knew the pain that I feel in not having been able to do what I so fervently desire, you will forgive me. But I hope these affairs will be over in a month from now, and you may count upon my making no delay, and that I shall travel without stopping. I entreat you, my very dear brother, to assure Mamma of this and of my obedience, and to let me know how you are, and how are Mamma and your dear family, in order to lessen my anxiety and impatience. You can imagine, my very dear brother, how inconsolable I should be, had I not the hope of shortly making up for this delay by staying with you all the longer. I am astonished that the Magdeburg merchant has not yet executed my letter of exchange: I beg you to keep it, and it shall be set right on my arrival. I have received notice that the pewter will soon be sent to you. I am ashamed of the delay, and that I have not been able ere this to fulfil my promise: I beg you to excuse me, and to believe that in spite of all my efforts I have been unable to succeed. You will agree with me when I am able to explain it by word of mouth. You may have no doubt that I shall hasten my journey: I am longing to see you more than you can imagine. I thank you very humbly for your good wishes for the New Year.[1] I for my part trust that the Almighty will give you and your dear family every kind of prosperity, and will soften by his precious blessings the trouble he has seen fit to bring upon you and me. You may rest assured that I shall always preserve the memory of the kindness you have shown to my late sister, and that these sentiments will continue as long as my life. Have the goodness to give my compliments to Mr. Rotth, and all my good friends. I embrace you and all my dear family, and I am with lifelong affection,

> Sir, your very honoured brother,
> Your very humble and obedient servant,
>
> GEORGE FRIDERIC HANDEL.

To Mr. Michael Dietrich Michaelsen,
  Doctor of Law, Halle, Saxony.

This letter was written in French, which was then the universal language of polite society. Handel, once settled in England, always spelt his second name in the way given here. The sermon preached at the funeral of Dorothea Sophia

---

[1] It is clear that the news of Handel's loss was considerably delayed. The letter above is dated 20th February 1719.

was published by the university printer of Halle and is extant, together with about a dozen poems upon her. Michaelsen seems to have done all he could for her. As she was in a consumption, he had bought a property near Halle, hoping that the country air might prolong her life, but she died before he was able to move to it.

At Canons Handel had not only to compose, but in his capacity of chapel-master had to train the choir and teach the principal singers his own peculiar style of music. But this did not fill all the time or energies of one gifted with so extra-ordinary a power for work, and he was soon called upon to act in another capacity. In 1719 the Government, being anxious to get rid of unredeemable annuities amounting to £800,000 per annum, offered them for sale. The South Sea Company and the Bank of England competed for their purchase, and the former bought at seven and a half million pounds, with the right of paying off the annuitants at eight and a quarter years' purchase. Subscriptions were opened by the South Sea Company; the whole nation engaged in specula-tion; dozens of bubble companies were started; the South Sea Company took proceedings against them and thus alarmed its subscribers, who soon found that it was the biggest bubble company of them all. The well-known crash came, and thousands of families were ruined.

Among the companies formed at this time was one for the promotion of Italian opera, founded by a committee of twenty noblemen in 1719. Though it proved eventually to be a failure, it was begun in all good faith. Fifty thousand pounds was privately subscribed, of which the king gave £1000, and the enterprise took the name of the 'Royal Academy of Music.' The names of some of the original members are given by Hawkins and Burney. The first year the Duke of Newcastle was governor and Lord Bingley deputy-governor. The directors were the Dukes of Portland

and Queensberry, Earls of Burlington, Stair and Waldegrave; Lords Chetwynd and Stanhope; Generals Dormer, Wade and Hunter; Sir John Vanbrugh; Colonel Blathwayt, who had as a child been a pupil of Alessandro Scarlatti, and at the age of twelve had astonished every one by his harpsichord playing; Colonel O'Hara, Brigadier-General Hunter, Conyers D'Arcy, Bryan Fairfax, Thomas Coke or Cole, William Pulteney, George Harrison and Francis Whitworth. Heidegger was engaged as manager. This enterprise was not intended to be run merely as a speculation, but was an effort in the cause of the best musical art, which had hitherto failed for want of adequate support.

It must be remembered that at this time there did not exist what we should call a musical public. The mass of the people were not sufficiently educated to appreciate anything of the nature of art; the middle classes, the landowners, were deeply prejudiced against music, considering that it was a foreign luxury which, if tolerated, would inevitably lead to a decadence of the British race. Italian opera was in 1720 cultivated only by the more intelligent and intellectual of the aristocracy. It became the fashion for the wealthy to have a box at the opera, and it was reserved for Handel, after years of incredible efforts, to establish, through his oratorios, a public in England which could be refined in manners and improved in morals by the highest productions of musical art.

The Royal Academy of Music set to work in earnest. Giovanni Battista Bononcini was invited to take up his residence in England as composer at the beginning of the second season, in November 1720, and soon afterwards Attilio Ariosti was brought from Berlin for this purpose. Bononcini's opera, *Thomyris,* had recently been fitted with English words by Haym, and performed with fair success under the management of MacSwiney at the theatre in Lincoln's Inn Fields, so that he was not unknown to English opera-goers. Handel was also engaged both as composer and impresario, for which purpose he sought and easily obtained leave of absence from the Duke of Chandos, who, though he may have been unwilling to let him go, could not refuse his taking part in an enterprise in which the king was interested. He at once set out for Dresden, where the Elector of Saxony, Frederick Augustus I, who was also King Augustus II of Poland, maintained an Italian company and had operas performed in the most perfect and splendid manner possible.

CHAPTER VI

THE HEY-DAY OF OPERA

Applebee's Weekly Journal of 21st February 1719 announces that 'Mr. Hendel, a famous Master of Musick, is gone beyond sea, by order of his majesty, to collect a company of the choicest singers in Europe for the opera in the Haymarket.' He must therefore have started immediately after sending the letter quoted in the last chapter to his brother-in-law, in which he said he could not leave for another month. He first went to Düsseldorf, where he engaged Benedetto Baldassari, an eminent tenor singer, and then visited Hanover. In the autumn he was at Dresden, where he found a large company of the best Italian singers, who, with Lotti, were celebrating the wedding of the elector with the Archduchess Maria Josepha of Austria. Here he after a time succeeded in engaging Margherita Dura-stanti, who according to Gerber was specially excellent in male characters, and Senesino, an artificial soprano, whose real name was Francesco Bernardi. They were not imme-diately available, however. *Applebee's Weekly Journal* announces on 31st December 1719 that 'Signor Senesino, the famous Italian eunuch has arrived, and 'tis said that the company allows him two thousand guineas for the season.' Other singers engaged by Handel from the Dresden company were Berenstadt, a German born and trained in Italy; Boschi, a bass whom he had met at Naples and who had sung in *Rinaldo* in 1711 [1]; Signora Salvai, and a tenor called Ber-selli. During this visit to Dresden he played on the harpsichord

[1] According to Julian Marshall in Grove's *Dictionary of Music and Musicians.*

before the elector, who presented him with a hundred ducats as a mark of his appreciation of his wonderful powers. The gift was made in February 1720, but Handel had probably played some time previously.[1] The well-known challenge of Bach to Marchand had taken place at Dresden in 1717. Bach had been promised a reward, but it was purloined by a court official, and never reached him. The nature of these two great artists, who had so much in common in their lofty view of the profession they were called upon to exercise, differed essentially in money matters. Bach was satisfied with a bare living wage, sufficient to maintain himself and his numerous family in decent comfort of the artisan standard. Handel earned and saved many thousands of pounds, which he devoted to the highest possible uses—the furtherance of the art of music and the relief of the unfortunate.

Handel took the opportunity of being in Germany to pay the promised visit to his mother and brother-in-law at Halle. The exact time of his being there is unknown, but in the autumn of 1719 Bach journeyed from Cöthen to visit him there and found that he had that very day set out for England.

Too much has been made of this and a later similar incident. The biographers of Bach are apt to hint that Handel was not anxious to meet Bach, while those of Handel endeavour to explain that Bach might have taken more trouble to get to Halle in time, if he was really anxious to meet him. But journeys were slow and laborious in those days. Bach was very eager to learn all that he could of his art and, admiring Handel greatly, took some trouble to meet him. Handel, an excessively busy man, was not living a quiet life of study, and was probably not disposed to give up perhaps a whole day to a possibly dull interview with a learned cantor, who knew nothing of the excitements of operatic life. There is no reason to find fault with either. Any busy professional man, to

[1] Chrysander, ii. 18.

whom time is of the utmost importance, will sympathize with Handel, while the quiet, earnest student, not overburdened with this world's goods or excitements, will have an equal sympathy with Bach.

Handel appears to have returned to England some time before November 1719, and the meetings of the directors of the new Academy began in that month. Besides composers and singers, the Royal Academy engaged an Italian poet, Antonio Rolli, to write words for the operas, and to act as 'Italian Secretary to the Academy.' The Academy proposed to give fifty representations during the season, which began on 2nd April 1720 at the King's Theatre in the Haymarket. The prices of tickets for subscribers were ten guineas on delivery of the ticket, and two further payments of five guineas each, but a reduction was to be made in case less than fifty representations took place. A difficulty arose from the fact that a company of French comedians had been for a long time in possession of the theatre, but it was got over by an arrangement by which they were to have the house for half the week and the Royal Academy for the other half.

The Academy was at once attacked by Steele, who started a newspaper in defence of English plays. On 1st March 1720 this paper, *The Theatre,* announced: 'Yesterday, South Sea 179; Opera Company, 83½. No transfer.' On 8th March: 'At the rehearsal on Friday last, Signior Nihilini Benedetti (i.e. Benedetto Baldassari) rose half a note above his pitch formerly known. Opera Stock, from 83½ when began; at 90 when he ended.' Again: 'This Signior announced in recitative style to the assembled opera directors, that he was not accustomed to play any part below that of a Sovereign or Prince of the blood; and therefore it was allowed him that Tigranes, which was his part in Handel's *Radamisto,* should be raised from a simple officer to a prince.'[1]

[1] Quoted from Chrysander, vol. ii, p. 30.

Shares were sold at £100, each coupon entitling the holder to a seat for the time the company should last. The prices of the ordinary seats were ten shillings and five shillings, but they were raised or lowered according to circumstances. The season opened with *Numitor,* composed by Giovanni Porta of Venice, which was performed five times, and was followed on 27th April by *Radamisto,* written by Haym, the music composed by Handel specially for the Academy. Burney says: 'The composition of this opera is more solid, ingenious and full of fire than any drama which Handel had yet produced in this country.' The opera had been announced for 26th April, but was postponed in order to allow the French comedians to play, 'by particular desire of several ladies of quality.' Mainwaring tells us that

the applause it received was almost as extravagant as his *Agrippina* had excited; the crowds and tumults of the house at Venice were hardly equal to those at London. In so splendid and fashionable an assembly of ladies (to the excellence of their taste we must impute it), scarce indeed any appearance of order or regularity, politeness or decency. Many who had forced their way into the house with an impetuosity but ill-suited to their rank and sex, actually fainted through the heat and closeness of it. Several gentlemen were turned back who had offered forty shillings for a seat in the gallery, after having despaired of getting any seat in the pit or boxes.

Although the Academy had made a rule of allowing none of the audience on the stage, it broke it and advertised: 'To be admitted on the stage, one guinea.' The opera ran for ten nights and was performed many times in subsequent seasons. Handel subscribes himself in the book of words 'His Majesty's most faithful subject,' but he was not a subject of George until 1726, when he was naturalized by a private Act. Great pains were taken with the engraving and printing of this opera, which was published by the author and corrected by him. The printer was Richard Meares, at the Golden

Viol, who says in his advertisement that 'he presumes to assert that there hath not been in Europe a piece of music so well printed and upon so good paper.' In 1721 forty-one pages of additional songs were published by Meares, and presented gratis to purchasers of the opera.

There was a general consensus of opinion that *Radamisto* was by far the finest opera that had yet appeared on the London stage, or perhaps any. Handel himself told Hawkins that he considered the arias 'Cara sposa' (in *Rinaldo*) and 'Ombra cara' (in *Radamisto*) to be the best he had composed. The work consisted of the usual alternations of recitative and aria, with a long final chorus sung by all the soloists. The story, taken from Tacitus' *Annals*, is merely strung together for the sake of opportunities for music; the dramatic effects are entirely dependent on the excellence of Handel's composition. Portions of it are adapted from the Latin motet *Silete, venti* and from the German Passion Music.

The part of Radamisto, originally written for soprano, was afterwards rewritten for contralto, and that of Tiridate, originally for a tenor, was transposed to bass for Boschi.

The work was performed at Hamburg in 1722 under the name of *Zenobia,* with a German translation, but the Italian arias were retained. A company similar to that of the Royal Academy was started at Hamburg on this occasion.

Radamisto was succeeded by Domenico Scarlatti's *Narciso,* under the direction of his pupil, Thomas Roseingrave, but it had no great success. But in November 1720 Bononcini was brought to London by Lord Burlington, and the second season began at the King's Theatre with that composer's *Astarto,* which was given thirty times. Bononcini, who was thirteen years older than Handel, thus at once met with a decided success, aided by a brilliant cast of singers, including Senesino, who was now well established in London, and the publication of his *Cantate e Duetti,* dedicated to the king in 1721, brought him in one thousand guineas. *Astarto* was shortly afterwards performed at Hamburg. Ariosti, who was known to Londoners by two operas performed in 1716, produced *Ciro* in 1721.

Rivalries soon began to appear. The aristocracy of those days would seem to have been never happy unless they could foster some kind of competition between musicians. We have seen that Handel had already competed as a performer with Domenico Scarlatti in Italy; it was now his fate to be the victim of a foolish and ignoble party warfare, which, beginning with what may have been a friendly competition, ended by ruining him. Bononcini's operas were undoubtedly for a time more favourably received than those of Handel, and the admirers of each were rapidly dividing into two rival parties. It was proposed that they should try their strength in an opera, of which one act was to be composed by Bononcini and another by Handel. But since a serious opera was unthinkable unless it had three acts at least, the services of Filippo Mattei, a violoncellist in the orchestra, who went by the name of Pipo, were called upon. Rolli wrote a libretto, and on 15th April 1721 the opera called *Muzio Scevola* was produced. The first act was by Pipo,[1] the second by Bononcini and the third by Handel. Each act had its own overture and chorus, and was therefore practically a complete short opera.

The issue was doubtful; the partisans of both Handel and Bononcini claimed the victory, though Burney and Hawkins say that it undoubtedly lay with Handel. The performance

[1] Burney, Mainwaring and Hawkins say that Ariosti was the coadjutor of Handel and Bononcini in *Muzio Scevola*, and Rockstro accepts their statement. A manuscript in the Dragonetti collection at the British Museum and a notice in Mattheson's *Musikalischer Patriot*, point to Mattei; Chrysander considered him more likely to have been the composer, because he thought Ariosti was not in England at the time. The matter is not of great importance.

anned into a flame the spirit of dislike towards Handel which was rising among the aristocracy. Burney says that the employment of the three composers on the same work was not done by way of competition, but merely to save time; and that it was a device often resorted to in Italy for this purpose. But whatever the cause, the result remained that the public took it as a contest. Both composers, however, continued to be employed by the Academy as long as it lasted.

Besides the difficulties arising from the rival factions supporting Handel and Bononcini, financial troubles began. Constant calls of five per cent on the subscribers are found in the advertisement columns of the newspapers of the time. In November 1721 new directors were chosen and a new financial scheme was arranged. It does not belong to our task here to follow the fortunes of the Royal Academy of Music to its untimely end, but only to refer to it in its relation to Handel. Besides operas, it occasionally gave concerts, at one of which, given on 5th July 1721 for the benefit of Durastanti, two new cantatas by 'Mr. Handel and Signor Sandoni' (at that time second cembalist at the opera) were announced, together with four songs and six duets by 'the famous Signor Steffani.'

The third season opened on 1st November 1721, and on 9th December *Floridante,* a new opera by Handel, set to words by Rolli, was brought out. Burney says that the overture was less pleasing to the public than others of Handel's because the subject of the fugue admitted of no countersubject. One can hardly imagine a modern audience influenced for or against a work by the technicalities of a fugue, and indeed it is difficult to believe anything of the kind of Handel's public. Bononcini followed four weeks later with *Crispo,* for which Rolli again supplied the libretto. It was performed seventy-eight times, and was succeeded by his *Griselda.* Meanwhile party strife was raging. The utter foolishness of it is shown by the fact that the Whigs espoused the cause of Handel and the Tories that of Bononcini;[1] as if the merits of composers had any connection whatever with political parties.

An epigram which was afterwards set as a 'cheerful glee for four voices' was written by John Byrom, a 'poet and stenographer,'[2] a physician, an amateur theologian, and a Fellow of Trinity College, Cambridge:

> Some say, compared to Bononcini,
> That Mynheer Handel's but a ninny;
> Others aver, that he to Handel
> Is scarcely fit to hold a candle.
> Strange all this difference should be
> 'Twixt Tweedledum and Tweedledee.

These lines were afterwards attributed to Swift. On the other hand Henry Carey, one of Handel's party, wrote:

> The envy and the wonder of mankind
> Must terminate, but never can thy lays;
> For when, absorbed in elemental flame,
> This world shall vanish, music will exist.
> Then their sweet strains, to native skies returning,
> Shall breathe in song of Seraphims and angels,
> Commix't and lost in Harmony eternal,
> That fills all Heaven!

One of Bononcini's admirers wrote of *Griselda*:

> Cast from her kingdom, from her Lord exiled,
> Griselda still was lamb-like, mute and mild.
> But Rolli's verse provoked the Saint to roar,
> She raved, she maddened, and her pinners tore.
> Till Bononcini smoothed the rugged strains,
> And sanctified the miserable scenes.

---

[1] According to Hawkins's *History*, vol. v, p. 276.

[2] He is thus quaintly described in Chambers's *Encyclopaedia*.

At each soft sound, again she felt her thought,
And all the nonsense dy'd beneath the note.
Appeas'd, she cried, it is enough, good Heaven!
Let Gaultier, and let Rolli be forgiven.

There is no doubt that though Bononcini's arias are now antiquated, their simplicity was more able to appeal to the general public of their day than the far more vigorous music of Handel. Bononcini's cause was warmly espoused by the Marlborough family, and when the duke died he was commissioned to write an anthem for the funeral. It was published by Walsh and is still extant. In the same year (1722) he published *Divertimenti da Camera, tradotti pel cembalo da quelli composti pel Violino o Flauto,* consisting of arrangements of his cantatas for violin and harpsichord. This had a large sale among his admirers.

The opera season lasted some seven to eight months in those days. That of 1721–2 closed on 16th June 1722 with a performance of *Griselda.* The chief singers engaged had been Senesino, Baldassari, Boschi, Anastasia Robinson and Salvai.

In the following season, on 12th January 1723, a new singer, Francesca Cuzzoni, appeared in a new opera, *Ottone,* by Handel. The words were by Haym, who had succeeded Rolli as secretary and poet. Burney considers this to be the best of Handel's operas. A duet, 'A' teneri affetti,' is written in what was at that time called the 'Lombardic style,' introduced by Vivaldi the violinist, consisting of continual syncopation. This style was used with good effect by Bach in the cantata *Freue dich, erlöste Schaar.* Of the song 'Affanni del pensier,' with its original scoring, Mainwaring relates that 'an eminent master' (probably Pepusch), who was not on good terms with Handel, said: 'That great bear was certainly inspired when he wrote that song.' The gavotte in the overture became at once popular and was played on every instrument from the organ to the salt-box of itinerant musicians.

Great difficulties had been experienced in getting Cuzzoni. She was certainly a finer singer than had yet appeared in London, but she had an uncertain temper, and was withal very ugly. Heidegger had engaged her at £2,000 for the season, had paid her £250, and she had promised to come in good time to rehearse Handel's new opera in the autumn of 1722. But she delayed coming and made every one anxious. Heidegger sent Sandoni, the second cembalist at the opera, to fetch her, and on the journey she suddenly married him. She finally arrived in London in the last week of December, a fortnight before the production of *Ottone*. The directors were able to charge four guineas for each seat when she performed.[1]

Handel had considerable trouble with Cuzzoni. She had as stubborn a temper as he had. In those days a composer was looked upon merely as the person who supplied a framework for the singer to elaborate at his or her own sweet will. Handel, however, rebelled against this traditional usage and insisted on having his music sung exactly as he had written it. During a rehearsal of *Ottone* she refused to sing 'Falsa immagine,' whereupon Handel seized her in his arms, saying: 'Madam, I know you are a very she-devil; but I will have you know that I am Beelzebub, the prince of the devils,' and made as though he would throw her out of the window. This action frightened her into compliance, and she sang the song exactly as it was written, with the result that she made one of her greatest successes with it.

For her benefit on 26th March she chose *Ottone*. Handel, to make up for his previous treatment of her, added three new songs and an entire new scene for her. The rush to hear her

[1] According to Malcolm, *Manners and Customs in London during the Eighteenth Century*; Rockstro, *Life of Handel*, p. 139, says five guineas.

on this occasion was so great that fifty guineas were paid for some of the seats. On 19th February 1723 a new opera by Ariosti, *Coriolano,* words by Haym, was produced with great success. A prison scene caused the ladies in the audience to weep. On 30th March Bononcini produced a new opera, *Erminia,* and on 14th May Handel brought out *Flavio,* which had eight representations, the last of which closed the season on 15th June. The composition was finished on 7th May, allowing just a week for rehearsals.

In July the opera company of the Royal Academy of Music paid a visit to Paris at the invitation of the Duke of Orleans and stayed there four months, under the conductorship of Bononcini. French society was entirely taken up with the merits of Italian music and the claims of the rival composers, as it was in London, where, Gay wrote to Swift,

the reigning amusement of the town, it is intirely music; real fiddles, bass viols, and hautboys; not poetical harps, lyres and reeds. There's nobody allowed to say, *I sing,* but an eunuch, or an Italian woman. Every body is grown now as great a judge of music, as they were, in your time, of poetry; and folks, that could not distinguish one tune from another, now daily dispute about the different stiles of Handel, Bononcini and Attilio [Ariosti]. . . . In London and Westminster, in all polite conversation, Senesino is daily voted to be the greatest man that ever lived.

Fielding, an admirer of Handel, writes in *Tom Jones:* 'It was Mr. Western's custom every afternoon as soon as he was drunk, to hear his daughter play on the harpsichord, for he was a great lover of music, and perhaps, had he lived in town, might have passed for a connoisseur, for he always excepted against the finest compositions of Mr. Handel.'

Opera was, as a rule, performed only two nights a week; on other nights various entertainments took place. Heidegger advertised 'Ridottos,' or masked balls, preceded by a concert given by the opera singers. These masked balls led to all kinds of improprieties, so that the Grand Jury of Middlesex took alarm. We learn from Malcolm (*Manners and Customs*) that the following presentment was made on 12th February 1723:

Whereas there has been lately published a proposal for six ridottos, or balls, to be managed by subscription, at the King's Theatre in Haymarket, we, the Grand Jury of the County of Middlesex, sworn to inquire for our sovereign Lord the King, and the body of this county, conceiving the same to be wicked and illegal practices, and which, if not timely suppressed, may promote debauchery, lewdness, and ill conversation; from a just abhorrence, therefore, of such sort of assemblies, which we apprehend are contrary to law and good manners, and give great offence to His Majesty's good and virtuous subjects, we do present the same, and recommend them to be prosecuted and suppressed as common nuisances to the public, as nurseries of lewdness, extravagance, and immorality, and also a reproach and scandal to civil government.

In consequence of this presentment the three last ridottos were given up, but they were renewed during the following season under the name of 'Balls.'

The fifth season, which opened on 27th November 1723, made a bad beginning. Ariosti's *Vespasiano,* produced on 14th January following, was so badly received that it threatened the very existence of Italian opera. Bononcini's *Farnace* and *Calfurnia* only served to cause so much dissension that opera stock was expected to fall; a call of five per cent was immediately made on the shareholders. Handel came to the rescue by hastily finishing his setting of a new libretto by Haym, *Giulio Cesare,* which was produced on 20th February 1724. Senesino made a great impression by his rendering of an accompanied recitative, 'Alma del gran Pompeo,' and in a song, 'Da tempesta.' During a subsequent performance a piece of machinery fell upon the stage just as Senesino had sung 'Cesare non seppe mai, che sia timore' ('Caesar knows not what fear is'), and the poor hero was so frightened that he trembled, lost his voice and began to cry.

This opera was published by Cluer and B. Creake in good style. The last opera of the season was a *pasticcio* called *Aquilio*, arranged by Ariosti.

Little is known of what Handel did between the opera seasons during those years of the Royal Academy, once he had left the service of the Duke of Chandos, though he was occupied to some extent by conducting private concerts for the Duke of Rutland, the Earl of Burlington and other members of the nobility. It would be a mistake to suppose that his time was fully taken up by the composition of operas, even when he produced more than one a season, for he composed with extreme rapidity. *Tamerlano,* the next opera to appear, at the opening of the sixth season, 31st October 1724, was completed in twenty days.

One incident of the summer of that year, however, is known. On 24th August Handel played the organ at St. Paul's Cathedral before his royal pupils, the Princesses Anne and Caroline. The instrument had been enlarged in 1720 and was considered to be one of the finest in Europe. In addition to instructing the princesses, he directed concerts for the royal family at the queen's library in Green Park, in which they and various aristocratic amateurs took part.

Tamerlano was

remarkable for the dramatic power exhibited in its closing scene, where the tyrant, Bajazet, who has taken poison, is tended by his daughter with such devoted affection that even Tamerlane is moved to pity. The tragic force of this powerful situation is irresistible. Its chief strength lies in the skill with which the composer leads up to the touching climax. So artistically is this accomplished that it would be difficult to find a similar catastrophe more effectively treated in any period of the history of art.[1]

---

[1] Rockstro, *Life of Handel,* p. 140.

It was published in score with English and Italian words.

In *Rodelinda,* which was produced on 13th February 1725, Cuzzoni made such a sensation that the brown silk dress, embroidered with silver, which she wore became the fashionable costume for the rest of the season. Another and far more objectionable fashion now arose of publishing the music of Handel's operatic songs with sacred words tacked on. The aria in *Rodelinda,* 'Dove sei, amato bene' ('Where art thou, my well beloved'), was turned by Preston into 'Hope, thou source of every blessing'; by Arnold, into 'Holy, holy, Lord God Almighty.' The fashion thus started soon took root. 'Rendi 'l sereno al ciglio' ('Smooth thy troubled brow'), in *Sosarme,* became 'Lord, remember David'; 'Non vi piacque' ('It did not please you'), in *Siroe,* became 'He was eyes to the blind'; 'Nel riposo,' in *Deidamia,* 'He was brought as a lamb,' and so on. 'The mania for putting everything into their prayers has betrayed the English into some most unworthy actions,' says Schoelcher. Fortunately, however, this mania has now died out, and when an operatic piece has to be sung in English a more or less acceptable translation is made use of in the present day.

But the religious mania was not the only thing from which Handel's music suffered, for low comedy and bacchanalian songs laid it under contribution. The famous gavotte in the overture to *Ottone* became a bacchanal, 'Bacchus, god of mortal pleasures, by Mr. Handel.' Words beginning, 'O my pretty Punchinello,' were adapted to a song in *Rodelinda,* 'Ben spesso in vago prato' ('Oft in fair meadow'), 'the music by Mr. Handel,' and the march in *Rinaldo* was introduced in *The Beggar's Opera.*

The whole of *Rodelinda* was published by Cluer in score, and also for the flute, soon after its appearance. It had few subscribers. Chrysander explains this by the fact that when Bononcini and Ariosti published operas they solicited subscriptions from house to house, a course to which Handel would never stoop.

During the time that Handel was busy as composer and manager of opera, others were performing his music elsewhere for their own profit, for there was no legal property in those days in literary or musical work. Walsh was busy pillaging and publishing the songs in *Acis and Galatea,* and the work itself was being constantly performed by different persons. Thus in 1731 Rich was performing it at his theatre in Lincoln's Inn Fields, and in 1732 a company at the New Theatre in the Haymarket was doing the same, with 'scenery, machines, and other decorations.' Handel's former cook, Waltz, who turned into an excellent bass singer and *viol da gamba* player, took the part of Polyphemus, while the Arnes, father, son and daughter, managed it. Poor Handel had no legal power to prevent these piracies; his only resource was to advertise a more complete performance of the work, with additions, and with Italian songs. He was obliged to take any course that might attract an audience, or he would not have inter-mingled Italian with English in a purely English work. 'He was fighting for bare existence against a band of sharpers, whose only care was how to fill their pockets most easily at his expense. The event proved that, in matters of worldly policy, he was considerably more than a match for his unscrupulous antagonists' (Rockstro).

CHAPTER VII

OPERA IN DECLINE

In 1724 the Royal Academy found that they could do without Bononcini, and therefore did not re-engage him. To make up for this, the Duchess of Marlborough settled on him a pension of £500 a year in order to keep him in England. He lived for some years longer in her house until he was forced to leave England, as will appear later.

About this time Handel became the tenant or owner of No. 57 Brook Street, Hanover Square, now No. 25, of which the rateable value was £35, and here he lived to the end of his life. It was a very suitable location for a composer, sufficiently removed from the noises of the town and yet within easy reach of the three theatres. It was also close to his parish church of St. George, Hanover Square, at which he was a regular attendant. He was a strict Lutheran, and he would often say that it was one of the great felicities of his life that he was settled in a country where no man suffers any molestation or inconvenience on account of his religious principles. The various Acts of Parliament directed against Romanists and Nonconformists were in reality not inspired by a spirit of intolerance against differences of religious opinion, but by political exigencies, and a foreigner who did not meddle with politics was in no way troubled by them.

[Handel was still assisted by the faithful Schmidt, now John Christopher Smith, whose son became his pupil about 1725, at the age of thirteen.]

The king went to Hanover in the summer of 1725, and

Handel hoped to have an opportunity of visiting his mother, who was now advanced in age. But his engagements were so pressing that he could not leave London. Like Bononcini, Ariosti was not re-engaged by the King's Theatre, so that Handel was now the only composer attached to the Academy. He wrote to his brother-in-law as follows:[1]

LONDON, *the* 22/11 *June* 1725.

SIR AND VERY HONOURED BROTHER,—Again I find myself very much in your debt through not having for a long time fulfilled my duty towards you in the matter of letters: nevertheless I do not despair of obtaining your generous pardon, when I assure you that it is not the result of forgetfulness, and that my esteem and friendship for you are inviolable, as you will have found, my very much honoured brother, by the remarks which are contained in my letters to my mother. My silence has rather been from a fear of troubling you with a correspondence which might weary you. But what has made me overcome these reflections, in inconveniencing you by the present letter, is that I would not be so ungrateful as to pass over in silence the kindness that you have shown towards my mother, by your assistance and consolation in her advanced age, without at least giving you some sign of my very humble thanks. You will not be unaware of how much everything regarding her affects me, and you will therefore be able to judge under what obligations I am to you. I shall esteem myself happy, my very dear brother, if I can persuade you to give me from time to time some news of yourself, and you may be assured of the sincere interest I shall feel, and of the faithful reply you will always obtain from me. I had hoped to be able to renew my intercourse with you by word of mouth, and to make a journey to your neighbourhood when the king goes to Hanover; but my endeavours have not been successful this time, and the position of my affairs deprives me of this happiness, though I still hope to have so great a pleasure some day. Meanwhile, it will be a very great consolation to me if I dare flatter myself that you will accord me some place in your memory, and honour

---

[1] The letter is in French.

me with your friendship, since I shall never cease being, with unalterable love and attachment,

Sir,

Your very honoured Brother,
Your very humble and
obedient Servant,

GEORGE FRIDERIC HANDEL.

I make my very humble respects to your wife,[1] and I tenderly embrace my dear godchild and the rest of your dear family; my compliments, if you please, to all my friends.

On 14th February 1726 Handel took the oath of allegiance in the House of Lords as a naturalized British subject, and was nominated 'Composer of Musick to the Chapel Royal' next to Croft.

On 12th March he produced *Scipione,* the composition of which was finished on 2nd March. The words were by Rolli. It opens with the well-known march in D. The Grenadier Guards claim that this march, which they still play, was specially composed for them by Handel before its introduction into the opera.[2] It was introduced in Gay's *Polly,* the sequel to *The Beggar's Opera.* The singers in *Scipione* were Cuzzoni, Constantini, Senesino, Baldi, Antinori and Boschi.

Not two months after, on 5th May, yet another new opera was produced, *Alessandro,* which ran continuously till 7th June, on which day the season closed. The composition was finished on 11th April, so that nearly a month, an unusual length of time, was allowed for rehearsals. This opera is important as being the first in which the famous Faustina Bordoni, who later became the wife of Hasse, appeared. She had long been expected. Negotiations had been carried on

---

[1] i.e. his second wife.
[2] Rockstro, *Life of Handel,* p. 143.

for years with her. Her reputation was enormous; and she was quite clever enough to see that by delaying her appearance she would not only increase the eagerness of the public, but would be offered higher terms. She was finally engaged at £2,500 for the season, Cuzzoni receiving £2,000. She was as good-looking as Cuzzoni was ill-favoured; she had a wonderful command of vocal dexterity and a knack of imperceptibly taking breath, so that she could apparently hold out a note for any length of time. Handel had the difficult task of writing for both Faustina and Cuzzoni in such a manner as to favour neither at the expense of the other. He caused them both to appear at once in a recitative for two voices, in which Roxana and Lisaura, the two mistresses of Alexander, expressed their love and their jealousy. He managed that the arias for each should be so suitable to their respective excellences that they each obtained equal applause; while in a duet each voice had alternately the principal part. His treatment was naturally not appreciated by the fops, who were anxious to see Cuzzoni sung down, but the result proved so attractive that the opera was given three times a week instead of only twice, which was the normal number of weekly performances. One of the secrets of Handel's success as a composer was his power of adapting his music to the peculiar qualities of each individual performer.

Senesino had another slight accident in this opera, which caused much laughter. In his prowess in leading his soldiers to the assault of Ossidraca he so far forgot himself in the heat of the combat as to stick his sword through one of the pasteboard stones of the town wall, and bear it in triumph before him as he entered the breach.[1]

Another contest was now on hand; not this time between rival composers, but between the two prima donnas, in spite of Handel's efforts to prevent it. The compass of their voices

[1] *World*, 8th February 1753.

seems to have been about the same, though Faustina's voice was lower, and all accounts agree as to the perfection of their singing. In those days, besides beauty of voice and expression, great technical skill was demanded of singers, especially in the performance of the 'divisions' and trills so familiar in Handel's songs. Moreover, singers were expected to add their own grace-notes and other ornaments to the melody written for them by the composer. Thus, Burney tells us of Cuzzoni that 'a native warble enabled her to execute divisions with such facility as to conceal every appearance of difficulty'; 'in a cantabile air, though the notes she added were few, she never lost an opportunity of enriching the cantilena with all the refinements and embellishments of the time. Her shake was perfect.' Of Faustina Burney says: 'She in a manner invented a new kind of singing, by running divisions with a neatness and velocity which entranced all who heard her. She had the art of sustaining a note longer, in the opinion of the public, than any other singer, by taking her breath imperceptibly. Her beats and trills were strong and rapid; her intonation perfect.'

Here then was plenty of opportunity for jealousy and petty rivalry, and the fashionable public encouraged it to the utmost. Not so Handel. His wish was to get the best singers together in order to obtain the most artistic performance possible. In *Alessandro* he gave each the same number of songs; each sang a duet with Senesino, and in a duet for the two ladies the composer so arranged the parts that each had the upper notes in turn, so that there could be no question of first and second singer. That he could make a respectable drama under these conditions would appear to be impossible; if he was able to do so, he gave another and striking proof of his genius.

But the supporters of opera did not demand dramatic proprieties. All they wanted was an opportunity of hearing the singers and pitting them against one another. Handel's efforts failed to keep the peace. The history of the Italian opera of those days shows a succession of miserable quarrels between rival composers, rival singers and rival parties.

A story is told to the effect that Cuzzoni had been made by her partisans to swear on the Gospels that she would never accept a less sum than Faustina, and that the directors, wishing to get rid of her, offered her £2,000 and Faustina £2,001, whereupon she left the kingdom; and another ridiculous report was circulated to the effect that she was under sentence of death by beheading for murdering her husband. But there is no truth in these stories, for both ladies continued to sing together under Handel's tuition for a long time. The rival parties hissed their opponents' protegée; epigrams appeared in the papers, of which the following is an example:

> Old poets sing that beasts did dance
> Whenever Orpheus played;
> So to Faustina's charming voice
> Wise Pembroke's [1] asses brayed.

A reply is found in an epigram on Cuzzoni:

> Boast not how Orpheus charmed the rocks;
> And set a-dancing stones and stocks,
> And tygers' rage appeased;
> All this Cuzzoni has surpassed;
> Sir Wilfred seems to have a taste,
> And Smith and Gage [2] are pleased.

The eighth Academy season opened on 7th January 1727 with Ariosti's *Lucio Vero,* a weak piece which had no success. On the last day of the month followed Handel's *Admeto,* which had a run of nineteen nights. The libretto is founded on the *Alcestis* of Euripides. The performers were Senesino, in the

[1] Lady Pembroke, who 'headed the Cuzzonists' (Grove).

[2] Sir Wilfred Lawson, Simon Smith and Sir William Gage were members of the Royal Academy.

part of Admetus, Boschi as Hercules, Faustina as Alcestis and Cuzzoni as the heroine of a counterplot. The music of *Admeto* was published by Cluer and stolen 'with his usual mastery' by Walsh.[1]

A performance on 6th May of *Astyanax* by Bononcini was stopped by hisses, yells and catcalls from the leaders of the best society in London, the voices of the two singers being drowned by the hubbub of the rival factions, who tried to uphold their respective claims to pre-eminence.

Henry Carey's *Satyr on the Luxury and Effeminacy of the Age* has the following passages:

> Cuzzoni can no longer charm,
> Faustina now does all alarm;
> And we must buy her pipe so clear
> With hundreds, twenty-five a year.

> And if a brace of powder'd coxcombs meet
> They kiss and slabber in the open street:
> They talk not of our Army or our Fleet,
> But of the warble of Cuzzoni sweet,
> Of the delicious pipe of Senesino
> And of the squalling trill of Harlequino;
> With better voice, and fifty times her skill,
> Poor Robinson is always treated ill:
> But, such is the good nature of the town,
> 'Tis now the mode to cry the English down.

> They care not, whether credit rise or fall,
> The opera with them is all in all.
> They 'll talk of tickets rising to a guinea,
> Of pensions, duchesses, and Bononcini;
> Of a new eunuch in Bernardi's place,
> And of Cuzzoni's conquest or disgrace.

Handel's friend Arbuthnot wrote a pamphlet, 'The devil

[1] Chrysander.

to pay at St. James's; or a full and true account of a most horrid and bloody battle between Madam Faustina and Madam Cuzzoni, also, of a hot skirmish between Signor Boschi and Signor Palmerini. Moreover, how Senesino has taken snuff, is going to leave the opera, and sing Psalms at Henley's Oratory.'

The reason why the eighth season had not opened until January 1727 was that the engagement of the two ladies had led to a new and unforeseen trouble. The funds of the Royal Academy were rapidly becoming exhausted by the enormous sums paid to singers, calls were constantly made on the subscribers, and it was necessary to offer every possible attraction to the public, when Senesino, the spoilt idol of society, finding that his performance was slightly less attractive than that of the two ladies, suddenly announced that he was ill and must retire to the Continent. Once having got away he made the greatest difficulties about returning in the following season, since he had now learned that the Academy were easily to be squeezed by any Italian singer whom they thought they could not do without. He did not return till after Christmas 1726, and the opera could not therefore open for the following season till then. Its place was taken by an Italian comedy company which was patronized by the king.

In 1726 an English version of *Camilla* by Bononcini's brother Marc' Antonio was tried by Rich (at which theatre is unknown) with English singers, but apparently without any great success. The audience would only listen to Italian singers: not for the sake of music, but because, being idle and extremely frivolous, it merely wanted something to get up rivalries about. People went to the opera much as they went to a prize-fight, a bear-garden or a cock-pit, in order to see human beings or animals or birds trying to get the better of one another.

The Royal Academy was sinking more and more into pecuniary difficulties. After the performance of *Admeto*, it called Bononcini and Ariosti again to its assistance, commissioning them each to write an opera. Bononcini produced *Astyanax* with the result we have already seen; and Ariosti produced nothing.

In the summer of 1727 George I set out for Hanover with two of his courtiers. His wife had recently died, after being for thirty-two years imprisoned in a castle on suspicion of adultery with a Swedish count. In her last illness she sent a letter to the king complaining of his ill-usage and summoning him to meet her within a year and a day before the tribunal of God, to answer for his conduct. This so alarmed him that he fell into a convulsion in his coach and died, in the vicinity of Osnabrück, before reaching Hanover.

On the accession of George II, in June 1727, Handel's income of £600 a year was confirmed for life, made up of the two pensions of £200 given him by Queen Anne and George I respectively and the salary of the same amount for his duties as music-master to the young princesses. He was also given the honorary title of 'Composer to the Court' in addition to that of 'Composer of Musick to the Chapel Royal' already held by him, for which he had no regular salary.[1]

The coronation took place at Westminster Abbey, on 11th October, on which occasion Handel's four coronation anthems, beginning with the well-known *Zadok the Priest*, were performed with a large orchestra. Unlike the operas, in which practically no chorus appeared, these anthems, like the *Te Deums*, consisted mostly of massive writing of five, six

---

[1] Handel, being now by naturalization a British subject, was able to hold these posts, for which fees seem to have been paid him on special occasions. Croft, who died in August, had received altogether £522 a year as court composer, organist, Master of the Children of the Chapel Royal, teacher of the royal children, etc. He was succeeded as Master of the Children by Bernard Gates, as organist by a Mr. Robinson and as composer (for two were employed) by Maurice Greene.

and seven vocal parts. The singers were all English, being members of the Chapel Royal and Westminster Abbey choirs. Twelve boys and thirty-five men were employed, the solos being sung by Francis Hughes, John Freeman, John Church, Samuel Wheely and Bernard Gates. The instrumental part was played by the opera orchestra, and a new organ was built for the occasion by Schröder. This instrument, which was a very fine one, was afterwards given to the abbey by the king. A double bassoon was used for the first time on this occasion. It had been designed and made by Stanesby, a flute maker, under the superintendence of Handel himself. It is called in Handel's scores *Basson-grosso*. Schoelcher, misunderstanding the expression familiar to organists, '16 feet tone,' is puzzled by imagining a bassoon sixteen feet high. The instrument was, of course, about sixteen feet long, but bent on itself to a convenient length, in the way familiar to all concert-goers.

The actual placing of the crown on the head of the new king was accompanied by 'instrumental music of every sort' (i.e. the full orchestra). At the conclusion of the ceremony was sung the fourth anthem, 'My heart is inditing of a good matter.' It is stated that the Bishop of London had selected and sent a list of texts to Handel for these anthems, and that Handel, taking offence at this, wrote to the bishop, saying: 'I have read my Bible well, and will choose for myself.'

On 30th October a court ball took place in celebration of the king's birthday, for which Handel, as composer to the court, provided a series of minuets, which were immediately published by Walsh.

The Royal Academy was now moribund. Subscribers, attracted by other pleasures, or disgusted with the riotous scenes which frequently took place, had fallen off in large numbers, and no one came forward in their place. The fund of £50,000 was exhausted and opera shares were unsaleable. Handel worked desperately to save the Academy from ruin. Thinking that a story taken from English history would attract the English people, he produced *Riccardo primo, Rè d'Inghilterra* on 11th November 1727, in which again the parts for Cuzzoni and Faustina were equally matched. The libretto was by Rolli.[1] But the disturbances experienced in the opera whenever these two performers appeared were beginning to have their natural result.

Handel still made further efforts to save the Academy from ruin. He produced *Siroe,* set to a libretto by Haym, after Metastasio, on 17th February 1728. It was performed nineteen times. *Tolomeo* (words by Haym) followed on 30th April, and here Handel obtained a novel effect of echo by making Senesino repeat Cuzzoni's phrases behind the scenes. The opera ran for seven nights only. All his efforts were unavailing. In addition to its internal squabbles, the Royal Academy was now being actively attacked from outside.

On 29th January 1728 John Gay's satire, *The Beggar's Opera,* had been produced at the theatre in Lincoln's Inn Fields. The music was arranged by Dr. Pepusch from the popular tunes of the day and from songs that had been current for generations.[2] The director was Rich. It proved irresistible to the fashionable society of the day and had a run of ninety nights, which went a long way towards ruining the Academy, already impoverished by the exorbitance of its singers and the quarrels of rival partisans. The libretto treats of thieves, murderers, receivers of stolen goods, highwaymen and other

[1] Rolli dedicated the libretto to the king, and was rewarded with the title of Court Poet.

[2] It is evident that Gay and Pepusch made their choice very easy by culling most of the material from d'Urfey's *Wit and Mirth.* This is clear from the fact that in the indications of the sources of the tunes, d'Urfey's words are generally quoted, not the original ones. Kidson, in *The Beggar's Opera,* gives Thompson's *Orpheus Caledonius* and Playford's *Dancing Master* as the other two main sources.—E. B.

disreputable characters, and it is at once a skit on the manners and customs of the aristocratic society of the time and on the rigid conventions of Italian opera. Pepusch composed an overture in the usual form of a slow movement followed by a fugue. A prologue is spoken by a beggar and a player, in which a discussion takes place as to what will best please the audience; and in an epilogue, spoken by the same characters, the conclusion is come to that the play must end happily since this is expected of every opera. The thing continued for more than a century to please the public, if one may judge from the number of editions that appeared. No less than twenty editions and arrangements are in the British Museum, ranging from 1728 to 1892.[1]

This glorification of crime is said by Hawkins to have fulfilled the prognostications of many that it would prove injurious to society:[2]

Rapine and violence have been gradually increasing ever since its first representation; the rights of property, and the obligation of the law that guards it, are disputed on principle; young men, apprentices, clerks in public offices, and others, disdaining the arts of honest industry, and captivated with the charms of idleness and criminal pleasures, now betake themselves to the road, affect politeness in the very act of robbery, and in the end become victims to the justice of their country; and men of discernment, who have been at the pains of tracing this great evil to its source, have found that not a few of those who, during these last fifty years, have paid to the law

---

[1] Thereafter *The Beggar's Opera* was not heard of in public until it was brilliantly revived by Nigel Playfair at the Lyric Theatre, Hammersmith, on 5th June 1920, with the music edited and rearranged by Frederic Austin. It then had a run which threatened to prove interminable.—E. B.

[2] It appeared to have no such effect on the more cynical audiences of 1920, who delighted in it simply as a witty play and an entertainment of surprising artistic vitality.—E. B.

the forfeit of their lives, have, in the course of their pursuits been emulous to imitate the manners and general character of Macheath [the hero of *The Beggar's Opera*].

This ballad opera proved the origin of a new type of English stage entertainment and was followed by a number of imitations, called the *Village Opera, Lover's Opera, Harlequin's Opera Quaker's Opera*, etc.

CHAPTER VIII

FROM OPERA TO ORATORIO

BONONCINI now published a pamphlet in Italian and English called *Advice to Composers and Performers of Italian Music,* which he issued gratis to any one asking for it. It was an attack on Handel's method, which, he said, consisted of overloading the songs with instrumental accompaniment and thereby ruining the voices. It was immediately answered by a friend of Handel in *Remarks on a pamphlet lately imported from Modena*[1] *called Advice to Composers and Performers of Vocal Musick.* The matter does not appear to have disturbed Handel very much.

The last performance given by the Academy was that of *Admeto* on 1st June 1728; it was to have been repeated on 11th June, but Faustina was taken ill. The whole company of singers now dispersed and by next year were engaged at two of the theatres in Venice. On 5th June the general court of the Royal Academy met, 'in order to consider of proper measures for recovering the debts due to the Academy, and discharging what is due to performers, tradesmen, and others; and also to determine how the scenes, cloaths, etc., are to be disposed of, if the opera cannot be continued. *N.B.*—All the subscribers are desired to be present, since the whole will be then decided by a majority of votes.'

This was the end. Abortive efforts were made to appoint a new body of directors in November and to meet in January; after this nothing more is heard of the Royal Academy of Music. It had given 245 performances of operas by Handel,

[1] Bononcini was born at Modena.

108 of operas by Bononcini, 55 of works by Ariosti and 79 of those by other composers.

But though the Royal Academy had ceased to exist, Handel did not give up hope. Heidegger was now the lessee of the King's Theatre, and Handel immediately went into partnership with him, risking the £10,000 he had saved by the hard work and economy of the past twenty years. Heidegger was to attend to the business part, Handel to the music. The king supported the undertaking with his annual subscription of £1,000, and there appears to have been a board of directors; but it is doubtful whether the undertaking, which was called the 'New Royal Academy of Music,' was on the same lines as the old one. It was, however, supported by some of the nobility as well as the king, for there was no other audience.

The first thing to do was to find singers, and Handel set off for Italy in January 1729. He visited Florence, Venice, Rome, Milan and other cities. [He heard many new operas by such composers as Porpora, Vinci, Hasse and Pergolesi, and he also became acquainted with the librettos of Metastasio, who was then, at the age of thirty-one, rising to fame.] On his way home he visited his mother in Halle, having previously forwarded a letter to his brother-in-law, Michaelsen, announcing his intended visit.[1] He reached Halle in June, and found that his mother was quite blind and paralytic, being only able to walk from one room to another with a stick. This was the last time he saw her, for she died on 27th December 1730, a few weeks before her eightieth birthday.

It was during this visit that Handel received an invitation from Bach to visit him at Leipzig, Bach being too ill to go to Halle and sending his son, Wilhelm Friedemann, as a messenger. But he would not leave his mother, as was only

---

[1] The letter is extant and is quoted in full by Rockstro, p. 161. [See also *Handel's Letters and Writings* (Cassell, 1935).—E. B.]

natural, and this fact explains the apparent incivility of his refusal of the invitation.

Two subsequent letters to Michaelsen are extant, in which he thanks him for the care taken with the funeral of his mother, and for forwarding a copy of the funeral sermon.

While in Rome, Handel was invited to visit Cardinal Colonna, who offered him a fine portrait of himself; but Handel, hearing that the Pretender was a guest at the house, refused the invitation and the portrait, since it would not be at all suitable for him to meet the enemy of his patron, George II.

In the *Daily Courant* of 2nd July 1729 we find the following notice:

Mr. Handel, who is just returned from Italy, has contracted with the following persons to perform in the Italian opera: Signor Bernacchi, who is esteemed the best singer in Italy; Signora Merighi, a woman of a very fine presence, an excellent actress, and a very good singer, with a counter-tenor voice;[1] Signora Strada, who hath a very fine treble voice, a person of singular merit; Signor Annibale Pio Fabri, a most excellent tenor, and a fine voice; his wife, who performs a man's part exceeding well; Signora Bertolli, who has a very fine treble voice, she is also a very genteel actress, both in men and women's parts; a bass voice from Hamburg, there being none worth engaging in Italy.[2]

Handel had engaged Gottfried Riemschneider, first bass in the cathedral of Hamburg, on his return journey. The company landed at Dover in September, and the theatre opened with Handel's new opera, *Lotario,* on 2nd December 1729; and this was followed by *Partenope* on 24th February 1730.[3]

[1] She was a contralto.

[2] Handel had also engaged 'some other persons of less account' (Hawkins, vol. v, p. 318), amongst whom was Commano, a bass.

[3] *Lotario* was published by Cluer's widow. After this Walsh became Handel's publisher. Both *Lotario* and *Partenope* were arranged from old and well-known opera librettos which had been set by many Italian composers.

Neither work was very successful, one of the reasons being that the new *prima donna,* Anna Strada del Pò, failed to please at first, mainly on account of her preternatural ugliness, which led to her being nicknamed 'The Pig' and made a satirist suggest that she would be a fit match for Heidegger. Handel, concluding that another leading singer was required to draw the public, engaged Senesino, through the good offices of Francis Colman, the English envoy at Florence. Senesino had been singing at Florence, and was engaged to sing in London for fourteen hundred guineas for the season. He made his reappearance in a revival of *Scipione* on 3rd November 1730 at the King's Theatre, and on 2nd February 1731 he sang the principal part in *Poro,* an opera which was very successful and was repeated in the four following seasons. [The libretto was that of Metastasio's *Alessandro nell' Indie,* which was then quite new.] During this season Handel revived *Rodelinda* and *Rinaldo,* the latter 'with new scenes and cloathes.' A change was also made in the singers: Signora Merighi was replaced by Campioli, a male contralto; Pio Fabri, the tenor, by Pinacci, and Commano by Montagnana. On 26th March 1731 some sort of an attempt at English opera was made by a stage performance of *Acis and Galatea,* without choruses, at John Rich's theatre in Lincoln's Inn Fields.

Handel was now hard at work again composing. The third season of the 'New Academy' opened on 13th November, but it was not until 15th January that he produced *Ezio* at the King's Theatre, following it up on 19th February with *Sosarme.* Though both were fairly successful, they failed to bring pecuniary profit to the partners. The libretto of *Ezio* was by Metastasio, that of *Sosarme* by Matteo Noris. *Ezio,* which contained the favourite aria 'Nasce al bosco,' was published by Walsh and stolen by Cluer's widow; *Sosarme* was published as soon as possible by Walsh in order to forestall Mrs. Cluer.

More lampoons now appeared, of which the following are examples:

> When smooth stupidity's the way to please,
> When gentle Handel's singsongs more delight,
> Than all a Dryden or a Pope can write.

And

> In days of old when Englishmen were men,
> Their music like themselves was grave and plain.

> .   .   .   .   .   .

> In tunes from sire to son delivered down,
> But now, since Britons are become polite,
> Since masquerades and operas made their entry,
> And Heydegger and Handell ruled our gentry;
> A hundred different instruments combine,
> And foreign songsters in the concert join
> And give us sound and show, instead of sense.

It will be remembered that while at Canons Handel had composed and privately performed a sacred masque called *Haman and Mordecai*. On 23rd February 1732 Bernard Gates, Master of the Children of the Chapel Royal, having by some means obtained the score, caused it to be performed privately by his boys at his own house as a birthday surprise for Handel, the part of Esther being taken by John Randall, afterwards a doctor and professor of music at the university of Cambridge. [John Beard, later the famous tenor, also appeared in it.] The orchestra was composed of amateurs who belonged to the Philharmonic Society.[1] A little later, Gates put his forces at the service of the Academy of Ancient Music, who gave the work on a much larger scale at the Crown and Anchor tavern in the Strand, and supplied an orchestra from their own members. The success of these experiments was

[1] Not the present Philharmonic Society, which was founded in 1813.

such as to induce some speculator to give the masque publicly in York Buildings, Villiers Street, on 20th April 1732.

This performance took place without Handel's sanction or participation, and in the state of the law as it then was he could not prevent it, if he had wished to do so. But that he should not be entirely a loser, he arranged a performance for his own profit, of which the following advertisement appeared in the *Daily Journal*:

By His Majesty's Command.—At the King's Theatre, in the Haymarket, on Thursday, the 2nd of May will be performed the sacred story of *Esther*; an oratorio in English, formerly composed by Mr. Handel, and now revised by him with several additions, and to be performed by a great number of voices and instruments.

N.B.—There will be no acting on the stage, but the house will be fitted up in a decent manner for the audience. The music to be disposed after the manner of the coronation service.

Tickets to be delivered at the same price.

An important feature of this revision was the change of the title to *Esther*; another the addition of some new words by Samuel Humphreys to Pope's original libretto; and Handel considerably augmented the orchestra, some of the music being now scored for violins in no less than five parts, violas, violoncellos and basses, two flutes, two oboes, two bassoons, harpsichord, harp, theorbo and organ; some of the choruses are in seven parts.

It was an enormous success, and seems to have completely suppressed the Villiers Street efforts. Colman mentions that 'Hester, an English oratorio, was performed six times, and very full.' The solo parts were sung in English by Strada, Bertolli, Senesino and Montagnana. The words 'There will be no acting,' refer perhaps to the performances by Gates, in which a certain amount of action was introduced; [but the real reason why the work was given in the manner advertised is that the Bishop of London, Dr. Gibson, refused to sanction the dramatic representation of Biblical characters on the stage.] Thus the first English oratorio came into being, and oratorios have continued to be performed without action to this day.[1]

Another performance of Handel's music without his participation was that of *Acis and Galatea* already referred to. The upholsterer, Thomas Arne, father of the celebrated Dr. Arne, gave the serenata 'with scenery, machines and other decorations,' and with action and choruses at the New Theatre [2] in the Haymarket, on 17th May 1732. [Young Thomas Augustine Arne conducted and his sister, Susanna Maria, who was eighteen, sang the part of Galatea.] This caused Handel to announce a performance for 10th June at the King's Theatre of the same work, as 'revised by him, with several additions, and to be performed by a great number of the best voices and instruments,' but without action. [The additions were some of the numbers from the earlier Italian *Aci*; the best voices belonged to a mixed cast of English and Italian singers.] Strada's husband now advertised:

Whereas Signor Bononcini intends, after the serenata composed by Mr. Handel hath been performed, to have one of his own, and hath desired Signora Strada to sing in that entertainment: Aurelio del Pò, husband of the said Signora Strada, thinks it incumbent upon him to acquaint the nobility and gentry, that he shall think

---

[1] An exception was made in 1833, when an oratorio called *The Israelites in Egypt*, made up of Rossini's and Handel's works on the same subject, was performed on the stage at Covent Garden with action, arranged by Rophino Lacy. Princess (later Queen) Victoria and her mother, the Duchess of Kent, attended, and the performance was very successful; but the Bishop of London objected, and further performances were suppressed. [A century or so later Mendelssohn's *Elijah* has been given with action more than once.—E. B.]

[2] Called also the 'Little Theatre.' It stood nearly on the same spot as the present Haymarket Theatre.

himself happy in contributing to their satisfaction; but, with respect to this request, hopes he shall be permitted to decline complying with it for reasons best known to the said Aurelio del Pò and his wife.

This announcement was construed by the gossips of the day into a political allusion, an attempt of the Pretender to open a correspondence with the Academy of Music. Aurelio, they said, stood for the Pretender, Del for the Devil, and Pò for the Pope. The performance of Bononcini's pastoral entertainment took place on the appointed day at Handel's theatre, for Handel seems to have been above the petty jealousies of the time.

[The year 1732 saw the appearance of some other than operatic music by Handel. He began the composition of a series of Sonatas for violin, flute or oboe (Op. 1) and supplied Rich with incidental music for a production of Ben Jonson's *The Alchemist* at Covent Garden, which was, however, mainly an adaptation of the dance tunes from the *Rodrigo* of 1707.]

The new tenor, Pinacci, did not stay for the fourth season of the 'New Royal Academy,' which opened on 4th November 1732. The company was now reduced to five Italian singers: Strada, Senesino, Bertolli, Celeste Gismondi, a new mezzo-soprano, and the splendid bass Antonio Montagnana, who had made his first appearance in a revival of *Poro* at the end of 1731. For them Handel composed *Orlando*, produced 27th January 1733. This fine opera has several remarkable points. In it the composer is said by Burney [1] to have used the diminished seventh for the first time,[2] though the passage he quotes does not contain this interval. In order to represent the ravings of madness, Handel used 5–8 rhythm, a novelty at that time, and he made use of two *violette marine*, a kind of *viola d'amore* invented by the brothers Castrucci, one of whom

[1] *History of Music*, vol. iv, p. 365.

[2] Mr. C. F. Crowder points out an instance in the aria 'Son contenta di morire' from *Radamisto* (1720).—E. B.

was the leading first violin of the orchestra at that time. Francis Colman remarks: 'Orlando very fine and magnificent.' Its ninety pages were engraved, printed and bound by Walsh in seventeen days. Floridante was revived, and the season closed with Bononcini's Griselda on 9th June 1733.

The success of Esther and Acis without action led Handel to see his way to a new kind of work which might answer if opera should fail, which it showed every sign of doing. But, faithful to his first love, he continued to struggle against adversity, which now closed in on him very fast. Orlando was the last opera in which Senesino sang for him. Senesino seems to have been anything but an admirable character. He was insolent, cowardly and quarrelsome. He had, while at Dresden, by his quarrels with the Capellmeister caused the break-up of the opera company before Handel engaged him; [1] he was publicly and violently caned behind the scenes by Lord Peterborough for his insolence to Anastasia Robinson at a rehearsal. But he served Handel's purpose and no doubt stood in awe of him. Yet he turned from Handel and joined the rival opera house in Lincoln's Inn Fields, organized by a party of music-lovers opposed to Handel. For this scheme Porpora was engaged as conductor, and all Handel's singers, except Strada, went over to the hostile camp.

Handel was now without enough Italian singers, but he was not yet beaten. There was no doubt whatever that as far as he was concerned Italian opera was at an end. But he had already in his Te Deum and in Esther proved his strength as a composer of massive choral music, for which there was no opportunity in opera, and he now resolved to try his fortune with oratorio, in which the solo singers would not take so important a place as the chorus. His friend Aaron Hill, moreover, in the following letter, gave voice to a growing

[1] Quantz, Autobiography, referred to by Rockstro, p. 181.

popular feeling that the English language was good enough for musical setting:

5th Dec. 1732.

To Mr. Handel.

Sir,—I ought sooner to have returned you my hearty thanks for the silver ticket, which has carried the obligation further than to myself; for my daughters are both such lovers of musick, that it is hard to say which of them is most capable of being charmed by the compositions of Mr. Handel.

Having this occasion for troubling you with a letter, I cannot forbear to tell you the earnestness of my wishes, that, as you have made such considerable steps towards it already, you would let us owe to your inimitable genius the establishment of musick upon a foundation of good poetry; where the excellence of the sound should be no longer dishonoured by the poorness of the sense it is chained to.

My meaning is, that you would be resolute enough to deliver us from our Italian bondage, and demonstrate that English is soft enough for opera, when composed by poets who know how to distinguish the sweetness of our tongue from the strength of it, where the last is less necessary. I am of opinion that male and female voices may be found in this kingdom capable of everything that is requisite; and, I am sure, a species of dramatic opera might be invented, that, by reconciling reason and dignity with musick and fine machinery, would charm the ear and hold fast the heart together. I am so much a stranger to the nature of your present engagements, that if what I have said should not be so practicable as I conceive it, you will have the goodness to impute it to the zeal with which I wish you at the head of a design as solid and imperishable as your musick and memory.

I am, sir, your most obedient and obliged servant,

A. Hill.

Handel set to work, therefore, not on English opera—this had already been attempted by others and had failed—but on a new oratorio. A French drama on the subject of Deborah was utilized by Humphreys for the poem. His attention had been called to it by a setting of *The Song of Deborah and Barak* by Dr. Greene, which had been recently performed.

Handel finished the oratorio of *Deborah* on 21st February 1733. It is in several respects a remarkable work. Thus the overture, instead of being, as was usually the case, entirely unconnected with the work, contained the music of one of the choruses in praise of Baal, while another portion of it forestalls the chorus of Israelites in answer to the Baal chorus. The opening number is a double chorus, as grand as any in *Israel in Egypt*. It is accompanied by three trumpets, three horns, two organs and two harpsichords, in addition to the usual strings and oboes. There is also another double chorus and one in six parts. Strada sang the part of Deborah. The prices were raised to a guinea for the boxes and half a guinea for the gallery. The *Daily Journal* announced on 17th March:

By His Majesty's command, *Deborah,* an oratorio or sacred drama in English, composed by Mr. Handel. The house to be fitted up and illuminated in a new and particular manner; and to be performed by a great number of the best voices and instruments. *N.B.*—This is the last dramatick performance that will be exhibited at the King's Theatre till after Easter.

But the work did not draw. The high price of the tickets was partly responsible for this, and it was lowered for the three or four subsequent performances. The cabal which had been long formed against Handel became more active. The strong feeling of animosity will be judged from a letter written by Rolli, the librettist of some of Handel's earlier operas, and the Italian Secretary of the Royal Academy, to the editor of *The Craftsman,* of which we give some extracts:

A New Opera Scheme

As I know your zeal for liberty, I thought I could not address better than to give you the following exact account of the noble stand lately made by the polite part of the world in defence of their liberties and properties, against the open attack and bold attempts of Mr. H——l upon both. . . . The rise and progress of Mr. H——'s power and fortune are too well known for me now to relate. Let it suffice to say, that he has grown so insolent upon the sudden and undeserved increase of both, that he thought nothing ought to oppose his imperious and extravagant will. He had for some time governed the operas, and modelled the orchestra, without the least control. No voices, no instruments, were admitted but such as flattered his ears, though they shocked those of the audience. Wretched scrapers were put above the best hands in the orchestra; no music but his own was to be allowed, though everybody was weary of it; and he had the impudence to assert that there was no composer in England but himself. Even kings and queens[1] were to be content with whatever low characters he was pleased to assign them, as is evident in the case of Signor Montagnana, who, though a king, is always obliged to act (except in an angry, rumbling song or two) the most insignificant part of the whole drama. This excess and abuse of power soon disgusted the town: his government grew odious, and his operas empty.

However, this, instead of humbling him, only made him more furious and desperate. He resolved to make one last effort to establish his power and fortune by force, since he found it now impossible to hope it from the goodwill of mankind. In order to do this, he formed a plan without consulting any of his friends (if he has any), and declared that at a proper season he would communicate it to the public; assuring us, the very same time, that it would be very much for the advantage of the publick in general, and of operas in particular. Some people suspect that he had settled it previously with Signora Strada del Pò, who is much in his favour: but all that I can advance with certainty is that he had concerted it with a brother of his own,[2] in whom he places a most undeserved confidence.

His scheme set forth in substance that the decay of operas was owing to their cheapness, and to the great frauds committed by the

---

[1] i.e. principal singers.

[2] Either Smith the elder, who was devoted to him, or his brother manager, Heidegger.

doorkeepers: that the annual subscribers were a parcel of rogues, and made an ill-use of their tickets by often running two into the gallery: that to obviate these abuses, he had contrived a thing that was better than an opera, called an oratorio, to which none should be admitted but by printed permits, or tickets of one guinea each, which should be distributed out of warehouses of his own, and by officers of his own naming, which officers could not reasonably be supposed to cheat in the collection of half-guineas; and lastly, that, as the being of operas depended upon him singly, it was just that the profit arising from hence should be for his own benefit. He added, indeed, one condition, to varnish the whole a little, which was, that if any person should think himself aggrieved, he should be at liberty to appeal to three judges of musick, who should be obliged within the space of seven years at farthest, finally to determine the same, provided the said judges should be of his nomination, and known to like no other musick but his. This extravagant scheme disgusted the whole town. Many of the most constant attenders of the operas resolved to renounce them, rather than go to them under such extortion and vexation. They exclaimed against the insolent and rapacious projector of this plan. The kings, old and sworn servants of the two theatres of Drury Lane and Covent Garden, reaped the benefit of this general discontent, and were resorted to by crowds in the way of opposition to the oratorio. Even the fairest breasts were fired with indignation against this new imposition.

Assemblies, cards, tea, coffee, and all other female batteries were vigorously employed to defeat the project, and destroy the projector. These joint endeavours of all ranks and sexes succeeded well; and the projector had the mortification to see but a very thin audience at his oratorios; and of about two hundred and sixty odd that it consisted of, it is notorious that not ten paid for their permits, but, on the contrary, had them given them, and money into the bargain, for coming to keep him in countenance. This accident, they say, has thrown him into a deep melancholy, interrupted sometimes by raving fits, in which he fancies he sees ten thousand opera devils coming to tear him to pieces; then he breaks out into frantic incoherent speeches, muttering, *sturdy beggars, assassination,* etc.

It is much questioned whether he will recover; at least if he does, it is not doubted but he will seek for a retreat in his own country, from the general resentment of the town.

The letter ends with an epigram in which Handel is represented as combining with Walpole to *excise* the whole nation, for 'of what use are the sheep if the shepherd can't shear 'em?'

But the opposition was not confined to scurrilous letters such as the above: tea parties were given during Lent, an unheard-of practice, the evenings being purposely selected on which oratorios were announced, with the express object of attracting the audience away from Handel's music, and no efforts were spared actively to oppose him.

Joseph Goupy, drawing-master to Frederick, Prince of Wales,[1] and scene-painter, attacked Handel by a caricature, under the title of 'The Charming Brute.' The story goes that Handel invited Goupy to dine with him at his house in Brook Street, but left him alone after dinner; Goupy, looking out of a back window, saw his host in another room, writing and surrounded by fruit and wine. Whereupon he went home and drew the pastel, which was reproduced with slight variations and had a wide circulation. Handel is represented in the form of a fat hog, seated on a beer barrel and playing on an organ to which are attached a ham and a fowl. The floor is strewn with oyster-shells, and a turbot rests on a pile of books. At his feet are some musical instruments, and a scroll bearing the words 'Pension, Benefit, Nobility, Friendship.' Æsop, standing behind the organ, holds a mirror to him that he may see what he is like. On his head is an owl and behind him are wine-bottles. Below are the words:

> The figure's odd—yet who would think
> Within this tunn of meat and drink,

---

[1] The court faction which adhered to the Prince of Wales, who was on extremely bad terms with the king and queen, supported the opposition opera in Lincoln's Inn Fields.—E. B.

There dwells a soul of soft desires,
And all that harmony inspires?

Can contrast such as this be found
Upon the globe's extensive round?
There can—yon hogshead is his seat,
His soul devotion is—to eat.

He was accused of profanity because he caused Bible words to be sung in the theatre. No efforts, however mean, however scurrilous, were spared by his enemies to ruin and disgrace him. But his obstinate Saxon nature rose superior to every-thing. Though eventually ruined in health, in fortune, and with his mind on the verge of giving way, he still, like Sir Richard Greville, 'fought on,' not knowing when he was beaten, till he finally overcame his enemies.

Deborah was repeated in March and April 1733, with the boxes reduced to half a guinea and the gallery to five shillings. Though, like *Esther,* it was performed without action, the reporters of the period were so little accustomed to the novelty that they record that the king and princess went to the Hay-market to 'see the opera of *Deborah*,' and refer to *Esther* 'as it is now acted at the Theatre Royal.' Besides these two oratorios, *Orlando* and *Floridante* were performed again this season. Strada continued to sing for Handel, almost the only Italian singer who kept faith with him, and the king, with part at least of the court, always warmly supported him.

CHAPTER IX

HONOURS AND STRUGGLES

EARLY in July 1733 Handel went to Oxford, having been invited by Dr. Holmes, the Vice-Chancellor of that university. Thomas Hearne of St. Edmund's Hall, one of those to whom music did not appeal, and who therefore took upon himself to despise the art and its professors, gives the following account of the visit:

1733, *July* 5. One Handell, a foreigner (who, they say, was born at Hanover), being desired to come to Oxford, to perform in musick at this Act,[1] in which he hath great skill, is come down, the Vice-Chancellor (Dr. Holmes) having requested him so to do, and, as an encouragement, to allow him the benefit of the Theater, both before the Act begins, and after it. Accordingly he hath published papers for a performance to-day, at 5*s.* a ticket. This performance began a little after five o'clock in the evening. This is an innovation. The players might as well be permitted to come and act.

July 6*th.* The players being denied coming to Oxford by the Vice-Chancellor, and that very rightly, tho' they might as well have been here as Handell and his lowsy crew, a great number of forreign fidlers, they went to Abbington, and yesterday began to act there, at which were present many gownsmen from Oxford.

July 8. Half-an-hour after five o'clock yesterday in the afternoon, was another performance, at 5*s.* a ticket, in the Theater by Mr. Handell for his own benefit, continuing till about eight o'clock.

N.B.—His book (not worth 1*d.*) he sells for 1*s.*

---

[1] A university ceremony.

Another account says:

Thursday, the 5th of July. About five o'clock the great Mr. Handel shewed away with his Esther, an oratorio, or sacred drama, to a very numerous audience, at five shillings a ticket.

Saturday, the 7th. The Chevalier Handel very judiciously, forsooth, ordered out tickets for his Esther this evening again.

Some of the company that found themselves but very scamblingly entertained at our dry disputations, took it into their heads to try how a little fiddling would sit upon them.

Such as cou'dn't attend before, squeezed in with as much alacrity as others strove to get out, so that ere his myrmidons cou'd gain their posts, he found that he had little likelihood to be at such a loss for a house, as, once upon a time, folk say he was.

So that, notwithstanding the barbarous and inhuman combination of such a parcel of unconscionable chaps, he disposed, it seems, of most of his tickets, and had, as you may guess, a pretty mottley appearance into the bargain.

[With these disparaging reports it is interesting to contrast a document unearthed in the library of the Liceo Musicale at Bologna on behalf of Mr. Newman Flower, and quoted by him in full. In it is mentioned that

the University of Oxford invited Handel to come and give a performance of an Oratorio or some solemn music . . . for a very generous fee, though not pretending to say generally what it should be. But they say it was sufficient for the transport of the whole orchestra there and back, as well as the pay of all the musicians, who were little short of 100, for all the time they were away from London, which was about a fortnight. They say the lowest player received a pound a day, and the singers much more according to the pay they required. Handel was so scrupulous in his choice of virtuosi for this performance that there was not a single poor performer; and for their part they competed so to shew their respect for the Master for being chosen on this occasion according to their merit and not by their engagements, that every one of them appeared so well dressed that it looked an orchestra of cavaliers.]

Both *Esther* and *Deborah* were given. The Utrecht *Te Deum* and *Jubilate* were performed on Sunday, 8th July, at the University Church, and on the following Tuesday

the company in the evening were entertained with a spick and span new oratorio called *Athaliah*. One of the royal and ample had been saying that, truly it was his opinion that the theater was erected for other guise purposes than to be prostituted to a company of squeeking, bawling, outlandish singsters, let the agreement be what it would. This morning, Wednesday, July 11th, there was, luckily enough, for the benefit of some of Handel's people, a serenata in their grand hall. In the evening *Athaliah* was served up again; but the next night he concluded with his oratorio *Deborah*.

The *Gentleman's Magazine* reports that *Athaliah* [1] was received at Oxford 'before an audience of 3,700 persons.'

He was offered the degree of Doctor of Music on account of this oratorio. The degree fees in those days amounted to £100; and on being asked why he refused the honour, he is reported to have said: 'What the devil I throw my money away for that which the blockheads wish? I no want.' Chrysander, however, thinks that it was refused more courteously, and that it was offered as a mark of honour, without payment. [2]

After the Oxford visit Handel went to Italy with Smith to

[1] The libretto, by Samuel Humphreys, was based on Racine's *Athalie*.

[2] According to Dent, 'it is inconceivable that a fee should have been demanded for an honorary degree.' A possible explanation, which does not seem to have occurred to any biographer, would be that it may have been suggested to him to pay £100 towards some charity or other worthy object out of the profits he had made at Oxford, and to take the degree in exchange as a special acknowledgment. This would not have been in the least unreasonable if it is true that, as the document at Bologna says, he cleared £4,000. O. E. Deutsch points out that Hearne's diary shows Handel to have refused the Oxford degree because he had declined the Cambridge degree before.—E. B.

engage a new company. He heard two male sopranos, the famous Farinelli and Carestini, but engaged only the latter, who was then about twenty-eight, Farinelli proving far too expensive to be brought to London at a risk. Duranstanti came back to London, and he also secured Scalzi and the two Negri sisters. Montagnana had deserted him and followed Senesino to the rival company, after having been engaged for the Oxford production of *Athaliah,* in which the part of Joad, the high priest, was specially written for him. When he failed Handel at the last moment, the part was taken by Waltz, the German bass who had sung Polyphemus in Arne's performance of *Acis,* and who had been Handel's cook.

The Duke of Marlborough and the Prince of Wales now set themselves to work with all their power to ruin Handel. The Prince of Wales had no particular object in doing so other than that of showing his dislike to his father, who had always been a supporter of Handel. The Duke of Marlborough and the 'Nobiltà Britannica,' as the aristocracy were called by Rolli in the dedication of his librettos, supported the opposition in every possible way. The Duchess of Marlborough had given Bononcini, besides the pension of £500 a year, a house in her stable-yard at St. James's, and had two concerts every week, in which no music but his was performed. Moreover, she helped him with the publication of his *Cantate e Duetti* by obtaining subscribers for him, and he made £1,000 by the transaction.

The fundamental cause of the quarrel (though not recognized) lay in the gradual change that was coming over the position of the art of music in the social world. It had been a mere amusement, and its professors were glad to obtain the patronage of the great. But the more advanced of its exponents were beginning to chafe under this indignity and to assert their rights as free men, who resented the patronage of those who were their inferiors in intellect, however much they might be their superiors by wealth and social position. The Bach family afford several instances of this upholding of the dignity of the musical profession in Germany, and Handel was now doing the same in England. The aristocracy resented the so-called insolence of a mere musician who stood upon his dignity. The quarrel came to a climax in Handel's case, and he eventually won the day; but Mozart after him had to endure much from the same cause, while every one knows that the battle had been won in the time of Beethoven, who would bow to no one and who was always treated with respect, in spite of his undoubtedly unpolished manners.

Senesino, as we have seen, deserted Handel in favour of the 'opera of the nobility.' He foresaw the coming ruin of the Handel-Heidegger partnership; he also saw that the oratorio with which it was being attempted to replace opera, owing to its preponderance of choruses, put the chief singer more or less into the shade. Handel was very angry at the desertion and said that he should never again sing in his theatre. It was thought that Senesino himself hired the theatre in Lincoln's Inn Fields, and the two theatres were referred to as 'Haymarket, Handel's House,' and 'Opera, Lincoln's Inn Fields, Senesino's House.'

Efforts were now made to force Handel to re-engage Senesino, in spite of his having distinctly said he would never allow him to sing for him again. To give way on this point would be to allow himself to be beaten by the aristocracy, and his proud spirit could not brook such a defeat. His patrons became indignant against the 'arrogant man,' and having given up their boxes at the Haymarket at the end of the 1733 season, they hired the theatre in Lincoln's Inn Fields, and began to seek singers from abroad. They succeeded in getting Cuzzoni, Montagnana and Farinelli. It is a curious fact that at this time, while male sopranos were very much in fashion, basses were thought little of and tenors were rarely employed.

Senesino became one of the chief attractions of the new opera company, while Handel had only Carestini, an artificial contralto of great reputation, to introduce as a new attraction.

Handel's rival, Bononcini, was, however, destined to write no operas for the new company. In 1731 a member of the Academy had received from Venice a book of compositions by Antonio Lotti, who was at that time organist of St. Mark's, and had selected from it a five-part madrigal, *In una siepe ombrosa,* for performance. This madrigal was at once recognized as having been produced four years previously at the Academy by Dr. Greene as a composition by Bononcini. Correspondence with Lotti ensued, which resulted in his proving to the satisfaction of all except Greene that he was the composer. Bononcini, being unable or unwilling to answer the charge of plagiarism brought against him, fell into disgrace and quitted England in 1733, never to return.

The newly established 'opera of the nobility,' having engaged Arrigoni and Porpora as composers, opened with *Ariadne* by Porpora on 29th December 1733. The rehearsal had taken place at the Prince of Wales's house, 'where were present a great concourse of nobility and quality.'

[In 1733 six Sonatas for two violins, flutes or oboes with harpsichord (Op. 2) were published by Walsh, who also brought out a pirated edition of a second series of Suites for harpsichord, consisting of 'lessons for Princess Anne.']

Handel opened on the king's birthday, 30th October 1733, before his opponents were ready, with *Semiramide.* The royal ball was given up for this occasion, and the king and court, including even the hostile Prince of Wales, attended the opera. This was followed by *Caius Fabricius,* in which Carestini made his first appearance, and in January by *Arbaces.* These were pasticcios,[1] arranged by Smith from the music of various composers, the words being written in by Handel.

On 26th January 1734 a new opera, *Arianna,* set to a libretto by Francis Colman, was produced with Carestini in the part of Theseus. The season was not successful, but Handel bravely struggled on. In March, on the occasion of the marriage of Princess Anne of England to the Prince of Orange, Handel produced at the Haymarket a serenata called *Parnasso in festa,* treating of the marriage of Thetis and Peleus, 'being an essay in several different sorts of harmony.' The modern newspaper puff is by no means a new invention, for we find in the *Daily Journal* an announcement that 'People have been waiting with impatience for this piece, the celebrated Mr. Handel having exerted his utmost skill in it.' The performance was attended by the king and queen, the Prince of Wales and the rest of the royal family, with the Prince of Orange. The music was mostly adapted from *Athaliah* to Italian words, while later on some of the original music of *Parnasso* was introduced into that oratorio. On the same occasion, besides an anthem, of which the music was copied from *Athaliah* by Smith, Handel writing in the new words, a Chandos anthem was performed at the Chapel Royal.

Between January and June 1734 there were performed at the King's Theatre *Arianna, Deborah, Sosarme, Acis* and *Il Pastor fido,* the last with large additions. In this year also were published the oboe Concertos.

On 18th May Handel gave his new version of the *Pastor fido* of 1712, 'intermixed with choruses, the scenery after a particular manner.' This was performed fourteen times. For all that, Handel's arrangement with Heidegger came to an end on 6th July 1734, owing to the increasing lack of support from which their enterprise suffered, and his adversaries at once took advantage of this by engaging the King's Theatre, which his former partner did not scruple to offer them.

Handel found a good friend in Dr. Arbuthnot, who helped to fight his battles for him. In 1734 he published *Harmony in an Uproar: a Letter to Frederick Handel, Esq.,* in which the composer is summoned to appear on trial to answer to the charges of certain misdemeanours.

Imprimis, you are charged with having bewitched us for the space of twenty years past. Secondly, you have most insolently dared to give us good musick and harmony, when we wanted and desired bad. Thirdly, you have most feloniously and arrogantly assumed to yourself an uncontrolled property of pleasing us, whether we would or no; and have often been so bold as to charm us when we were positively resolved to be out of humour. . . .

Have you taken your degrees? Are you a doctor? A fine composer, indeed, and not a graduate. . . . Why, Dr. Pushpin (Pepusch) and Dr. Blue (Greene) laugh at you, and scorn to keep you company. . . . You have made such musick as never man did before you, nor, I believe, never will be thought of again when you are gone, etc., etc.

Handel now went into partnership with John Rich for the purpose of producing Italian opera alternately with English drama at the fine new theatre that was just being completed in Covent Garden; but as it was not ready, they began at the smaller and less convenient theatre in Lincoln's Inn Fields.

The rival company had endeavoured to obtain the services of Hasse, who was then at Dresden. He said: 'Then Handel is dead,' and when he heard that this was not the case, refused to come to London to put himself in competition with so great a man, though he was afterwards persuaded to do so. The company produced operas by Hasse, Porpora and several others; but London could not support one opera, much less two, and the inevitable result was the final ruin of both.

After concluding the agreement with Rich, Handel paid a visit to the country, probably for his health's sake, and on 5th October he began the new season with *Arianna* at the Lincoln's Inn Fields theatre. On 9th November Handel and Rich moved to Covent Garden, where *Il Pastor fido* was revived, with a 'Prologue' called *Terpsichore*, as an opening piece for the new theatre. This was a kind of ballet, in which Apollo invites Terpsichore (Mademoiselle Sallé, a famous dancer) to dance. At Rich's request Handel supplied the music for this.

A pasticcio, *Oreste*, with dances, followed on 18th December, and on 8th January 1735 a new opera, *Ariodante*, came out. Yet another opera, *Alcina*, produced on 16th April, continued till the end of the season on 2nd July. Covent Garden was not a success, for the rival company had now secured a new attraction in the person of the greatest of all male sopranos—Farinelli. During Lent, when no opera might be given, the theatre was used for oratorios on Wednesdays and Fridays. *Esther* was re-arranged, *Athaliah* was performed for the first time in London, and Handel began the practice of playing organ concertos between the acts of the oratorios. The 'opera of the nobility' also tried oratorio. A work by Porpora, *David and Bathsheba*, was produced, but without success.

In 1735 Handel was in correspondence with Charles Jennens, a very wealthy amateur poet, about the words of an oratorio which the latter seems to have been preparing for him. He incidentally mentions that he was going to Tunbridge Wells, doubtless for his health, which was now giving way. He was at Tunbridge Wells in the autumn. The oratorio in question is supposed to have been *Saul*.

Mattheson wrote to Handel in 1735 asking particulars of his career for his *Ehrenpforte*. Handel answered on 29th July, thanking him and saying that 'it would be impossible for me to recall the events of my past life, since continual application to the service of this court and nobility prevents me from giving my attention to other matters.' Mattheson thereupon said he believed Handel thought that a present was expected from him.

Carestini now left London to fulfil engagements in Venice,

and Handel set to work on a new English work, *Alexander's Feast,* arranged for musical setting by his friend, Newburgh Hamilton, from Dryden's ode. This was completed in January 1736, and performed without action at Covent Garden on 19th February, the songs being sung by Strada, Cecilia Young, afterwards the wife of Arne, John Beard, the English tenor, and Erard, a bass. The ode had been arranged many years before by Newburgh Hamilton for Clayton, whose music was performed in York Buildings in 1711. Clayton's music had been a failure, but Handel's attracted no less than thirteen hundred persons, the receipts amounting to £450.

Walsh, who had published six Fugues for harpsichord by Handel, died on 13th March 1736, leaving to his children either £20,000 or £30,000 according to different accounts. He was a man of little education, but he had a keen scent where money was to be made by publishing popular musical works. If he could not publish them with the composer's partnership, he simply pillaged them, a proceeding which probably paid better, as he would then reap the whole instead of half the profits. His son, who continued the business, published for Handel. *Alexander's Feast* was published by him at a subscription price of two guineas. The cost of publication was greater than that of printing the operas, on account of the choruses. It was corrected by the composer, and a print of him, 'curiously engraved,' was given to the subscribers and encouragers of the work; but the publication was delayed for two years, when the composer's share of the profits amounted to £200.

The season was carried on with repetitions of *Alexander's Feast, Esther* and *Acis,* but proved a failure, in spite of Handel's bringing over a new singer, Gizziello (Conti), who made his first appearance on 5th May in *Ariodante* and sang on the 12th in *Atalanta,* which formed part of the festivities on the occasion of the marriage of Frederick, Prince of Wales, with Princess

Augusta of Saxe-Gotha, for which Handel had produced an anthem at the marriage ceremony on 27th April.

On 12th January 1737 *Arminio* was performed, but, meeting with little favour, it gave way to *Giustino* (16th January), which also had little success; but Handel was not to be beaten. Finding that operas no longer attracted the public, he gave regular performances of oratorios during Lent, with new concertos for the organ and other instruments, amongst other things reviving his early Italian work, *Il Trionfo del tempo,* in a new version.

But more defeats were in store for him. *Berenice,* produced on 18th May, failed to please, and the blow fell. The king, annoyed at the favour suddenly shown to Handel by the Prince of Wales after the wedding anthem and *Atalanta,* ceased his annual subscription of £1,000. Handel had spent the whole of the £10,000, the savings of many years, with which he began his management. He was deeply in debt, and was obliged to close his theatre. His health was entirely broken by the struggle; he suffered agonies from rheumatism; his mind gave way; on 13th April he had a stroke and his right arm and side became paralysed, so that he could no longer perform in public; and nervous prostration set in. The baths at Tunbridge Wells failed to do him good, though he was a little better in May, and began again to conduct his operas. But in the end he was forced to give up and go to the baths at Aix-la-Chapelle late in the summer.

The public had in reality become indifferent to opera. The novelty had worn off, and in the same year the rival house failed with a loss of £12,000. Farinelli, Senesino and Hasse, who had taken the place of Porpora and produced his *Artaserse* with success, quitted England, and London was left with the remainders of its ballad-operas, for which it had shown so strong a predilection. Covent Garden Theatre was now given over to performances of *The Dragon of Wantley,* a parody of *Giustino* by Carey, set to music by Lampe, Handel's bassoon player. Waltz played the part of the dragon. While Handel's finest operas were considered successful if they ran for sixteen or seventeen nights, this parody of one of them had a run of sixty-seven nights, while its libretto went into fourteen editions in one year.

CHAPTER X

RUINED HEALTH AND FORTUNE

HANDEL had a constitution of iron. He was with great difficulty persuaded to try the effect of the baths at Aix-la-Chapelle, but when he went there

he submitted to such sweats, excited by the vapour baths, as astonished every one. After a few essays of this kind, during which his spirits seemed to rise rather than sink under an excessive perspiration, his disorder left him; and in a few hours after the last operation he went to the great church of the city, and got to the organ, on which he played in such a manner that men imputed his cure to a miracle. Having received so much benefit from the baths, he prudently determined to stay at Aix-la-Chapelle till the end of six weeks from the time of his arrival there, and at the end thereof returned to London in perfect health.[1]

[There is a tradition that at Elbing, a town in East Prussia, documents were discovered, according to which the choruses for a cantata celebrating the five-hundredth anniversary of the foundation of Elbing were composed by 'Handel of London' during his stay at Aix. The music, if indeed it was ever composed, has not been traced.[2]]

[1] Hawkins, *History of Music,* vol. v, p. 326.
[2] According to Dent it is impossible 'to suggest any reason why the authorities of this remote place should have applied to Handel for a composition.' It is just possible, however, as Aix was not more inaccessible from Elbing than from London, that he may have met one of its prominent citizens there, who would naturally have seized the opportunity of offering him such a commission. —E. B.

The *London Daily Post* mentions that 'Mr. Handel, the composer of Italian music, returned on November 7th, greatly recovered in health.' He was certainly back in England soon after 29th October 1737, when Heidegger, collecting together the remains of the two defunct Italian opera companies, opened a season on his own account at the King's Theatre, for which he asked Handel to write two new operas and compile a pasticcio.

As the law stood at the time, Handel could have been sent to prison by his creditors; but his reputation for integrity and honesty was such that they all trusted him to discharge his debts as soon as he should be able, except Aurelio del Pò, the husband of Strada, who insisted on immediate payment.

Queen Caroline died on 20th November 1737, and Handel, who had begun the opera of *Faramondo* for Heidegger five days earlier, was obliged to abandon it for a funeral anthem. This was performed at the Chapel of Henry VII in Westminster Abbey on 17th December. The score of *The Ways of Zion do Mourn,* which occupies eighty pages of print, was composed in five days. The choirs of the Chapel Royal, Westminster Abbey, St. Paul's and Windsor took part in it; there were one hundred instrumentalists and eighty vocalists.

The death of the queen delayed the production of *Faramondo* to 3rd January 1738. It was a failure, in spite of the first appearance made in it by Caffarelli, a great male soprano new to England, and Handel tried with equally bad success the pasticcio *Alessandro Severo* on 25th February, and *Serse,* a comic opera on the subject of Xerxes,[1] on 15th April. But the tide was now at its lowest. Handel's misfortunes brought about a reaction in his favour. The public admired his courage and the strength of his character. His friends persuaded him to give a benefit concert, which he did much against his will.

[1] Containing the famous air, 'Ombra mai fù,' known as the 'Largo.'

This was advertised as an 'Oratorio,' but it in reality consisted of a number of extracts from his favourite works in the form of an ordinary concert. He also played a concerto on the organ. The theatre being crowded, seats were placed upon the stage and were occupied by no less than five hundred persons of rank. Every one seemed to wish to do the master honour, and the receipts, estimated by Burney at £800 and by Mainwaring at £1,500, were amply sufficient to pay off del Pò.

A month later a statue was erected to him in Vauxhall Gardens by Jonathan Tyers, the lessee of that place of entertainment. This statue, which was acknowledged to be an excellent likeness, was the first important work of Roubiliac and established his reputation. Handel gave many sittings for it, and the cost was £300. It was placed in a niche specially prepared for it, and on 2nd May was unveiled at a great concert of Handel's music, which was attended by a very large audience.[1]

Handel's music was very popular at Vauxhall and other public places. The following anecdote appears in the *History of the Parish of Marylebone*: [2]

While Marylebone Gardens were flourishing, the enchanting music of Handel, and probably of Arne, was often heard from the orchestra there. One evening, as my grandfather and Handel were walking together and alone, a new piece was struck up by the band. 'Come, Mr. Fountayne,' said Handel, 'let us sit down and listen to this piece. I want to know your opinion of it.' Down they sat, and after some time the old parson, turning to his companion, said: 'It is not worth listening to—it's very poor stuff.' 'You are right, Mr. Fountayne,' said Handel; 'it is very poor stuff. I thought so myself when I had just finished it.' The old gentleman, being

---

[1] It is now in the entrance hall at Messrs. Novello's in Wardour Street.—E. B.

[2] J. T. Smith, 1833.

taken by surprise, was beginning to apologize, but Handel assured him there was no necessity, that the music was really bad, having been composed hastily and his time for the production limited, and that the opinion given was as correct as it was honest.[1]

Handel, in spite of his failures, was by no means without admirers at this time. Besides Walsh, who had a portrait of him engraved, as we have already seen, they included Pope, Fielding, Hogarth, Smollett, Gay, Arbuthnot, Colley Cibber, Hughes and others. All his operas were published, whether they were successful or not. George II made a point of attending all the performances of his oratorios, even when the audiences were very thin. 'What, my lord,' said someone to Lord Chesterfield, who was seen coming out of Covent Garden theatre one evening, 'is there not an oratorio?' 'Yes,' said Lord Chesterfield; 'they are now performing, but I thought it best to retire, lest I should disturb the king in his privacy.' Princess Anne, on her departure after her marriage to the Prince of Orange, expressed her concern for her former music-master, and the Prince of Wales grew less and less hostile to him.

One of the results of the Italian opera was that many musicians, foreign and English, were attracted by the possibilities of reward to settle in London. The profession naturally became overcrowded. The weaker members, the old and infirm, the families of those who died, were pushed out of the competition, and found themselves starving.

Amongst the numerous oboe players who were thus attracted was one named Kytch, who had come from Germany, but becoming unable to support himself, had died of starvation in the street, while his two young sons made a miserable living by driving milch asses. Festing, a violinist, afterwards leader of the orchestra at Ranelagh Gardens, struck with pity at the

[1] Letter from the Rev. J. Fountayne.

sight of these boys, after raising a subscription to relieve the immediate wants of the family, induced Dr. Greene to help him to organize a permanent fund for the relief of similar cases. They were immediately joined by Handel, Dr. Boyce, Dr. Arne, Christopher Smith, Carey, Edward Purcell (son of the great Purcell), Leveridge, Dr. Pepusch and others, who in 1738 established a 'Fund for the support of Decayed Musicians and their Families.' Out of this grew the present Royal Society of Musicians of Great Britain. Handel, it will be seen, came forward at a time when he was himself in monetary distress to help others who were more unfortunate, and sank all his differences with Greene, Arne, Pepusch and others in the cause of charity. How nobly he continued to support the 'Fund' for the rest of his life will appear in the course of this histroy.

[This was not the only charity in which Handel took an active share. Like Hogarth, he showed much interest in the Foundling Hospital, founded by Captain Coram in 1740, an institution to which he was to present an organ and of which he was to become a governor later.]

On 20th March 1739 *Alexander's Feast* was performed with various concertos for the organ and a new concerto specially composed for the benefit of the Fund for Poor Musicians. This took place at the King's Theatre. Not only was the house full, but many gave subscriptions over and above the price of the tickets. Heidegger gave £20 and Handel gave the theatre and his own services. He could do no more. He was still deeply in debt, and he gave his services in circumstances under which he could quite reasonably have claimed some of the profits for himself.

Heidegger failed in 1738. He had advertised that he would continue the opera if two hundred subscribers came forward; but they did not, and London was now without an opera.

Handel wrote seven Sonatas for two violins, flutes or oboes and harpsichord (Op. 5) in 1738 and published the first six organ concertos (Op. 4) in October.

To all lovers of music: whereas there are six concertos for the organ by Mr. Handel published this day, some of which have been already printed by Mr. Walsh, and the others done without the knowledge or consent of Mr. Handel: this is to give notice, that the same six are printing, and will be published in a few days, corrected by the author.—J. WALSH.

In 1739 Handel took the King's Theatre for the performance of oratorio twice a week, and from this time he gave twelve performances every year during Lent. The first oratorio he gave here was *Saul*, which had occupied him from 3rd July to 27th September 1738. It contains the longest of Handel's overtures. At the end of the second of the four movements the organ, which is used throughout as a solo instrument, is given an empty space in the score, marked *organo ad libitum*. Here Handel gave an extempore performance. The third movement, a fugue, contains brilliant organ solo passages. The oratorio was performed 'with several new concertos on the organ,' but some numbers are marked in the book of words as having to be omitted.

On 4th April 1739 *Israel in Egypt* was performed 'with several new concertos on the organ.' This work had been composed in twenty-seven days during the previous year, being completed on 11th October 1738. It does not seem to have been successful, and was repeated on the 11th 'in a shortened form, intermixed with songs.' These songs were Italian ballads; and the oratorio was preceded at both performances by the *Funeral Anthem* as a lamentation for the death of Joseph. The audience, accustomed to a lighter form of art, could not tolerate the succession of massive eight-part choruses. A letter, however, appeared in the *London Daily*

Post from one of the audience, begging for a repetition of the work, and shortly afterwards a paragraph: 'We are informed that Mr. Handel, at the desire of several persons of distinction, intends to perform again his last new oratorio of *Israel in Egypt,* on Tuesday next, the 17th inst.' It had thus three perform-ances in its first year. A fourth was advertised, but given up. 'This day, the last new oratorio called *Saul,* and not *Israel in Egypt,* as by mistake was advertised in yesterday's bills and papers; with a concerto on the organ by Mr. Handel, and another on the violin, by the famous Signor Piantanida, who is just arrived from abroad.' It had one performance in 1740, 'with a new concerto for several instruments, and a concerto on the organ,' and then was shelved till 1756.

In *Israel* Handel did not use a text by a modern writer, but chose words from Scripture itself. The second part was written first, and called 'Moses' Song, Exodus, chapter xv.' The first, or historical part, was added afterwards. Of the borrowing in which Handel indulged to so great an extent here, and which indeed became a habit with him from this time onward, we will speak later. The oratorio was per-formed by the Academy of Ancient Music on 10th May 1739 under the title 'The Song of Moses and the Funeral Anthem for her late Majesty, set to music by Mr. Handel,' and it was also given in Oxford.

A pasticcio, *Jupiter in Argos,* composed in April 1739, was advertised for 1st May, but it is doubtful whether the per-formance ever took place.

In November Handel was again in the theatre in Lincoln's Inn Fields, when 'a new ode, with two new concertos for several instruments, preceded by *Alexander's Feast,* and a concerto on the organ,' were announced for St. Cecilia's Day, 22nd November 1739. It was also announced that 'the passage from the fields to the house will be covered for better conveniency.'

The words of the 'new ode' were by Dryden. St. Cecilia's
Day was at that time honoured by musical performances on
a grand scale, which had been first instituted by Purcell and
his master, John Blow. They took the form of concerts in
the theatres or a performance of the *Te Deum* in cathedrals
and churches. Purcell's *Te Deum and Jubilate* in D were composed for a performance in honour of St. Cecilia in 1694.
Cecilia societies were founded in most of the important towns
in England, and odes were written by the best poets. Thus
Dryden wrote *Alexander's Feast, or the Power of Music* and *A
Song for St. Cecilia's Day,* and Pope, who, though having no
ear for music, was not so crass as not to respect an art so closely
allied to his own, wrote a fine *Ode on St. Cecilia's Day,* in
praise of music, which Greene set to music as his Doctor's
exercise. Pope, who had a genuine admiration for Handel's
genius, wished him to set this ode, and employed Belchier, a
friend of both, to negotiate. But Handel would have nothing
to do with it, saying: 'It is the very thing my bellows-blower
has set already for a Doctor's degree at Cambridge.' Christopher Smith asked why Pope, who was absolutely insensible
to music, had praised Handel in his *Dunciad*; Pope said: 'That
merit in every branch of science ought to be encouraged; that
the extreme illiberality with which many persons had joined
to ruin Handel, in opposing his operas, called forth his indignation; and though nature had denied his being gratified by
Handel's uncommon talents in the musical line, yet when his
powers were generally acknowledged, he thought it incumbent
on him to pay a tribute due to genius.'

Pope one day asked Arbuthnot, of whose knowledge in
music he had a high idea, what was his real opinion in regard
to Handel as a master of that science. The doctor immediately
replied: 'Conceive the highest that you can of his abilities,
and they are much beyond anything that you can conceive.'

In February 1740 there was a great frost, and we read that

'In consideration of the weather continuing so cold, the serenata called *Acis and Galatea* will be put off for a few nights further, of which due notice will be given.' Opera seems now to have entirely given way to oratorio, for the season was occupied with several performances each of *Alexander's Feast, Ode for St. Cecilia's Day, Acis, Saul, Esther* and *Israel in Egypt*. [There was also a new work, *L'Allegro, il Pensieroso ed il Moderato*, adapted from Milton by Charles Jennens, who wrote the third part entirely himself. It was produced on 27th February, but, owing to the intense cold, wretchedly attended.]

In the same year (21st April) there were published twelve *Concerti grossi* in seven parts, for four violins, viola and violoncello, with a thoroughbass for the harpsichord (Op. 6), the seven Sonatas or Trios (Op. 5) having been issued on 3rd March 1739. The latter was sold to subscribers at two guineas, and was under 'His Majesty's royal licence and protection.'

Although this season again proved unsuccessful, Handel, in spite of his troubles and his debts, gave a performance on 28th March of *Acis* and Dryden's Ode 'for the Musical Fund benefit.' The bitter persecution of his enemies continued, and extended even to tearing down his play-bills as fast as he could put them up. But he must have received some consolation in the efforts of poets to sing the praise of the man who had gone through so much and had borne himself so well in the fight. Newburgh Hamilton writes:

To Mr. Handel on his setting to musick Mr. Dryden's *Feast of Alexander*.

> Let others charm the list'ning scaly brood,
> Or tame the savage monsters of the wood;
> With magick notes enchant the leafy grove,
> Or force ev'n things inanimate to move:
> Be ever your's (my friend) the god-like art
> To calm the passions, and improve the heart;

. . . . .

That artist's hand (whose skill alone could move
To glory, grief, or joy, the Son of Jove)
Not greater raptures to the Grecian gave,
Than British Theatres from you receive:
That Ignorance and Envy vanquished see,
Heav'n made you rule the world by Harmony.

.   .   .

Had Dryden lived, the welcome day to bless
Which cloth'd his numbers in so fit a dress;
When his Majestic Poetry was crowned
With all your bright magnificence of sound;
How would his wonder and his transport rise?
Whilst famed Timotheus yields to you the prize.

Handel found it hard to give up his beloved opera entirely. On 22nd November 1740 he produced *Imeneo,* or *Hymen,* which was withdrawn after two representations, as he had by this time no company left who could give an adequate performance of Italian opera. His last opera, *Deidamia,* completed on 20th November 1740 and produced on 10th January the following year, was withdrawn after three performances. After this he abandoned opera for ever. On 8th April 1741 he gave a farewell concert.

Some of the songs from *L'Allegro* were published by Walsh on 15th March 1740 at four shillings, and a second collection of the songs was published in May at three shillings, the two collections containing the whole of the songs in the three parts of the work. Walsh also published the six organ Concertos (Op. 7) that year.

CHAPTER XI

THE LATER ORATORIOS

IN 1741 Charles Jennens, who had now become one of Handel's most intimate friends, selected for him from Scripture the words of an oratorio on the subject of the Messiah.[1] Handel had been invited by the fourth Duke of Devonshire, then Lord Lieutenant of Ireland, to pay a visit to Dublin, where many performances of his works had taken place, and where he was held in great esteem. He therefore resolved to offer *Messiah*, on which he was engaged, 'to that generous and polite nation' in aid of certain charitable societies, for every charitable work interested him. We learn by the autograph score in the Royal Library that it was begun on 22nd August 1741, that the first part was finished on 28th August, the second part on 6th September, the third on 12th September, and that the 'filling-in' was completed by 14th September. The composition of the whole, therefore, occupied twenty-two days. On 29th October he finished another oratorio, *Samson*, with the exception of three numbers.

He is supposed to have left London about 4th or 5th November, but he did not arrive in Dublin until the 18th. He probably performed the journey by easy stages. Burney, who was then at school at Chester, relates that he saw him smoke a pipe over a dish of coffee at the Exchange Coffee-house. He was detained at Chester (near which was the place of embarkation for Ireland) by contrary winds for several

---

[1] Or rather, he had them selected for him by Pooley, his chaplain, and then complacently passed them off as his own work.—E. B.

days, and during this time he applied to Mr. Baker, organist of the cathedral, to know if there were any choir-men who could sing at sight, for he wished to try some of the choruses which he intended to perform in Ireland. A time was appointed at the Golden Falcon Inn, where Handel was staying. But alas! on trial of the chorus, 'And with His stripes we are healed,' poor Janson (a printer and the principal bass of the choir), after repeated attempts, failed so egregiously that Handel let loose his great bear upon him; and, after swearing at him in four or five different languages, cried out, in broken English: 'You scoundrel! did you not tell me that you could sing at sight?' 'Yes, sir,' said the printer, 'and so I can, but not at *first sight*.'

The account of the visit to Ireland is very interesting, and has been fully recorded by Horatio Townsend. A new concert room, capable of accommodating an audience of six hundred persons, had recently been erected in Fishamble Street, then a fashionable quarter. Here took place the meetings of the Musical Academy, an amateur society consisting of members of the aristocracy only. Lord Mornington [1] was the president and leader of the band; Lord Belamont and Dean Burke were violoncellists; Lord Lucan played the flute; Lady Freke, the Right Hon. W. Brownlow and Dr. Quin the harpsichord. Though the meetings were mostly private, the society performed once a year for charities, when the public were admitted on payment.

Faulkner's Journal of 21st November 1741 announces that 'last Wednesday the celebrated Dr. Handel arrived here, in the packet boat from Holyhead . . . to perform his Oratorios, for which purpose he hath engaged Mr. Maclaine, his wife, and several others of the best performers in the musical way.' Maclaine was an excellent organist. Later on we read: 'Last

[1] Afterwards doctor and professor of music at Dublin University. He was the composer of the well-known double chant in E flat.

Tuesday arrived in the Yacht from Park Gate, Signora Avolio, an excellent singer, who comes to this kingdom to perform in Mr. Handel's musical entertainments.' *Messiah,* however, was not performed yet. Several public 'entertainments' took place at the new music hall, the first being on 23rd December, at which *L'Allegro* was performed, interspersed with the usual two grand concertos and an organ concerto, and considered 'superior to anything of the kind in the kingdom before.' The same music was repeated in January, by command of the Duke and Duchess of Devonshire, and was followed a week later by *Acis* and other works. By this time the entertainments had become so popular that it was found necessary to regulate the traffic, to hire a convenient room for the footmen and to make a new passage for sedan-chairs.

The choruses were sung by members of the Philharmonic Society, the Musical Academy and such members of the choirs of both cathedrals as would give their services. Altogether eight of these concerts took place before *Messiah* was performed, and great enthusiasm prevailed. Handel had been naturally anxious that his works should be performed to the best advantage. Before leaving London he had stipulated that the trained choirs of the cathedrals should take part. This stipulation was agreed to by the authorities for charity concerts only, since it was found that promiscuous singing at concerts led to imaginary or real abuses. He had been some five months in Dublin, and the enthusiasm for him had reached the highest pitch, when the following notice appeared in *Faulkner's Journal,* 27th March 1742:

For the relief of the prisoners in the several gaols, and for the support of Mercer's Hospital, and the Charitable Infirmary, on Monday the 12th of April will be performed at the Musick Hall in Fishamble Street, Mr. Handel's grand new oratorio, called *The Messiah,* in which the gentlemen of the choirs of both cathedrals will assist, with some concertos on the organ by Mr. Handell. Tickets to be had at the Musick Hall, and at Mr. Neal's in Christ Church Yard, at half-a-guinea each. *N.B.*—No person will be admitted to the rehearsal without a rehearsal ticket, which will be given gratis with the ticket for the performance when pay'd for.

On 10th April a further notice requested the ladies to come without hoops on the day of the performance, 13th April, which they did. This enabled seven hundred persons to attend, and the receipts amounted to about £400, of which £127 was given to each of the three 'great and pious charities.' The three Dublin papers concurred in praising the oratorio:

The best judges allowed it to be the most finished piece of music. Words are wanting to express the delight it afforded to the admiring, crowded audience. The sublime, the grand, and the tender, adapted to the most elevated, majestic and moving words, conspired to transport and charm the ravished heart and ear. It is but justice to Mr. Handel that the world should know he generously gave the money arising from this grand performance to be equally shared by the Society for relieving prisoners, the Charitable Infirmary and Mercer's Hospital, for which they will ever gratefully remember his name; and that the gentlemen of the two choirs, Mr. Dubourg, Mrs. Avolio and Mrs. Cibber, who all performed their parts to admiration, acted also on the same disinterested principle.

'At the particular desire of several of the nobility and gentry' a second performance took place on 3rd June. In order to keep the room as cool as possible, a pane of glass was removed from the top of each window. This was Handel's last performance in Dublin. On 12th August he embarked on a Chester trader, with 'several other persons of distinction,' to go to Parkgate, and reached London in due course.

His visit to Dublin was one of the pleasantest episodes in his stormy career. Here he found peace and, what is more to an artist, complete appreciation of his works. He fully intended to renew his acquaintance with the friendly Irish public in the following year, but events happened which prevented his ever going to Dublin again.

Handel was not certain as to his movements on his return to London. In a letter to Mr. Jennens of 9th September he says:

The report that the direction of the opera next winter is committed to my care is groundless. The gentlemen who have undertaken to meddle with harmony cannot agree, and are quite in a confusion. Whether I shall do something in the oratorio way (as several of my friends desire), I cannot determine as yet. Certain it is, that this time twelvemonth I shall continue my oratorios in Ireland, where they are going to make a large subscription already for that purpose.

Samson, at any rate, was almost ready, and he added the two numbers which completed it on 12th October 1742. The first performance took place at Covent Garden Theatre on 18th February 1743, the part of Samson being sung by Beard, Manoah by Savage, Micah by Mrs. Cibber and Delilah by Mrs. Clive. The only foreign singer employed was Signora Avolio. The trumpet obbligato in 'Let the bright seraphim' was played by Valentine Snow. The old hostility had not quite died out. Horace Walpole writes:

Handel has set up an oratorio against the opera, and succeeds. He has hired all the goddesses from the farces, and the singers of roast beef from between the acts at both theatres, with a man with one note in his voice, and a girl without ever an one, and so they sing and make brave hallelujahs, and the good company encore the recitative, if it happens to have any cadence like what they call a tune.

Dubourg, the famous Dublin violinist, joined him, and *Faulkner's Journal* endeavoured to encourage Handel by a friendly notice; but the season again seems not to have been very successful. *Samson* was performed eight times, *Messiah* three times (the first performance in London was on 23rd

March 1743), and *L'Allegro* and the Cecilia Ode once each. None of the London papers seems to have noticed any of these performances, and the season was concluded with *Samson* on 30th March.

Between 3rd June and 4th July Handel wrote *Semele,* and then began the *Te Deum* and Anthem, solemnly sung in the presence of George II at St. James's Chapel on 27th November 1743 in honour of the victory of the British army under the personal command of the king over Marshal de Noailles and the Duc de Grammont at Dettingen on 27th June..

'By particular desire' Handel set to work to arrange for twelve subscription oratorio performances for Lent 1744. The subscription price was four guineas, and the composer engaged to give two new oratorios, besides some of his former ones. The first of the two new works was 'an English opera, but called an oratorio, and performed as such,'[1] at Covent Garden on 10th February. Its name was *Semele* and it was set to a libretto by Congreve, written in 1707 and revised for Handel, with words for a new song, 'Where 'r you walk, by Pope. The second was *Joseph and his Brethren,* in which a pupil of Handel, Signora Galli, made her first appearance on 2nd March.[2] It is said that Handel's power of teaching singers was at least equal to his power of composing music for them.

From June to October he was in correspondence with Jennens about a new oratorio called *Belteshazzar,* but the name was afterwards changed to its present form, *Belshazzar.* Handel found it too long. It would, he said, occupy more than four hours, though he had retrenched the music as far as possible. As the conceited Jennens would not curtail his words, Handel caused them all to be printed, but cut out some two hundred

---

[1] i.e. without action.

[2] The first in a work by Handel. She had already come before a London audience in Galuppi's *Enrico* in 1743, and was known in Italy before that.—E. B.

lines in the performance. It came to a hearing on 27th March 1745, but previously to this, on 5th January, he had performed a 'musical drama' called *Hercules*, composed during the correspondence on *Belshazzar*.

When Handel had failed in 1737, a new opera company was started at the King's Theatre in the Haymarket under Lord Middlesex, who carried it on at a loss for some years. This opposition society now failed, and Handel was therefore able to take the King's Theatre again in the autumn of 1744; but though unable to support a rival opera, his enemies were by no means inactive. They resorted to the old trick of giving balls and card parties on the nights of his oratorios, although the season was Lent, and succeeded in making his audiences so thin that he was forced to give up his enterprise again, for the proceeds of his Irish visit had been devoted to the payment of his former creditors. But it was not at all in keeping with his character to give in to misfortune. He returned to the battle next season at Covent Garden, where he gave twenty-four subscription performances. The subscription was to be eight guineas for a box ticket for the season, the performances to take place every Saturday till Lent, when they were to be twice a week.

Deborah, with a concerto on the organ, was given on 24th November, and a new work, the *Occasional Oratorio*, was first heard on 14th February 1746. The 'occasion' it celebrated was the suppression of the Jacobite rebellion under the Young Pretender, Charles Edward. It borrowed much music from *Israel in Egypt* and contained a quotation of Arne's 'Rule, Britannia.' Handel also wrote two smaller topical works, a song for the Gentlemen Volunteers of the City of London, sung at Drury Lane on 14th November 1745, and a 'Song of Victory over the Rebels,' published in the *London Magazine* for July 1746. Hawkins says that he frequently played to houses that would not pay his expenses, and Burney mentions a Lady Brown, who gave very fine concerts and distinguished herself as a persevering enemy of Handel. A famous mimic and singer named Russell was engaged by certain ladies to set up a puppet-show in opposition to the oratorios of Handel, but he was not properly supported, became bankrupt and was thrown into prison, where he lost his reason. Thereupon his patronesses subscribed £5, on payment of which he was admitted to Bedlam, where he naturally became hopelessly mad and died in the utmost misery. We have seen how narrowly Handel escaped the same horrible fate. [There is good reason to suppose that he would have gone mad had he been thrown into the debtors' prison, for there is some evidence, including a letter from Lord Shaftesbury, that ever since his paralytic stroke and all through his financial troubles he had 'been a good deal disordered in the head.'] Smollett, who was a friend of Handel, writes:

> Again shall Handel raise his laurel'd brow,
> Again shall harmony with rapture glow;
> The spells dissolve—the combination breaks,
> And Punch, no longer Frasi's rival, squeaks.
> Lo! Russell falls a sacrifice to whim,
> And starts amaz'd, in Newgate, from his dream;
> With trembling hands implores their promis'd aid,
> And sees their favour like a vision fade![1]

The result of these machinations was that Handel had to close his theatre after the sixteenth performance and was once more deeply in debt.[2]

[On 25th March 1746 Handel appeared at a concert with Gluck, who visited England in the autumn of the preceding year, at the age of thirty-one. Handel on this occasion played an organ concerto of his own. He was on friendly terms with

[1] Smollett, *Advice: a Satire.*
[2] He had, however, as Professor Dent reminds us, his regular income of six hundred pounds a year from the court.—E. B.

the younger composer, although he declared his music to be detestable. Too much has been made, however, of his remark that Gluck knew no more counterpoint than his own cook, seeing that the cook was Waltz, the bass singer, who may quite possibly have been a good enough musician to have more than a smattering of counterpoint. For the rest, the fact remains that Gluck really was weak in that particular.]

The tide was again about to turn. Handel resolved to attempt no more subscription performances, but to open Covent Garden Theatre to all comers and not to bind himself to any definite number of works. He had become acquainted with a learned antiquarian and scholar, Thomas Morell, a Doctor of Divinity, and he now proposed to him the feats of Judas Maccabaeus as a good subject for an oratorio. Morell took to the idea, provided a libretto, and Handel, setting to work on 9th July 1746, had finished the composition by 11th August—thirty-three days. It is said that the subject had been suggested to Handel by the Prince of Wales to celebrate the return of his brother, the Duke of Cumberland, after the victory at Culloden on 16th April, and the words were dedicated to the prince by the author.

The oratorio, which was produced on 1st April 1747, appealed not only to the political feelings of the time, but the Jews flocked to hear the exploits of their national hero drama-tized. The result was an immediate success; and that it was lasting is shown by the fact that Handel himself performed the work thirty-eight times. Rockstro points out that in the chorus 'We never will bow down to the rude stock and sculptured stone,' with its magnificent finale, 'We worship God, and God alone,' 'Handel preached a sermon in his own resistless language to which neither Jew nor Christian could listen unmoved.'

Lucio Vero, a pasticcio made up of songs pirated from various operas by Handel, was performed in 1747 at the Italian opera and afterwards published by Walsh. It was found necessary to use his music and his name to attract an audience to the rival theatre, and this was not the first occasion that such measures were taken, for in 1734 his opera, *Ottone,* and in 1743 *Roxana* (another name for *Alessandro*), had been performed in the theatre that was opened for the avowed purpose of ruining him.

On 1st June 1747 Handel began *Alexander Balus,* and finished it on 4th July, and on the 30th of this month he began *Joshua,* which was finished on 19th August. Dr. Morell was the author of the words of both oratorios. In later years Haydn, after hearing the latter work performed, said to Shield that 'he had long been acquainted with music, but never knew half its powers before he heard it, as he was perfectly certain that only one inspired author ever did, or ever would, pen so sublime a composition.' He particularly referred to the chorus in *Joshua,* 'The nations tremble.' Both works were performed at Covent Garden in March 1748 (9th and 23rd).

Handel was now sixty-three years old, but he was as indefatigable as ever. As soon as the season was over, he set to work on two more oratorios, *Solomon* in May and June, and *Susanna* in July and August. These two works came to a performance during the following season, *Susanna* on 10th February and *Solomon* on 17th March. The score of *Solomon* is written on all kinds of paper, from which Schoelcher concludes, doubtless quite wrongly, that Handel's affairs were still in an unsatisfactory condition, and that he could not afford to buy even the necessary music-paper.[1]

On 7th October 1748 the peace of Aix-la-Chapelle was signed, and Handel was called upon to provide music for the festivities that took place on 27th April 1749. The most important item in these celebrations was a display of fireworks

[1] The scores were usually written in oblong books of ten staves to the page.

in Green Park. A wooden 'machine' was erected, 114 feet in height and 410 feet in length, representing a Doric temple, from a design by the Cavaliere Servandoni, a famous designer of theatrical settings. A band of a hundred musicians played an 'Overture' by Mr. Handel, a royal salute of 101 brass cannons was fired, the fireworks commenced, and unfortunately set fire to the temple, whereby the Royal Library narrowly escaped destruction. A rehearsal of the music had previously taken place at Vauxhall Gardens, before an audience of twelve thousand. The crowd was so great that it blocked all wheeled traffic on London Bridge for three hours, such was the power of Handel's music to attract. The composition consists of a number of short movements scored for three trumpets, three pairs of drums, three horns, three oboes, two bassoons, serpents, strings and side-drums. There were three players to each trumpet and horn part, twenty-four oboe players, twelve bassoonists, and the string and side-drum and serpent [1] players seem to have made up the number to a hundred as mentioned in the papers. The work became very popular and was frequently played at concerts.

A few days after the performance in Green Park, Handel gave a second performance of the *Fireworks Music,* with other pieces, including an anthem specially composed (Foundling Anthem), in the chapel of the Foundling Hospital, in the presence of the Prince and Princess of Wales. Tickets were sold at half a guinea; the king gave £2,000, an anonymous donor £50, and the proceeds were devoted to finishing the chapel. For this generosity Handel was immediately enrolled as one of the governors and guardians of the hospital.

---

[1] This was the only work in which Handel employed the serpent, a kind of bass cornet. He did not like the tone of it, and a story is told that one day, hearing a bad player performing on it, he said: 'What the devil be that?' On being told it was a serpent, he said: 'Oh, the serpent; aye, but it be not the serpent that seduced Eve.'

[On 8th January 1750 Handel finished incidental music to a dramatic piece by Smollett, based on the *Alcestis* of Euripides, to be staged at Covent Garden by Rich. But it was withdrawn and he used nearly all the music for the interlude, *The Choice of Hercules,* which he finished on 5th July.] On 16th March of the same year a new oratorio, *Theodora,* was produced, 'with a new concerto on the organ.' It was not a success, and Handel endeavoured to fill the house by giving away tickets to professional musicians who were not performing. This led to two of them asking for tickets for a performance of *Messiah*; whereupon Handel broke out in a rage: 'Oh, your servant, meine Herren, you are damnable dainty; you would not go to *Theodora*; there was room enough to dance there when that was perform!'

It is rather pathetic to see how devoted Handel always remained to this unfortunate oratorio, which never attracted the public. Before one performance he said to an intimate friend: 'Will you be here next Friday night? I will play it to *you.*' On another occasion he heard that someone had engaged to take all the boxes, in case it was again performed; whereupon he remarked: 'He is a fool; the Jews will not come to it, as to *Judas Maccabaeus,* because it is a Christian story; and the ladies will not come because it is a virtuous one.' Burney heard him say, when the house was very empty: 'Never mind; the music will sound the better.'

CHAPTER XII

THE LAST YEARS

HANDEL must by this time have paid off his creditors, for in 1750 he presented the Foundling Hospital with a fine organ and opened it with a performance of *Messiah* on 1st May. The tickets were sold at half a guinea each, and the proceeds given to the hospital. It was calculated that the chapel could hold about a thousand persons, the ladies coming without hoops and the gentlemen without swords; yet so great was the demand for seats that Handel gave a second performance a fortnight later, to which those who had bought tickets and had not been able to find room were admitted, besides others who desired to come.

Rockstro gives the specification of the organ, which is interesting as showing the kind of instrument in use at that time. It had three manuals, but no pedals. It was built by Morse of Barnet. The natural keys were black, the sharps being white.[1] The compass of the Great and Choir was from GG to E in alt, that of the Swell from fiddle G to the same note. There were twenty-one stops, arranged as follows:

GREAT: Double-stopped Diapason, Open Diapason 1, Open Diapason 2, Stopped Diapason, Principal 1, Principal 2,

[1] This was not an unusual feature in the organs of those days. The picture by Thornhill in the Fitzwilliam Museum shows Handel playing on a keyboard of this kind; a fine three-manual organ by Father Smith, belonging to the Mercers' Company, had the same arrangement of the keys. The organ that preceded the present one in Sevenoaks Church also had a similar arrangement of the keys.

Flute, Twelfth, Fifteenth, Bock-flute, Sesquialtera of 3 ranks, Trumpet.

CHOIR: Dulciana, Stopped Diapason, Principal, Fifteenth, Vox humana.

SWELL: Open Diapason, Stopped Diapason, Trumpet, Cremona.

This organ was replaced by a new one in 1854. The movement in favour of the now universal 'equal temperament' for keyed instruments had already begun in Germany, but had not yet reached England, and in order to enlarge the range of keys available, Handel caused four out of the five sharps to be doubled, so that there were separate sounds for G♯ and A♭, A♯ and B♭, C♯ and D♭, D♯ and E♭, the only sharp left single being F♯, which had to serve for G♭. It is not impossible that had Handel been as scientific a musician as Bach, he would have adopted equal temperament, and thus saved the duplication of sounds.[1]

From 28th June to 5th July 1750 Handel was engaged in composing *The Choice of Hercules,* and he then paid a short visit to Germany. The *General Advertiser* of 21st August announces that 'Mr. Handel, who went to Germany to visit his friends some time since, and, between the Hague and Haarlem, had the misfortune to be overturned, by which he was terribly hurt, is now out of danger.' There seems to be no further record of this visit to Germany, except a remark of

---

[1] For the uninitiated it may be explained that it is impossible with only twelve sounds in an octave to have all keys in tune. If a few keys are tuned perfectly, the remainder will be so harsh as to be unendurable. 'Equal temperament' puts all keys equally out of tune, but so slightly as to be unappreciable, and the composer has all keys equally at command. Bach's forty-eight Preludes and Fugues in all major and minor keys were written to prove the possibilities of equal temperament.

Forkel's that on Handel's third visit to Halle, Bach (who had wished to meet him) was dead.

On 21st January 1751 Handel began his last new work, *Jephtha,* which was not finished, however, till August. It is signed 'G. F. Handel ætatis 66, Finis Agost. 30, 1751.' The work was interrupted in February by illness, which drove him to Cheltenham for the sake of the waters after the completion of the second act. The third act was begun on 18th June and continued till 17th July, when his illness again seized him, and he was forced to stop work till 13th August. By this time his sight had begun to fail and was rapidly becoming worse. Yet he gave two performances of *Messiah* in April and May 1751, 'with an extempore on the organ.' His sight was too far gone to allow of his playing any longer from notes. *Jephtha* was produced on 26th February 1752.

He now placed himself in the hands of Samuel Sharp, the surgeon at Guy's Hospital, who found that he was suffering from incipient cataract. Hawkins says that

his spirits forsook him, and that fortitude which had supported him under afflictions of another kind deserted him in this, scarce leaving him patience to wait for that crisis in his disorder in which he might hope for relief. . . . Repeated attempts to relieve him were fruitless, and he was given to expect that a freedom from pain in the visual organs was all that he had to hope for the remainder of his days. As he could now no longer conduct his oratorios, he called upon Smith, the son of his amanuensis, to assist him, while he was forced to confine himself to extempore voluntaries on the organ.

He underwent three painful operations with no result.[1] [One of them was performed by the famous John Taylor, who had already operated unsuccessfully on Bach.] The

[1] The treatment consisted in forcing a needle through the eyeball. Anaesthetics were not in use in those days.

Theatrical Register informs us that on 3rd May 1752 he was couched by William Bramfield, surgeon to the Princess of Wales. This was the last operation, and for a few days his sight was restored, but it again left him and never returned.

He was at first quite overwhelmed by his misfortune, but gathering courage he sent for his pupil, the younger Smith, from France, and together with him began a new season on 9th March 1753. At first Smith played the organ, but Handel soon recovered sufficient courage to play his concertos from memory, and afterwards extempore.

At the performance of *Samson* this season many of the audience were moved to tears during the singing of

> Total eclipse, no sun, no moon,
> All dark amidst the blaze of noon.

at the sight of the old blind composer sitting near the organ. Burney says that to see him led to the organ at seventy years of age, and afterwards conducted towards the audience to make his accustomed obeisance, was a sight so truly affecting and deplorable to persons of sensibility as greatly to diminish their pleasure in hearing his performance.

Schoelcher has shown that Handel must have been able to see a little at intervals during his blindness. A pencilled correction in his handwriting is found in a score of *Jephtha*, made by Smith in the year 1758, and he was able to write his signature to all the four codicils to his will. The pencilled note of music is written with a trembling hand and is higher than the line on which he wished to place it, and in the duplicate signatures to the codicil of 1757 the letters are wide apart and very distinct.

But though Handel ceased to conduct after he became blind, an organist, John Stanley, who had lost his sight when two years old, was announced in 1753 to conduct the performance of *Alexander's Feast* and to play a concerto on the organ at the King's Theatre for the benefit of the Smallpox Hospital. In those days the conductor sat at the harpsichord, accompanied the recitatives, filled in the harmonies, and apparently kept the band together by playing some chords if they got out. Spohr, who conducted the Philharmonic Society in 1820, insisted on conducting after the continental manner with a baton, and he says that no one after this was seen seated at the piano during the performance of symphonies and overtures. It would be as impossible for a blind man to conduct, in the modern sense, as for a deaf man to do so, but it would be quite possible for a blind man, gifted with unusual memory, to control the band from the harpsichord.

Little is known of the next few years of Handel's life beyond the fact that his enemies were now silenced and that he and Smith continued to give performances of oratorios. In the evening of his life these became attractive enough to enable him not only to pay all his debts but to amass another fortune of £20,000. He was neither lavish nor parsimonious. He at all times lived within his means and in ordinary comfort. When his fortune increased he was enabled to give more in charity and to give his services more frequently in the same cause. He had an enormous appetite, due probably to the immense strain to which he subjected his physical powers during the production of his works. His only recreation before he was blind was to visit picture galleries; every other hour of the day, and, judging from the prodigious rapidity with which he produced his works, most of the night also, were given up to the most strenuous labour. With his income he might easily have kept a carriage, but he lived a perfectly simple life until his blindness forced him to employ a hackney coach.

He continued to work till the very end. In 1757 the *Triumph of Time and Truth,* a new version of the Italian *Il Trionfo del tempo* of 1708, which he dictated to Smith, was performed at Covent Garden. In 1758 it was repeated, with nine new pieces dictated by the composer. The Italian words of Cardinal Panfili were translated into English by an unknown author, the recitatives were to a great extent recomposed.

As his health deteriorated, Handel suffered increasingly from fits of terrible depression. In the beginning of 1759, Mainwaring says, 'He was very sensible of the approach of death, and refused to be flattered by any hopes of a recovery.' He lost his great appetite; yet he worked on. In February he gave *Solomon*, 'with new additions and alterations.' In March *Solomon, Susanna, Samson, Judas Maccabaeus* and *Messiah*. The season was the most prosperous he had ever had. On 6th April *Messiah* was performed at Covent Garden for the last time in the season. He was seized with faintness during the performance and went home to his bed, never to rise from it again. On 11th April he added a fourth codicil to his will. He was perfectly aware that death was upon him and wished that he might expire on Good Friday, 'in hopes of meeting his good God, his sweet Lord and Saviour, on the day of His resurrection.' Burney says, on the authority of Dr. Warren, who attended him in his last illness, that he died before midnight on Good Friday, 13th April 1759; but the *Public Advertiser* of 16th April says: 'Last Saturday, and not before, died at his house in Brook Street, Grosvenor Square, that eminent Master of Music, George Frederick Handel, Esq.'

In confirmation of the fact that the correct date is 14th April a letter is extant from James Smyth, a perfumer of Bond Street, an intimate friend of Handel's, to Bernard Granville, of Calwich, Derbyshire, which runs as follows:

17th April 1759.

DEAR SIR,—According to your request to me, when you left London, that I would let you know when our good friend departed this life—on Saturday last, at eight o'clock in the morning, died the great and good Mr. Handel. He was sensible to the last moment; made a codicil to his will on Tuesday; ordered to be buried privately in Westminster Abbey, and a monument not to exceed £500 for him. I had the pleasure to reconcile him to his old friends; he saw them, and forgave them, and let all their legacies stand. In the codicil he left many legacies to his friends; and among the rest, he left me £500, and has left to you the two pictures you formerly gave him. He took leave of all his friends on Friday morning, and desired to see nobody but the doctor, and apothecary, and myself. At seven o'clock in the evening he took leave of me, and told me we should meet again. As soon as I was gone, he told his servant not to let me come to him any more, for now he had done with the world. He died as he lived, a good Christian, with a true sense of his duty to God and man, and in perfect charity with all the world.[1]

The funeral took place at Westminster Abbey, on 20th April, at about eight o'clock in the evening. Though it was private, no less than three thousand persons attended, and a sermon was preached by the dean, Dr. Zachary Pearce, Bishop of Rochester. Music by Croft, his former colleague, was sung by the choirs of the Abbey, the Chapel Royal and St. Paul's.

Roubiliac took a cast of the composer's face after death and from it made the well-known monument in the Abbey. It is said by Hawkins to be the best likeness of all the many portraits of him that were produced.

Handel's will, written in his own handwriting, is now in private possession. It is given in full by Schoelcher, Rockstro and others, and a facsimile of the original will, dated 1st June 1750, without the codicils, was published by Messrs. Novello in a special number of *The Musical Times* for 14th December 1893.

He left his savings to his niece and goddaughter, Johanna

[1] *Autobiography and Correspondence of Mrs. Delany*, vol. iii, p. 549.

Friederike Floerken, of Gotha, the daughter of Dr. Michaelsen, who was also co-executor with George Amyand, merchant of London, subject, however, to the following legacies:

£2,000 to Christopher Smith, his old friend and secretary.

£1,000 to the Royal Society of Musicians.

£500 each to his servant John Duburk and his friend James Smyth, the perfumer.

£600 for his monument in Westminster Abbey.

£300 each to the five orphan children of his cousin Georg Taust, Pastor of Giebichenstein.

£300 each to his cousins Christiana Susanna Handelin,[1] and Rachel Sophia; Thomas Harris of Lincoln's Inn Fields; the widow of his cousin Magister Christian Roth.

£200 each to Dr. Morell; George Amyand; Reiche, Secretary of Affairs of Hanover.

£100 each to John Hetherington, of the Middle Temple; Matthew Dubourg, the violinist; Newburgh Hamilton; Mrs. Palmer, widow, of Chelsea; Thomas Bramwell, his servant.

Fifty guineas each to Benjamin Martyn, of New Bond Street; John Cowland, apothecary; John Belchier, surgeon; Mrs. Mayne, widow, of Kensington; Mrs. Downalan, of Charles Street, Hanover Square.

It will be seen that of the £20,000 a sum of £9,260 was divided between his personal friends, his widowed and orphan relations, the Royal Society of Musicians, and his servants, the bulk of the property going to his niece at Gotha.

To Christopher Smith he also left his large harpsichord, his little house organ and his music books. To John Rich his great organ, standing in Covent Garden Theatre; to the Foundling Hospital a full score and all the parts of *Messiah*;

---

[1] German surnames took female endings in those days.

to Charles Jennens two pictures by Denner; and to Bernard Granville of Calwich, in Derbyshire, two Rembrandts.

His furniture, of which an inventory is extant, was sold for £48 to his servant John Duburk. It is probable that at the time of his pecuniary troubles he had been obliged to sell a good deal and had never troubled to replace it. He had been in his later years exceedingly anxious about his future fame and had offered £3,000 to Smith to renounce his claim on the promised manuscripts, in order that they might be deposited in the university of Oxford. Smith could not be persuaded to agree, and Handel, held to his moral obligation, having sacrificed what he regarded as his means of continuing his memory, to his promise. He also requested that the dean should allow of his being buried in Westminster Abbey and left directions that the price of his monument should be paid out of his estate.

During his life he gave no less than eleven performances of *Messiah* at the Foundling Hospital, and a twelfth was advertised for 3rd May 1759, with his name as conductor, but owing to his death Christopher Smith took his place. The hospital benefited by the eleven performances to the extent of £6,935 and after his death continued to perform the work till 1768, realizing £1,332. For the next eight years John Stanley undertook the direction and realized £2,032, so that the hospital benefited by *Messiah* altogether to the extent of £10,299.

Smith refused an offer of £2,000 for the manuscripts made by the King of Prussia and would neither part with them nor allow them after his death to go out of the country. The mother of George III gave him a pension of £200 a year, and George III continued it after her death, in return for which Smith gave the king all the manuscripts, the harpsichord and a bust by Roubiliac.

These manuscripts are now in the Royal Library at the British Museum; the bust is at Windsor Castle. The fate of the harpsichord was for many years unknown: it was supposed to have gone to Winchester and to have been owned by Dr. Chard, organist of the cathedral there, and finally to Messrs. Broadwood, who presented it to the South Kensington Museum. But recent research has discovered at Windsor Castle a fine Ruckers harpsichord, dated 1612, which A. J. Hipkins identifies with every appearance of certainty as the one bequeathed by Handel to Smith.

CHAPTER XIII

HANDEL'S FAME AND CHARACTER

AFTER Handel's death his fame, as is usually the case, increased enormously. His oratorios were constantly performed. *Messiah,* as we have seen, added very considerably to the funds of the Foundling Hospital. In 1784 his birth was commemorated on an enormous scale. Under the conductorship of Joah Bates, an enthusiastic amateur, 525 vocal and instrumental musicians [1] gave performances lasting five days in Westminster Abbey and the Pantheon. A three days' festival had been advertised, but the demand for tickets was so enormous that it was found necessary to extend it to five days.

The programmes were taken entirely from the works of the master; Burney wrote an important *Sketch in Commemoration of Handel*; and after paying the expenses of the festival £6,000 was given to the Royal Society of Musicians and £1,000 to Westminster Hospital. The festival was repeated at intervals during subsequent years until 1791, when the number of performers reached 1,068.

In 1825 a similar festival took place at York. The centenary of Handel's death was celebrated in 1859 at the Crystal Palace under Sir Michael Costa with a choir of 2,700 and an orchestra

---

[1] 95 violins, 26 violas, 21 violoncellos, 15 double basses, 6 flutes, 26 oboes, 26 bassoons, double bassoon, 12 trumpets, 12 horns, 6 trombones, 4 drums, 59 sopranos, 48 altos, 83 tenors, 84 basses, with an organ specially built for the occasion. Seventeen vocal soloists are included in these figures.

of 460, a large organ being built for the purpose. The success of this experiment was so great that [until well into the twentieth century] these gigantic performances were repeated every three years under the name of the 'Handel Festival.'

Handel's music was much admired in Germany. In 1745 he was made the first honorary member of Mizler's Society for Musical Science, which had been recently founded at Leipzig. Bach did not join the society until two years later. Most of Handel's operas were performed in Germany soon after they appeared in London, though as a rule only in Hamburg, and after his death many of the oratorios were given in that country, though not so frequently as in England. After a time, however, they seem to have been more or less neglected. Then, chiefly owing to the efforts of Chrysander, they steadily won their way back to public favour. The *Zeitschrift der internationalen Musikgesellschaft* for October 1900 gives an interesting catalogue of performances of Handel's oratorios in various German towns from 1889 to 1900. *Messiah* has been given nineteen times; *Deborah* fifteen; *Hercules, Acis, Esther, Israel in Egypt, Judas Maccabaeus,* four times each; the Utrecht *Jubilate* three; *Samson* and *Saul* twice each; and the Cecilia Ode once; altogether sixty-two performances in eleven years.

Of Handel's personal character the reader will have gathered something from the biographical portion of this book. It is clear that he was obstinate and determined in the face of opposition, honourable and upright in all money transactions. That he was overflowing with compassion towards the unfortunate is shown by the numerous performances he gave in the cause of charity, even when he was himself in difficulties. He had deep sympathy with widows and orphans. He was one of the founders of the Royal Society of Musicians. For its benefit he performed *Acis and Galatea* in 1740; he gave it his *Parnasso in festa* and bequeathed it £1,000. His abounding charity and uprightness of conduct show that religion was a reality with him, and that it affected his whole life.

Like all gentlemen of the first half of the eighteenth century, he was in the habit of swearing a great deal. Later writers have professed to be much shocked by this 'profane' habit, quite forgetting that what we call 'bad language' was as general a habit in conversation as the 'slang' which has taken its place at the present day. It is not at all impossible that writers of the end of the twentieth century may be as much shocked by the 'slang' and 'bad English' of the nineteenth as modern writers are by Handel's perfectly harmless 'bad language.' His temper was, like that of most musicians, very irritable and not improved by the unworthy treatment he received from his enemies. But, except in one instance, he is not known to have borne ill-will against those with whom he had differences. The one instance is that of John Christopher Smith, his old university friend, who joined him at Anspach and for many years acted as his treasurer and concert agent. Smith's son, also named John Christopher, was sent to school in Soho Square, but at the age of thirteen, when he began to show considerable musical talent, Handel took him to his house, made him his pupil and afterwards employed him as copyist, becoming a faithful friend to him. Meanwhile Smith senior continued to be Handel's treasurer till four years before the latter's death, when they went to Tunbridge Wells together and there quarrelled over some trivial matter.

Handel then took the younger Smith by the hand and said he was going to put his name in the place of that of his father in his will. Whereupon Smith declared he would never play for Handel again, for it would look as if he had undermined his father in Handel's favour. Handel relented and increased the elder Smith's legacy from £500 to £2,000; but the quarrel does not seem to have been made up in spite of this, for three weeks before Handel's death, when he asked the son to receive the sacrament with him, Smith asked how he could communicate when he was at enmity with his former friend, whereupon Handel was immediately reconciled.[1]

It would seem, therefore, that Handel's sense of moral obligation was such that, though he could not forgive, he would not deprive of his just reward the man who had served him so well.

His personal appearance is described by Hawkins and Burney. Hawkins, vol. v, p. 412, says:

He was in his person a large made, and very portly man. His gait, which was ever sauntering, was rather ungraceful, as it had in it somewhat of that rocking motion which distinguishes those whose legs are bowed. His features were finely marked, and the general cast of his countenance placid, bespeaking dignity attempered with benevolence, and every quality of the heart that has a tendency to beget confidence and insure esteem. Few of the pictures extant of him are to any tolerable degree likenesses, except one painted abroad from a print whereof the engraving given of him in this volume is taken. In the print of him by Houbraken, the features are too prominent; and in the mezzo-tint after Hudson there is a harshness of aspect to which his countenance was a stranger; the most perfect resemblance of him is the statue on his monument, and in ʼt at the true lineaments of his face are apparent.

Burney, who frequently played the viola in his orchestra, describes his general look as somewhat heavy and sour; but when he smiled it was like the sun flashing out of a black

[1] *Anecdotes of Handel and Smith,* by Rev. J. C. Coxe. 1799. The account says that Handel was immediately reconciled and left Smith senior £2,400, having before given him £1,000 and all his manuscript music, etc. The original legacy of £500 was in reality increased by £1,500 by codicil in 1756: three years, not three weeks, before the death. Schoelcher, p. 352, overlooking the above account, says that the manuscripts, etc., were bequeathed to his *pupil,* Christopher Smith. It is evident that they were bequeathed to the elder Smith, and inherited from him by the younger.

cloud. He dressed handsomely in gold-laced coat, ruffles,[1] cocked hat and sword.

Anecdotes of Handel have been told over and over again and are well known to his admirers; but we are obliged to repeat some of them here in order to make the account complete and because they throw interesting side-lights on his character.

He liked occasionally to take a boat and go for a row on the Thames. There is an amusing account in the *Somerset House Gazette,* vol. i, 1823, by Ephraim Hardcastle, of a breakfast party, probably in 1751, to which Handel came uninvited with a 'notable appetite' after having been on the water. Ephraim Hardcastle had an uncle named Zachary, a merchant, who, after he retired from business, lived in Paper Buildings in the Temple, and there received on intimate terms the most distinguished painters, poets and musicians of his time. This Zachary Hardcastle had invited Pepusch, Arne and Colley Cibber to breakfast at nine o'clock, and to accompany him to hear a competition for the post of organist at the Temple Church. While the company were awaiting Arne, a knock was heard at the door, and Handel entered.

'What! my dear friend Hardcastle! you are merry by times! What, and Mr. Colley Cibbers and Doc⸺ Pepusch! Well, that is comical. Pray let me sit down a moment.

'Upon my word, that is a picture of a ham. It is very bold of me to come and break my fast with you uninvited; and I have brought along with me a notable appetite; for the water of old Father Thames, is it not a fine bracer of the appetite?'

'Pray, did you come with oars or scullers, Mr. Handel?' said Pepusch.

'How can you demand of me that silly question, Dr. Pepusch? What can it concern you whether I have one waterman or two watermans—whether I pull out my purse for to pay one shilling or two? Diavolo! I cannot go here,

[1] The late Dr. W. H. Cummings possessed one of these.

I cannot go there, but someone shall send it to some news-paper, as how Mr. George Frederick Handel did go sometimes last week to break his fast with Mr. Zac. Hardcastle; but it shall be all my fault if it shall be put in print, whether I was rowed by one waterman or by two watermans.'[1]

'Well, gentlemen,' said Zachary, 'it is ten minutes past nine. Shall we wait more for Dr. Arne?'

'Let us give him another five minutes,' said Colley Cibber; 'he is too great a genius to keep time.'

'Let us put it to the vote,' said Dr. Pepusch.

'I will second your motion with all my heart,' said Handel. 'I will hold up my feeble hands for my old friend Gustus (Augustus), for I know not who I would wait for over and above my old rival, Master Tom (Thomas Pepusch). Only, with your permission, I will take a snack of your ham and a slice of French roll, or a modicum of chicken, for to tell you the honest fact, I am all but famished; for I laid me down last night without my supper, at the instance of my physician; for which I am not inclined to extend my fast any longer.

'If you please, do me the kindness to cut me a small slice of ham.'

Dr. Arne was now announced, and the party began breakfast.

'Well, and how do you feel yourself, my dear sir?' said Arne.

'Why, by the mercy of Heaven and the waters of Aix-la-Chapelle, and the attentions of my doctors and physicians and oculists, of late years, under Providence, I am surprisingly better, thank you kindly, Mr. Gustus. And you have also been doing well of late, I am pleased to hear.'

'So, sir, I presume you are come to witness the trial of skill at the old Round Church? I understand the amateurs expect a pretty sharp contest,' said Arne.

[1] Handel hated trivial questions, saying: 'If a man cannot think but as a fool, let him keep his fool's tongue in his own fool's mouth.'

'Contest!' echoed Handel, laying down his knife and fork; 'yes, no doubt; your amateurs have a passion for contest. Not what it was in our remembrance. Hey, my friend? Ha, ha, ha!'

'No, sir, I am happy to say those days of envy and bickering and party feeling are gone and past. To be sure we had enough of such disgraceful warfare; it lasted too long.'

'Why, yes, it did last too long; it bereft me of my poor limbs; it did bereave me of what is the most precious gift of Him that made us and not we ourselves' (his reason). 'And for what? Why, for nothing in the world but the pleasure and pastime of them who having no wit, nor no want, set at loggerheads such men as live by their wits, to worry and destroy one another as wild beasts in the Coliseum in the time of the Romans.

'Gustus, do not you remember as it was almost only of yesterday, that she-devil, Cuzzoni, and that other precious daughter of iniquity, Beelzebub's spoiled child, the pretty-faced Faustina? Oh! the mad rage that I have to answer for, what with one and the other of these fine ladies' airs and graces. Again, do you not remember that upstart puppy, Senesino, and the coxcomb, Farinelli? Next, again, my some-time notable rival, Master Bononcini, and old Porpora? ha, ha, ha! all at war with me, and all at war with themselves. Such a confusion of rivalships, and double-facedness, and hypocrisy, and malice, that would make a comical subject for a poem in rhymes, or a piece for the stage, as I hope to be saved.'

The narrative ends here. It gives an interesting picture of Handel's private intercourse with his friends.

Dr. Morell having complained that the music of one of his airs did not suit the words, Handel lost his temper and cried out: 'What, sir, you teach me music? The music, sir, is good music. It is your words is bad. Hear the passage again. There; go you, make words to that music.'

A singer found fault with his method of accompanying,

saying that if he accompanied him in that way he would jump from the stage on to the harpsichord and smash it. 'Oh,' said Handel, 'you will jump, will you? Then let me know when you will jump and I will advertise it in the bills, and I shall get more people to see you jump than to hear you sing.'

When in Dublin, Dubourg, the famous violinist, having to play an extempore cadenza, had wandered far away from the key and, getting bewildered, was at some difficulty in returning. At length, when he arrived at the orthodox shake, which always terminated a cadenza, Handel said in a voice which was heard all over the theatre: 'You are well come at home, Mr. Dubourg.'

Handel was twice nearly married; on the first occasion the mother of the lady objected to her daughter marrying a 'mere fiddler.' On the death of the mother, the father came forward and said that there was now no objection to the marriage; but Handel, whose professional pride had been outraged, said it was now too late. It is said that the lady went into a decline and died. On another occasion he had wished to marry a lady of means and position, who, however, made it a stipulation that he should give up his profession. He remained single.

Handel, like all musicians of the first rank, looked upon his art as something higher than a mere amusement and recreation. After the first performance in London of *Messiah*, Lord Kinnoul complimented him on the 'noble entertainment' he had given the audience. 'I should be sorry, my lord,' said Handel, 'if I have only succeeded in entertaining them; I wished to make them better.' There is no doubt that the composition of *Messiah* affected him deeply. He was found sobbing while writing the music of 'He was despised and rejected of men,' and his servant, when bringing him his chocolate, was often astonished 'to see his master's tears mixing with the ink as he penned his divine compositions.'

After he had lost his sight, his surgeon, Mr. Sharp, recommended Stanley, the blind organist, as a person who, from his wonderful powers of memory, would be able to take his place at the organ in oratorios. Handel burst into a loud laugh, and said: 'Mr. Sharp, have you never read the Scriptures? Do you not remember that if the blind lead the blind, they will both fall into the ditch?'

Burney says he was impetuous, rough and peremptory in his manners and conversation but totally devoid of ill-nature or malevolence. There was an original humour and pleasantry in his most lively sallies of anger and impatience, which, with his broken English, were extremely laughable.

He was well read and had a competent knowledge of Latin, English, French and Italian, besides his own language. He used all five languages in the dates, etc., of his compositions; thus the oratorio *Jephtha* is 'angefangen, 21 Jan^r. 1751'; Jephtha enters 'solus'; the English word 'Symphony' is applied to the instrumental piece in the second act. The beginning of Act III is dated in French, 'Juin 18'; and its completion in Italian, 'Agost 30, 1751.' For the last twenty years of his life he always used astronomical signs to indicate the days of the week. When excited his language was most amusingly polyglot.

A clergyman named Felton, an amateur composer, had published a set of organ concertos, and finding them well received, he endeavoured to get Handel's name on the subscription list of a second set. The request was conveyed to him one morning while he was being shaved. Handel got up in a fury, and, with his face covered with lather said: 'Damn yourself and go to the Devil! a parson make concertos? why he no make sermons?'

As his old friends died off, he made few new ones and retired more and more from society. He then acquired a habit of talking loudly to himself so that he could be overheard. In Hyde Park he was heard commenting on a pupil who had run away from him: 'The devil; the father was deceived, the mother was deceived, but I was not deceived; he is a damned scoundrel, and good for nothing.'

Handel had as clear a conception as Beethoven of the distinction that comes from greatness of mind, as opposed to that which comes from mere birth or social position or wealth. 'Such as are not acquainted with his personal character,' says Hawkins, 'will wonder at his seeming temerity in continuing so long an opposition which tended but to impoverish him; but he was a man of a firm and intrepid spirit, no way a slave to the passion of avarice, and would have gone greater lengths than he did rather than submit to those [1] whom he ever looked upon as his inferiors.'

'Kings and princes,' said Beethoven, 'can, to be sure, make professors, privy councillors, etc., and confer titles and orders, but they cannot make great men, minds which rise above the common herd: these they must not pretend to make, and therefore these must be held in honour!'

At a private rehearsal of a duet in *Judas Maccabaeus* at Giulia Frasi's, Burney, who was humming the second part over the shoulder of Handel, made a mistake. He came in for a tremendous explosion of wrath, but summoned up courage to suggest that the manuscript might perhaps be wrong. Handel instantly, with the greatest humility, said: 'I beg your pardon, I am a very odd dog; Master Smith [2] is to blame.'

Carestini sent back the air 'Verdi prati' in *Alcina,* saying it did not suit his voice. Handel, who knew better than any one else how to suit a particular voice, lost his temper, rushed to Carestini's house and said: 'You dog! don't I know better than yourself what is best for you to sing? If you will

[1] i.e. the nobility.

[2] Smith, it will be remembered, made all the fair copies of Handel's works.

not sing all the song what I give you, I will not pay you one stiver.' [1]

If the Prince of Wales was late in coming to a concert, or if the ladies of the court talked during it, his rage used to become uncontrollable, and he would swear and call names in the presence of royalty; whereupon the princess would say to the talkative ones: 'Hush, hush, Handel is in a passion.' [2]

During an oratorio he was very excitable; he would utter the word 'Chorus' in a most formidable voice, as a warning for them to rise. He wore an enormous white wig, which nodded or vibrated when things went well; when it did not nod, observers knew that he was out of humour.

He was extremely sensitive to sound and could not tolerate the tuning of the orchestra, which was therefore done before he arrived at the theatre. A foolish practical joker one evening got into the orchestra and untuned all the instruments. The Prince of Wales arrived, and Handel gave the signal to begin *con spirito,* when such a discord arose, that the enraged musician

---

[1] Usually quoted from Burney in the excessively bad English which it is hard to believe Handel really spoke. This case is particularly suspicious, as Handel must have spoken to Carestini in Italian.—E. B.

[2] The detestable habit of looking upon instrumental music as a mere cover for conversation, which even now has not died out in certain social circles in England, seems formerly to have obtained in various parts of Europe. In Italy, for instance, poor Corelli was once so disturbed by it that he laid down his violin, saying he 'feared to interrupt the conversation'; and Beethoven, while playing a duet with Ries at the house of Count Browne, at Vienna, being disturbed by the conversation of a young nobleman with a lady, suddenly lifted Ries's hand from the instrument, saying in a loud voice: 'I play no longer for such hogs.' This has been brought against him as a breach of good manners, but surely the insult to the musicians was at least an equal breach of good manners.

started from his seat, overturned a double bass, seized a kettle-drum, threw it at the leader of the orchestra and lost his wig. He advanced bareheaded to the front of the orchestra, but was so choked with passion that he could not speak. Here he stood staring and stamping amidst general convulsions of laughter, until the prince personally, with much difficulty, appeased his wrath and prevailed on him to resume his seat.

A tradition states that one day, dining at a tavern, he ordered dinner for three and, getting impatient, asked why it was not brought up. The landlord said he was waiting for the company. 'I am the company,' said Handel, 'bring up the dinner *prestissimo*.'

He had a great liking for Father Smith's organ at St. Paul's, and at one time used often to play the concluding voluntary at afternoon service. He would then retire with the painter Goupy, Hunter, a scarlet dyer, and his secretary, J. C. Smith, to the Queen's Arms tavern, where he would play the harpsichord while he smoked and drank beer.

Concerning his organ playing an amusing story is told of his endeavouring to 'play the people out' at a country church. The people were so lost in admiration that they would not go; whereupon the country organist, getting impatient, said: 'You cannot play them out, let me show you how'; and on his taking Handel's place at the organ, the congregation rapidly disappeared.

Messiah was only partly published during his lifetime, and he gave manuscript copies to the Dublin Charitable Musical Society, the Royal Society of Musicians and the Foundling Hospital. The governors of the last-named institution, misunderstanding the purport of the gift, thought that they were to have the exclusive right of performing it for ever. They drew up a bill to be presented to Parliament confirming their legal rights in this matter and showed it to Handel, who became furious. 'The devil!' said he, 'for what shall the Foundlings put mine oratorio in the Parliament? The devil! Mine music shall not go to the Parliament.'

He took immense pains in preparing his concertos for performance: every key of his harpsichord was by constant practice hollowed out like the bowl of a spoon. This is supposed to be the instrument now at Windsor Castle, but its keyboards have been renewed.

When the rupture took place between Bononcini and the Academy of Ancient Music, Dr. Greene, who stuck to Bononcini, left it and took with him the boys of St. Paul's Cathedral. He then established concerts at the Devil tavern, near Temple Bar; whereupon Handel said: 'Poor Dr. Greene has gone to the devil.'

The fugue subject in the overture to *Muzio Scevola* is in G minor, the answer being, therefore, properly in D minor and involving a somewhat harsh progression from G to F natural. Handel boldly wrote F♯ in the answer, and was at once condemned by the critics as having broken the rules of fugue. Geminiani, hearing this accusation, exclaimed: 'True, but that semitone is worth a world.'

Amongst the small-minded attacks of his enemies was a paragraph in some of the daily papers in 1753 announcing that Mr. Handel was preparing his own Funeral Anthem, to be performed in the chapel of the Foundling Hospital. The governors, being very indignant at this, wrote to him, hoping that one who had done so much for the charity might be spared for a long life.

He undertook the entire education of the son of his friend and treasurer, John Christopher Smith, sending him to Mr. Clare's Academy in Soho Square and, after himself teaching him the rudiments of music, engaging Pepusch and Roseingrave, organist of St. George's, Hanover Square, to continue his musical education when he himself had no longer leisure to give him instruction.

Handel not only made use of the works of other composers, but availed himself of any source that might be useful. For instance, some of his songs were suggested by the notes of street criers; a piece of music paper among the Fitzwilliam manuscripts contains a tune used by one John Shaw, to the words 'Buoy any matches; my matches buoy,' evidently taken down with a view to future use.

Of English organists he said: 'When I first came I found among the English many good players, but no composers; now they are all composers and no players.'

When George III was a child, Handel, noticing that he listened very attentively to his harpsichord playing, asked him if he liked the music. The little prince was very enthusiastic in his love for it, whereupon Handel said: 'A good boy, a good boy; you shall protect my fame when I am dead.'

One of the stories told by his enemies is to the effect that Handel, having invited some of the principal performers in the oratorio to dine with him at Brook Street, cried out: 'Oh! I have the thought,' and left the table. One of the company at last peeped through the keyhole, and found that the composer was not writing down his 'thoughts,' but enjoying a bottle of Burgundy, of which he had received a hamper as a present from Lord Radnor, while his guests were given port. Schoelcher does not believe this story, and it is so similar to that told by the painter Goupy that it may well be regarded as a mere elaboration of a single occurrence. Handel was just as human as any other man. It is well known that one of his failings was an insatiable delight in the pleasures of the table. If he did not share his Burgundy with his guests, it was certainly a gross breach of good manners; but faults in manners are not confined to great geniuses. They have been known even in those who, having no brains and no absorbing work, are in a better position to give proper attention to the ordinary civilities of life.

Handel, like Beethoven after him, had little respect for potentates as such. When the King of Prussia, Frederick the Great, was about to visit Aix-la-Chapelle, and had expressed a wish to hear Handel, he quitted the place rather than expose himself to solicitations he had determined not to comply with, or to commands which he could not resist. He had a true artist's horror of exhibiting his powers as a mere curiosity.

CHAPTER XIV

THE OPERAS

THERE is no doubt that Handel's Italian operas were equal to anything that had been composed by Italians up to the time they came into existence, and superior to the work of many of his Italian contemporaries. Handel spent several years in Italy as a student, knew more about the voice than most singing masters, had a strong sense of dramatic fitness and, in addition, a colossal genius for original composition. But it was not only his power of composition that helped him: he had also a most remarkable talent for adapting himself to circumstances, and for producing real works of art under the most unfavourable conditions.

In order to understand what these conditions were, it is necessary to inquire into the state of Italian opera at that time. The first attempts at producing true dramatic music, as opposed to the old madrigal and other more or less contrapuntal forms, had been made about the year 1600 [by a group of artists attached to Count Bardi in Florence, including the composers Caccini, Peri, Galilei and Corsi, and the poet Ottavio Rinuccini. The first great creative musician who exercised himself on opera was Monteverdi.] The two outstanding new features of early opera were the aria for solo voice and the recitative, or narrative form of music. The movement rapidly spread over Italy, where numerous opera houses sprang up. It was taken up by the courts of Germany and France and in course of time reached England.

In Italy opera was cultivated by the people, but in other

countries it became merely an expensive amusement for rulers and for a cultivated nobility.

Good voice, delivery and expression, though indispensable, were not the only essentials demanded of singers. Enormous powers of execution were expected of them as a matter of course. They had to be capable not only of singing the so-called 'divisions' written for them by composers, but also to be able to invent others for themselves, to add the 'ornaments' which were then universal in slow movements, and to sing shakes clearly and rapidly on any note. The form of the opera soon became highly conventionalized, the main object being to give each character an opportunity for display. There were almost invariably three acts, each divided into scenes. Every scene had to end with an aria. The audience, who came only to hear its favourite singers, would not tolerate choruses, and the only place for a so-called chorus was at the end of the last act, when all the characters had to appear at once and sing some simple quartet or trio, doubling the parts if necessary, usually in the form of a gavotte or other dance, though in some cases in that of a madrigal. Duets, trios and quartets were introduced only when absolutely necessary to carry on the action, and the singing in two, three or four-part harmony, even in a duet, trio or quartet, was avoided as much as possible. Everything was done to exalt the solo voice, the only thing the audience cared to hear.

The opera was expected in all circumstances to end happily, whatever tragic situations might have occurred earlier. This is satirized in *The Beggar's Opera*, where the Player and Beggar enter at the moment the chief character is about to be executed and arrange that the opera should end happily: '. . . in this kind of Drama 'tis no matter how absurdly things are brought about—so—you Rabble there—run and cry, A Reprieve!— let the Prisoner be brought back to his Wives in Triumph. All this we must do, to comply with the Taste of the Town.'

The Opera of the Time

The scenes consisted of recitative followed by an aria, and the arias were of several classes: *aria cantabile,* a slow movement, into which the singer was expected to throw pathos and to introduce extempore ornamentation; *aria di portamento,* of a more strongly marked rhythm than the former; *aria parlante,* expressing violent emotion; *aria di bravura,* or *d'agilità,* intended to exhibit the powers of the singer in the display of difficult 'divisions'; *aria d'imitazione,* in which a flute or a horn imitated birds or the sounds of the chase, etc., besides many subdivisions of these classes and hybrids called *arie di mezzo carattere.*

The performers were the *prima donna* (first woman), a soprano; *seconda donna* (second woman), soprano or contralto; *terza donna* (third woman), contralto; *primo uomo* (first man), who had to be an artificial soprano; *secondo uomo* (second man), an artificial soprano or contralto; *terza uomo* (third man), tenor; *ultima parte,* when employed, was a bass.

The opera began with an overture, the form of which had been established by Lulli and was adopted by Handel for all his operas and oratorios. It had nothing in common with the modern overture, in which a foretaste of the music of the opera itself is given. It consisted of a *maestoso* movement followed by an *allegro,* generally of a light fugal texture, and frequently there was a third movement in the form of a minuet, gavotte or jig, or even a succession of dances followed the fugue.

Nearly all the arias took the *da capo* form cultivated by Alessandro Scarlatti, namely a long section in the principal key, followed by a shorter section in a related key and rounded off by a repetition of the whole of the first section. Each performer had to sing one or more songs in each of the three acts; no performer might sing two arias in succession, nor might two arias of the same class be sung one after the other. Recitative was either *secco* (dry), that is with only the basses and harpsichord for accompaniment, or *stromentato,* i.e.

accompanied by the strings. The *prima donna* and *primo uomo* had each a 'scena' to themselves in the course of the opera.

Singers, petted and spoilt by an idle aristocracy and as a rule persons of little culture, had by Handel's time become overbearing and conceited beyond description in their behaviour towards composers, who were expected to humour their every whim. The voice was everything to them, the music simply a vehicle for its display. Dramatic exigencies were flagrantly disregarded in order to allow them every opportunity for gaining applause. Jealousies were frequent. One of Handel's cleverest devices was the writing of the duet in which the two *prime donne*, Cuzzoni and Faustina, were given absolutely equal parts, so that neither could say that she had sung second to the other.

Handel was not a reformer like Gluck and Wagner. He took the opera as he found it and simply embellished it by means of his great genius. He was content to work on the forms that he found established, trusting for success to the employment of the best singers and instrumentalists that could be obtained.[1] He paid his singers handsomely, and when he

[1] There can be no doubt that his failure with the later operas was due to his conservatism as well as to adversity: '. . . the whole style of Italian opera was changing during the second quarter of the century. Handel had continued to develop his own style, based on the grand manner of old Scarlatti . . . in Italy, Scarlatti's style had already become old-fashioned before his death in 1725, and opera was moving on towards the lighter and flimsier manner of Galuppi, who first came to London in . . . 1738' (Dent). Even where Handel did apparently try to suit the new taste, he was unsuccessful: 'In choosing the libretto of *Serse* [his one comic opera], Handel seems to have made a desperate attempt to keep up with the taste of the day. . . . But the humour of *Serse*, diverting as it is to the modern historical student, is neither the musical nor the dramatic humour of 1737 [*sic*, should be 1738]; the plot bears

could no longer afford this, in the time of his bankruptcy, he somehow managed to arrange that at any rate his instru-mentalists should still be the best obtainable, and that they should be well paid for their services. We have the names of some of them: Matthew Dubourg, who was his first violinist, and who had led the band at Dublin for him, was a pupil of Geminiani and a famous player; Valentine Snow, his first trumpeter, for whom his many difficult solo trumpet parts were written; Caporale, his first violoncello, is mentioned by Fétis for his beauty of tone; Weideman, his flautist; Clegg, probably a pupil of Dubourg, and in his time a well-known violinist; Powell, a harpist; the brothers Castrucci, violinists, pupils of Corelli, who also played the *violetta marina* parts in *Orlando*; [1] Lampe, his bassoonist, for whom Handel is said to have caused a double bassoon to be made by Stanesby, was also a composer, employed by Rich to write two operas for the Covent Garden theatre, *Amalia,* 1732, and *Roger et Jean*; but he was best known by two burlesques, *The Dragon of Wantley* and *Margery*. He was also the author of a treatise on thorough-bass.

The orchestration of Handel's operas would probably seem monotonous to an audience accustomed to the brilliancy of modern instrumentation. Bach wrote counterpoint for each

no resemblance whatever to the Neapolitan comic operas of Vinci and Pergolesi, but rather recalls the very early operas, based on Spanish comedies, composed by Alessandro Scarlatti in the 1680's' (ibid.).—E. B.

[1] Fétis says that one of the Castrucci brothers served as a model for Hogarth's caricature, 'The Enraged Musician.' [Hogarth intro-duced other portraits of Handel's musicians into his satirical paint-ings. The singer in the fourth picture of the *Marriage à la Mode* is a caricature of Carestini, and the flute player who looks over his shoulder is Weideman. Cf. the reception scene in Strauss's *Rose Cavalier.*—E. B.]

individual instrument and voice, and his cantatas are, as a rule, in as many contrapuntal parts as there are instruments or voices employed. Handel's use of the orchestra was different. Laying a foundation of strings and harpsichord, to which he added oboes, often in unison with the violins, and bassoons with the string basses, he only introduces other instruments for special effects. Thus in a march trumpets and drums are invariably used; horns were also occasionally added. In a pathetic song, *flauti*, i.e. the *flûte-à-bec*, would be employed. In other places we find the *flauto traverso* (approximating to the modern flute); the *viola da gamba*, theorbo, harp, organ (it will be remembered that he owned a large organ which stood in Covent Garden theatre), *violetta marina* (a kind of *viola d'amore*, with sympathetic strings); *viola di braccio* (the ordinary viola); *violetta haute-contre* and *taille* (names for first and second viola); *cornet* (a wooden instrument covered with leather, with a trumpet mouthpiece); *flageolet* (a small *flûte-à-bec*); recorder (bass flute).

Often he would make all the violins play in unison, with nothing but the chords on the harpsichord between them and the bass; at other times he would use violas and basses only, as in 'Habbiate pazienza' in *Almira*. Again he would divide his violins into two, three, four or even five parts, and his violas also into several.

In the same opera, in order to give due effect to a song in which Fernando laughs at Osman for having his sword snatched away, the accompaniment consists of two oboes and a bassoon only. A great deal of expense was lavished on the machinery [1] of the theatre, and instrumental bands frequently appeared on the stage. In the third act of *Almira*, a band of oboes, a band of trumpets and drums, a band of cymbals,

---

[1] In *Rinaldo* a black cloud appears covered with horrible monsters spouting fire and smoke, with a great noise. We have already referred to the live birds in this opera.

drums and 'crossflutes,' a hurdy-gurdy and bagpipe, march in succession across the stage. Frequently an aria is accompanied by violins, or even the whole orchestra, in unison with the voice, without any bass. Solos for oboe, bassoon, violin or violoncello often occur in the songs, demanding considerable skill. There must have been a good solo violoncellist at Florence in 1707, for there is a difficult violoncello part in *Rodrigo*. The style, as we have seen, is like that of Corelli.

Handel was fond of imitative effects. The jumping of frogs, the 'Hailstone' chorus and the plague of flies in *Israel in Egypt* are well-known examples. In *Rodrigo* he represents the words 'La mia costanza' (my constancy) by a note sustained through nearly six bars by the voice, with an elaborate violin accompaniment. Handel, like Bach, felt the limitations of unequally tempered keyed instruments. He had no hesitation in modulating as far afield as he wished, but took care to silence the harpsichord or organ, leaving the strings alone to play in unusual keys.

In *Agrippina* he first divides his violins into three parts—Violino I, Violino II, Violino III—and uses muted violins with *pizzicato* basses and two flutes, which effect was also used by Bach in his cantata, *Freue dich, erlöste Schaar*. In the same opera he extemporized on the harpsichord in the ritornels of one of the songs. He afterwards wrote down the music of these extempore pieces, which are to be found in the Fitzwilliam Museum.

The well-known march in *Rinaldo* is scored for no less than four trumpets in addition to the strings, oboes and drums. Handel was very fond of the trumpet, and never lost an opportunity of introducing it. In *Il Pastor fido* the *violone grosso*, an exceptionally large double bass, appears for the first time. It is given solo passages besides a duet with the bassoon. In *Radamisto* horns occur for the first time, and they are frequently used in all subsequent works.

The aria 'Affanni del pensier' in *Ottone*, so frequently alluded to as one of the most beautiful songs, owes its effect as much to its delicate orchestration as to its melody. We quote a few bars:

In *Giulio Cesare* four horns with two different crooks are used, thus anticipating modern custom. The harp, *viola da gamba* and theorbo have very florid *obbligato* parts in music prepared by Cleopatra to soften the heart of Caesar.

In the second version of *Rinaldo* two harpsichords were used, and in *Orlando* two of the second violin players were ordered to strengthen the first violins in certain passages. In *Terpsichore* the theorbo played with 'les orgues doucement.'[1] In *Giustino* a bass flute is employed. In *Deidamia* a march is played by a band of horns, trumpets and drums on board a ship in which Nestor and Ulysses are about to embark.

The foregoing account of Handel's orchestration may appear dry and technical to the amateur reader, but we have given it in order to show that Handel was as skilful in his use of the orchestra as in his counterpoint. The operas were mounted with the greatest possible brilliancy, the orchestra was large and varied, and the composer was just as careful in the choice of suitable instrumentation as any modern composer could be.

His operas have disappeared from the stage, [and although attempts have been made to revive some of the best of them, especially in Germany, it cannot be pretended that they are ever likely to attract the public again, however interesting they might be to connoisseurs.] Handel, in his operas, was essentially a man of his own times. He made no effort to advance the art; he simply took the forms he found ready-made and adorned them with all the beauty and solidity he was capable of producing, which far surpassed the operatic efforts of his contemporaries. He did not anticipate future developments: his effort was to attract his own public by the best possible art that he could give them.

[1] This does not mean, as the author originally said, that 'apparently there was more than one organ in the theatre': in French a single organ is often called 'les orgues,' much as in Elizabethan England a virginals would be called 'the virginals.'—E. B.

The subject-matter of the operas is perhaps another bar to their acceptance. They deal with classical subjects in a way that reduces them to stereotyped patterns, and although countless people are capable of appreciating Euripides's treatment of the Alkestis legend or Shakespeare's of the history of Julius Caesar, it is hardly likely that they would care to see the same subjects treated with all the conventionality and formality of an eighteenth-century entertainment.

A third obstacle is that the vocal parts were written to suit the powers of special singers and were invariably altered when it was necessary that they should be sung by others. It is scarcely possible that singers could be found to execute the more difficult songs nowadays, to say nothing of the fact that artificial male sopranos are an extinct species. And even if they could, Handel is no longer among us to alter and adapt his music to their special powers. [It may be thought curious that the oratorios can still be heard, although they do not differ essentially from the operas except that they are more or less abundantly interspersed with choral numbers. But this is precisely what makes the difference. An oratorio is produced only when a choral society wishes to perform it, and it is noticeable that those of Handel's oratorios in which the choral portions are not conspicuous are almost as much neglected as the operas. The latter, on the other hand, contain far more purely instrumental music, which should make them acceptable for occasional concert performances, at any rate for the sake of affording lovers of music an unusual experience. On the whole, however, although in Handel's own time the operas were little more than concerts in costume, and were readily accepted as such, it is hardly reasonable to ask modern audiences to take again to a form of dramatic music without dramatic action. We must resign ourselves to hope for an occasional chance to hear a historical revival of one of Handel's operas and to regard them as a storehouse of hundreds of splendid arias for concert performance.   But that storehouse ought to be drawn upon far more frequently than it is at present, for it contains inexhaustible treasures of noble songs, all stamped with the hall-mark of the same genius, yet endlessly varied.]

CHAPTER XV

CHORAL AND INSTRUMENTAL WORKS

FROM what has been said in the foregoing chapter, it might be inferred that we considered Handel's music to be out of date and antiquated. This we believe is true of the operas as a whole, but not of single pieces from them. With the oratorios we are on entirely different ground. To Handel an oratorio meant an opera on a sacred or secular subject, sung without scenery and without action, and therefore relying entirely on the power of the music to attract the audience. For it must always be remembered that Handel was not, like Bach, writing exactly as his genius drove him, and caring little for whether he pleased his hearers or not, as long as he reached his own lofty ideal. Handel also had the highest possible ideal, but it was to attract the public by the very best music they were capable of appreciating.

In oratorio, then, he set to work in quite a different way from that followed by him in opera. The more or less obsolete instruments were discarded, and he relied on the orchestra of violins, violas, violoncellos, double basses, flutes, oboes, bassoons, horns, trumpets, trombones and drums, besides the organ and harpsichord. He no longer made journeys to Italy to find the latest attraction in the way of singers, and that abomination the artificial soprano, so attractive to the aristocracy, soon ceased to be employed. The operas depended on soloists for their effect, the oratorios more on massive choruses. Moreover, the subjects were for the most part taken from scriptural history instead of from classical antiquity. These works began to attract the general public, even when the aristocracy held aloof from them. They were no longer merely idle and expensive amusements: they were performed chiefly in Lent and struck deeply into the religious feeling of the people.

In the dramatic oratorios the hero appears and sings in person, surrounded by other characters. *Messiah,* on the other hand, is an epic poem in which the singers describe the events impersonally. Although treating of the same subject as Bach's Passion music, the construction of *Messiah* is entirely different. In Bach's Passion the Evangelist narrates the events, which are emphasized by the chorus, who represent Jews, apostles, etc., and the Saviour Himself speaks. The music for the soloists and the congregation represents the emotion that is aroused by the events narrated. In *Messiah* the congregation takes no part, the soloists are impersonal, and they and the chorus carry on the narrative by means of passages of Scripture bearing on the story. The Passion music is a religious service: *Messiah* is a sermon.

The overture, in E minor, is in the same form as all the other operatic and oratorio overtures, but it is of an exceedingly grave character. The fugue was at first objected to as not sufficiently dignified for its position, but succeeding generations have discovered that it, like all Handel's religious music, particularly expresses the pious exaltation of mind that the audience naturally experience. It is said that the overture concluded with a minuet in E major when played apart from the oratorio.

A tenor voice sings prophetic passages from the book of Isaiah, telling of the coming events: 'Comfort ye my people, saith your God. Prepare ye the way of the Lord, make straight in the desert a highway for our God. Every valley shall be exalted, and every mountain and hill made low, the crooked straight, and the rough places plain.' Then the chorus answers: 'And the glory of the Lord shall be revealed.'

A bass voice now sings, from the prophets Haggai and Malachi: 'Thus saith the Lord of Hosts; I will shake the heavens and the earth; and the desire of all nations shall come: The Lord whom ye seek shall suddenly come to His temple. But who may abide the day of His coming? and who shall stand when He appeareth?' The chorus sing: 'He shall purify the sons of Levi, that they may offer unto the Lord an offering in righteousness.' The prophecy is concluded with another passage from Isaiah, sung by a contralto voice in recitative and accompanied by the continuo:[1] 'Behold, a virgin shall conceive and bear a Son, and shall call His name Emmanuel, God with us.'

Prophecy now ceases for a time; the singer and the chorus address the prophet, saying: 'Get thee up into the high mountain; lift up thy voice with strength; say unto the cities of Judah: Behold your God.'

A bass voice now foretells that 'Darkness shall cover the earth, and gross darkness the people; but the Lord shall arise, and His glory shall be seen upon thee, and the Gentiles shall come to thy light. The people that walked in darkness have seen a great light; and they that dwell in the shadow of death, upon them hath the light shined.' The chorus sings: 'For unto us a Child is born, unto us a Son is given.' The fervour excited by these words finds its expression in the well-known florid passages of the chorus, which are to be sung *mezzo forte,* while at the words 'Wonderful, Counsellor! the mighty God!' the full orchestra and organ enter *fortissimo.*

Prophecy is now concluded, and we are taken to the plains of Bethlehem, where shepherds are heard playing one of the

[1] The author said 'the organ'; but the practice of playing the continuo parts in accompaniments for vocal solos on that instrument, though it still persists, is to be deprecated. The pianoforte, though an anachronism, is preferable, but the proper instrument is the harpsichord.—E. B.

airs used by the *pifferari* of southern Italy at Christmas.[1]
An angel appears who brings them good tidings: 'For unto
you is born this day a Saviour, which is Christ the Lord.'
And suddenly there was with the angel a multitude of the
heavenly host, praising God, and saying: 'Glory to God in
the highest, and peace on earth.' A soprano air follows
bidding the daughter of Zion rejoice: 'Behold, thy King
cometh; He is the righteous Saviour; He shall speak peace
unto the heathen.' 'The eyes of the blind shall be opened;
the ears of the deaf unstopped; the dumb shall sing; He
shall feed His flock as a shepherd. Come unto Him ye
that are laden, and ye shall find rest unto your souls.' The
chorus sing: 'His yoke is easy, His burthen is light.' This
ends Part I.

Part II brings us into the presence of the Saviour. The
chorus, in a solemn *largo,* bids us 'Behold the Lamb of God
that taketh away the sin of the world'; the contralto voice
describes in heart-rending accents how 'He was despised and
rejected of men; a Man of sorrows and acquainted with grief.'
The chorus, always in solemn *largo,* sings: 'Surely He hath
borne our griefs and carried our sorrows: the chastisement of
our peace was upon Him'; then, in a powerful fugue, 'and
with His stripes we are healed.' Another chorus follows:
'All we like sheep have gone astray; and the Lord hath laid
on Him the iniquity of us all.' The tenor sings: 'All they
that see Him laugh Him to scorn'; the chorus in mocking
accents follows with 'He trusted in God that He would
deliver Him; let Him deliver Him if He delight in Him.' A
tenor recitative describes how 'Thy rebuke hath broken His
heart: He looked for some to have pity on Him, but there was

[1] The 'pastoral symphony,' also adopted by Bach in the 'Christmas
Oratorio,' follows an Italian convention in drawing upon these
folk-tunes, which were used by Corelli, Alessandro Scarlatti and
others.—E. B.

no man; neither found He any to comfort Him. He was cut off out of the land of the living.'

Now comes the soprano solo bringing comfort: 'But Thou didst not leave His soul in hell, nor didst Thou suffer Thy holy one to see corruption.' The chorus hereupon take up the joyful strain of 'Lift up your heads, O ye gates, and the King of Glory shall come in: let all the angels of God worship Him.' The catastrophe is over; the Saviour has risen and ascended to heaven. The bass sings: 'Thou art gone up on high, Thou hast led captivity captive, and received gifts for men.' Now follow the good tidings to the Gentile world. 'The Lord gave the Word; great was the company of the preachers.' The soprano voice comments: 'How beautiful are the feet of them that preach the gospel of peace.' The chorus sings: 'Their sound is gone out into all lands, and their words unto the ends of the world.'

But the world is not yet ready to receive the glad tidings. The magnificent bass aria 'Why do the nations so furiously rage together,' with its tumultuous accompaniment, well represents the anger of the rulers of the earth, who 'rise up and take counsel together against the Lord and His anointed.' The chorus in their turn take counsel against the rulers: 'Let us break their bonds asunder, and cast away their yokes from us.' The tenor voice addresses the Saviour: 'Thou shalt break them with a rod of iron, and dash them in pieces like a potter's vessel.' The climax is reached; the heathen are subdued, and the chorus burst into shouts of 'Hallelujah, for the Lord God Omnipotent reigneth; the kingdom of this world is become the kingdom of our Lord and of His Christ, and He shall reign for ever and ever.' This ends the second part. The work that the Saviour came to do is accomplished. It is now for man to do his part.

Part III opens with the confession of faith: 'I know that my Redeemer liveth, and that He shall stand at the latter day upon the earth: for now is Christ risen from the dead, the first fruits of them that sleep.'

'Since by man came death, by man came also the resurrection from the dead . . . in Christ shall all be made alive.'

How this is to be brought about is described in the bass solo with its magnificent trumpet *obbligato*: 'The trumpet shall sound, and the dead shall be raised incorruptible.'

The chorus sings: 'Thanks be to God who giveth us the victory through our Lord Jesus Christ,' and the oratorio ends with a pæan of praise: 'Worthy is the Lamb that was slain, to receive power and riches, and wisdom and strength, and honour and glory, and blessing,' followed by one of the great masterpieces of musical art, the 'Amen' chorus.

Messiah towers above all the other oratorios of Handel's in the estimation of the English people. The highest ideals of the Christian religion are here set forth and enhanced by music which in its strength, its sincerity and its entire fitness to the subject appeals to learned and unlearned with equal force. The massive choruses, the powerful solos and recitative in which the highest skill of composer and performer are called forth, drive home to every hearer the truths of religion more powerfully than the finest oratory can do.

Handel wrote *Messiah* in the very midst of his misery and bankruptcy. The 'things of this world' seemed to have no effect on the workings of his genius, or it is possible that they drove him to concentrate his powers more than ever on his lofty subject. That he was deeply moved by it is well known.

The work was completed in twenty-four days. Like Mozart, when he began to write, Handel worked at white heat to the end; but there is evidence that the actual composition had been more or less worked out in his own mind before it was put on paper, for in the Fitzwilliam Museum there are some preliminary sketches for *Messiah* and other works. It is well known that Mozart completed all his works in his head

before he began writing them down, and it is probable that
Handel would destroy his sketches as so much waste paper
when a work was completed, and that those which still exist
must have escaped his notice.

Messiah is a household word with all English people,
whether music-lovers or not, and even those who are tempera-
mentally incapable of appreciating Handel's music (for no
music in the world appeals to all alike) usually acknowledge
its greatness. We have heard the 'Hallelujah' chorus, with
its frequent reiteration of the single word 'Hallelujah,' described
as irreligious; to us it seems to suggest vividly the sudden and
spontaneous cries of joy of a multitude who are greatly moved
by an event which concerns them very deeply. Handel was
in an intense state of religious exaltation when he wrote it,
saying afterwards: 'I did think I did see all Heaven before
me, and the Great God Himself.' The 'Hallelujah' chorus
in *Judas Maccabaeus,* representing the organized welcome of an
earthly hero coming home from war, is of an entirely different
character.

There is scarcely a single oratorio in which Handel did not
follow the practice common in those days of borrowing from
some of his own previous works, and *Messiah* is no exception
to this rule. Four of its choruses, namely 'His yoke is easy,'
'He shall purify,' 'For unto us,' and 'All we like sheep,' as
well as the duet 'O, death! where is thy sting?' are partly or
wholly taken from several of his chamber duets.

The compiler of the words, or rather the man who passed
for the compiler, Charles Jennens, was not satisfied with
Handel's setting of *Messiah.* Writing to one of his friends in
1740 he says: 'I shall show you a collection I gave Handel,
called *Messiah,* which I value highly, and he has made a fine
entertainment of it, though not so good as he might and ought
to have done. I have with great difficulty made him correct
some of the grossest faults in the composition. But he retained

his overture obstinately, in which there are some passages far unworthy of Handel, but much more unworthy of the *Messiah*.' Handel took the criticism much more mildly than he was wont to do. He wrote to Jennens: 'Be pleased to point out those passages in the *Messiah* which you think require altering'; and he made many alterations and improvements from time to time.

The other oratorios, with the exception of *Israel in Egypt*, are entirely different in plan from *Messiah*. They are, as we have said, dramatic works, in which the characters appear in person; the choruses are generally sung by Israelites, Philistines, priests and augurs, nymphs and swains, virgins, etc. The treatment is the same whether the oratorio is concerned with a sacred or classical story, and the work differs from an opera only in the absence of scenery and action, which are left to the imagination of the audience, in the preponderance of massive contrapuntal choruses, and in the simpler orchestra-tion. [Some of these concert works, such as *Semele* or *Hercules*, are entirely secular, being concerned with classical subjects. Others, like *Susanna*, are sacred only in so far as they treat of a subject drawn from the Bible. Both types of work, secular or semi-sacred, are entirely operatic according to the musico-theatrical notions of the day; some are indeed very strongly dramatic—*Belshazzar* and *Hercules*, for instance. The oratorios merit far more detailed discussion than can be given to them here. It is in a way unfortunate that they should be so numerous. One hardly knows where to begin examining them and, having begun, it would be exceedingly difficult to stop enlarging upon their endless beauties and their countless points of interest.

It is this wide choice, too, which is partly responsible for the deplorable fact that but a single one of Handel's oratorios is regularly performed. It is inconceivable that choral societies should not occasionally toy with the idea of giving another of his masterpieces a hearing; but they consider this and that, find themselves bewildered by the wealth and variety of the choice, and in the end fall back on *Messiah*. It may therefore be as well to mention no more than the four works singled out as examples above, all of which are well worth a revival, as indeed two of them have already proved.[1]]

We now have to deal with one of the most difficult problems that confront the student. Handel, like Bach, constantly borrowed from his own earlier works, adapting new words to music previously used. This was a common habit in those days. Another apparently recognized practice was the use of fugue or variation subjects or ground basses, by whomsoever composed, as the basis of new compositions. No one seems to have objected. Bach uses fugue themes by Legrenzi, Corelli and Albinoni without acknowledgment; Handel uses the subject of the Goldberg variations, and the well-known subject of Bach's great G minor organ fugue was undoubtedly suggested to him by a sonata of Reinken. It was constantly used as a theme for candidates for organ appointments to extemporize upon. We can therefore set aside the criticism that delights in finding 'coincidences' and attributes to accident all resemblances between a fugue subject of Handel and another by someone else.

But Handel was in the habit of appropriating whole sections of oratorios, operas, etc., by other composers, altering the words, rescoring and generally improving the music with all

---

[1] *Susanna,* a work full of particularly lovely music, seems to have been entirely ignored in the nineteenth century. It looks as though the subject of Susanna and the Elders, though admissible in painting, was felt to be not quite nice for people who went to an oratorio in order to attend a religious rather than an artistic function. Perhaps that was natural in the times of the bathing-machine, but there is no longer the slightest excuse for setting false prudery above true artistic perception.—E. B.

the effects his genius was capable of and then incorporating it into his own oratorios, operas, etc., without any acknowledgment.

The greater part of the choruses in *Israel in Egypt* are adapted from a manuscript eight-part *Magnificat,* which Rockstro, from an examination of the paper, watermark and handwriting, assigns to a period between the years 1737 and 1740. The manuscript is unfinished and undated; Handel was usually most careful to date both the beginning and end of his compositions. Now in 1857 a mysterious copy of this *Magnificat* was discovered in the library of the Sacred Harmonic Society, bearing the inscription 'Magnificat del Rd. Sigr. Erba.' It was at once concluded that Handel had 'borrowed' his *Israel* from one of two composers, Giorgio Erba, a violinist who published some sonatas in 1736, or Dionigi Erba, a celebrated maestro and composer who flourished at Milan about 1690. The letters 'Rd.' seem to imply that the owner or composer was a priest, and no priest of this name is mentioned as a friend of Handel. Chrysander attributes the composition to Dionigi of Milan. Rockstro thinks that the expression *del* instead of *dal* shows that that particular copy of the work *belonged* to the Rev. Signor Erba, and that it was not *by* him. But this cannot be borne out. [Sedley Taylor [1] has shown that the designation 'del' was quite frequently used by Italian composers to designate authorship and does not carry the meaning of mere ownership with which Rockstro (and Macfarren too) had tried to explain away Handel's plagiarism —as his practice would be called to-day.]

If this were the only instance of borrowing wholesale from another composer, it need not trouble us much. But from a serenata by Stradella he borrowed part of 'The people shall hear,' 'He gave them hailstones,' 'And believed the Lord,'

---

[1] *The Indebtedness of Handel to Works by Other Composers,* pp. 90-1.

'He spake the word,' 'He led them forth,' and from a canzona by J. C. Kerl, 'Egypt was glad when they departed.' From five Italian duets by G. C. M. Clari he borrowed five portions of *Theodora*: 'Come, mighty Father,' 'To Thee, thou glorious Son of worth,' 'How strange their end,' the second movement of the overture, and 'Descend, kind pity.' From eight pieces for the harpsichord by G. Muffat [1] were taken the first movement of the overture, the flute aria, the chorus 'From Harmony' and the organ aria in the Cecilia Ode; portions of the first, fifth, eighth, ninth, tenth and twelfth of the *Concerti grossi*; the introduction (which takes the place of the overture) and march in *Joshua*; parts of the overture of *Theodora*; march in *Judas*; the fugue in the overture to *Samson*. From a *Te Deum* by F. A. Urio (1682) ten numbers of the Dettingen *Te Deum* and parts of *Saul*. From the oratorio *Jephte* by Carissimi part of *Samson*, and from a mass by Habermann portions of *Jephtha*.

Handel was recognized among his contemporaries as a man of the highest honour and integrity, and many modern writers have exercised themselves a good deal over these 'borrowings,' which, from their being unacknowledged, seem to amount to nothing less than thefts. But if we look into the matter closely we shall see that these thefts were perfectly compatible with the spirit of the age. Property in literary works was not recognized. Every publisher, every performer, was practically at liberty to make what use he could of a composer's works. When Handel found that his clavier pieces were being published without his sanction and in an inferior form, he had no idea of going to law in the matter. We have seen that many of his compositions were pillaged, as a matter of course, by Walsh; yet this did not prevent him from employing Walsh. The law would not have protected him, and it had probably never occurred to any one at that time that such things should

[1] Published in 1739 or thereabouts, not in 1727 as other authorities have it, or even 1735 as Chrysander conjectures.—E. B.

be a matter of legislation. He took the only course open to him, of republishing the works himself in a more correct form. Everyone used everyone else's compositions as he liked. No one ever thought until the beginning of the nineteenth century that wrong was being done. If this practice had been recognized as theft, what a splendid chance there would have been for Handel's numerous enemies. They could have brought an indictment against him of being unable to compose music for himself and appropriating the labours of others.

If it be said that Erba, being an unknown composer, could be robbed by Handel with comparative safety, the same cannot be said of Clari, who was a contemporary of his, and whose works were well known and admired by the greatest masters of the time; nor of Muffat, another contemporary, whose *Componimenti musicali per il cembalo* were published in 1727 and considered his masterpiece; much less of the great Carissimi.

But, it will be said, Bononcini was obliged to leave England owing to the odium incurred by his appropriation of Lotti's madrigal. The cases are not quite on all fours. Handel, following a practice of his day, did not merely copy out the music of others: he made it the basis of far richer and more effective music than they could do. He adapted it to other words, rescored it to a great extent and so made it his own. Bononcini simply copied out the madrigal word for word and note for note, without improving or altering it, and this was considered a theft. Moreover, he attempted to use the stolen work for the purpose of impressing the Academy of Ancient Music. The other practice was no more than an enlargement, as it were, of the custom of using fugue subjects of others for new fugues, etc. That the practice was not even more resorted to may probably be attributed to the fact that there were no other composers (in England at all events) who could improve on the works of the Italian and German musicians.

Three manuscript copies of Urio's *Te Deum* exist. One of these, in the British Museum, has the following note:

This curious score was transcribed from an Italian copy in the collection of Dr. Samuel Howard, Mus.D., organist of St. Bride's and St. Clement Danes. It formerly belonged to Mr. Handel, who has borrowed from hence several verses in the Dettingen *Te Deum*, as well as some other passages in the oratorio of *Saul*, T. B.[1] This copy was written by John Anderson, a chorister of St. Paul's, 1781.

It is evident from the above note that some twenty years after Handel's death his practice of borrowing was noticed without comment. On another copy of Urio's work, now in the library of the Conservatoire at Paris, is written this remark:

Mr. Handel was much indebted to this author, as plainly appears by his Dettingen *Te Deum*, likewise a duett in *Julius Caesar*, and a movement in *Saul* for carillons, etc., etc.—J. W. Callcott, May 16, 1797.

We may hazard the opinion, then, that it is undeniably proved that Handel did borrow largely from other composers without acknowledgment; that what he borrowed he practically made his own by the exercise of his genius; and that it never once occurred either to him or to any of his friends or enemies that in so doing he was acting dishonourably. It was clearly a case of the survival of the fittest. If Erba or Urio or Clari had attracted the public more than Handel, we should have heard of them rather than of him; and he would not have thought of adapting the music of others if he could not have made it more attractive than it was already.

[Professor Edward J. Dent propounds an ingenious and very plausible theory:

No one seems to have noticed hitherto, that Handel's 'borrowings' begin in 1736 on a small scale, and become more frequent in 1737,

---

[1] Thomas Bever, Fellow of All Souls, Oxford,

after which they develop into a regular habit. It seems only natural therefore to connect them with Handel's mental collapse; it became acute in the spring of 1737, but it may well have been approaching in the previous year.

There is no need to go so far as to suggest that Handel suffered from moral insanity and was incapable of distinguishing between right and wrong; but it is quite conceivable that his paralytic stroke affected his brain in such a way that he may sometimes have had a difficulty in starting a composition. . . . Indecision is a common symptom of overstrained nerves, and any one who has attempted musical composition or taught it to students will understand the hesitation and uncertainty which often attends the first writing down of a musical theme, although, once the initial idea has been settled, the continuation and development of it may proceed without difficulty.

Another explanation of Handel's curious habit of pilfering, at which, indeed, Professor Dent hints in passing, is that he may have taken a particular pleasure in improving other people's work. It is worth remembering that he had no pupils for composition except the younger Smith, who may not have satisfied all the desire to teach which a composer with so great a technical mastery cannot have failed to feel.]

Various names were given to the smaller vocal works; *Acis and Galatea* was called a 'masque,' 'pastoral' and 'serenata' in different editions. It was, as we have seen, composed for the Duke of Chandos and performed at Canons about 1720. It was revised in 1732 for a performance at the King's Theatre, Haymarket, and again in 1733 for the Oxford Act.

The *Acis and Galatea* of 1720 was an English play; the serenatas of 1732 and 1733, mostly sung in Italian, were a combination of the Canons *Acis* with the *Aci, Galatea e Polifemo,* composed at Naples in 1708, with additions; and in 1740 Handel returned to the original masque of 1720, but divided it into two acts, adding a chorus, 'Happy we,' to end the first act. Between the acts a concerto was played on the organ by Handel or some other. The part of Damon was sung by a tenor at Canons, but afterwards was put into the treble and marked 'for the boy,' and many of the soprano solos in the oratorios are intended for 'the boy.' The choruses of *Acis* are in five parts, soprano (boys), three tenors and a bass, like the Chandos anthems, but at later performances he apparently caused the first tenor part to be sung by contralto voices. The orchestra was a small one, consisting of two oboes, two violins, basses and harpsichord. To these were added in some of the solos, a piccolo, two flutes, and in the chorus, 'Happy we,' a viola. The work differs from a secular oratorio in having scenery on the stage, and from an opera in the importance and length of the choruses.

Handel spared no pains in altering, rewriting and adapting his works to varying times and circumstances. No work was ever complete and finished; nearly every new performance saw it provided 'with additions and alterations.' Except in the case of *Messiah* he looked upon all performances as 'entertainments' of a high order which must be varied to suit the particular singers and each particular public.

The *Concerti grossi* were very popular and took the same place at concerts as the symphonies of later composers. The orchestra consisted of a *concertino* of two solo violins and a solo cello, a body of string instruments and figured bass. To these oboes, bassoons and flutes were occasionally added.

The concerto usually began with a slow, moderate or *maestoso* movement. Then came an *allegro* and an *adagio* in which the solo violins and cello were expected to exhibit their skill in ornamentation of the given themes. This was followed by an *allegro* of fugal character, and there was usually a final movement in triple time. But there are exceptions to the above plan, as in the third of the concertos for strings alone (Op. 6), where a *Polonaise andante* takes the place of the usual *adagio* and by a rare exception the *fugato* movement is omitted.

Another concerto (Op. 6, No. 7) ends with a hornpipe. [The *Concerti grossi,* long unaccountably neglected,[1] have come into their own again as splendid concert works full of dignity, varied invention and magnificent workmanship.]

There exists in the Fitzwilliam Museum an incomplete 'overture' for two clarinets and *corno di caccia.* The clarinet, or little trumpet (clarino), was invented about 1690 at Nuremberg, but it had not come into use as an orchestral instrument during Handel's lifetime. The *corno di caccia,* or hunting horn, was frequently used by Bach.

The organ Concertos are partly original and partly arrangements of other works. The second set of six were pirated by Walsh from the orchestral concertos and arranged for the organ. There is also extant a single movement in D minor for two organs and orchestra. The general construction of these concertos follows the plan of those for orchestra.

The accompaniment consists of two oboes or two flutes, one, two or three violin parts, violas, cellos and double basses. No. 6 of the first set is for harp or organ. The organ plays the same notes as the orchestra in the *tutti,* and the solo portions consist for the most part of florid passages ('divisions') for the right hand, with single notes for the left. Rarely are there more than two parts, and the orchestra, if it accompanies at all, only plays a few notes here and there. Pedal organs were practically unknown in England at that time; it is remarkable

---

[1] Perhaps the following remark made by the author in the original edition may help to explain the attitude of many nineteenth-century musicians towards Handel's instrumental works, difficult as it is to understand: 'These concertos, popular as they once were, would be no more acceptable to the general public of to-day than the operas. The succession of movements in the same key, the monotony of the orchestration, and the small range of modulation would pall, though there is plenty of spirit and verve in the actual themes.' —E. B.

that neither Smith nor Harris, who had learned their art in Germany and France, ever built a pedal organ in England.[1] Perhaps expense, want of space and insular prejudice may have been against them.

The Concertos have the appearance of being composed for small chamber organs. There are none of the massive effects that are found in the works of Bach and the German school; all the *forte* passages are played by the orchestra in conjunction with the organ, which is practically treated like a harpsichord, where the chief effects are produced by arpeggios and runs rather then by sustained sounds. [In modern performances various adaptations are generally used, made either by some editor or by the organist himself, who interprets the solo part, with more or less taste, according to the size of the hall and the orchestra, the capabilities of his instrument and, in some cases, the caprice of the moment.]

The first Concerto of Op. 7 shows that there must have been somewhere in England an organ with pedals, for its *andante,* which is on a ground bass, has a passage of thirty-three bars without the orchestra for 'organo a 2 clav. e pedale,' in which the ground bass is given to the pedals on a separate stave.

We learn from Mattheson that Handel, in his youth, surpassed him on the pedals, and from Burney that on his first arrival in England he used to go to St. Paul's Cathedral to play on the organ *for the exercise it afforded him in the use of the pedals.* It is evident, therefore, that pedals had been added to this organ by the year 1710, and it is not impossible that Handel might have had them temporarily added to the manuals of some of the organs on which he played at public entertainments, and as no one but he could use them, with the above exception, he omitted printing a part for them in his published Concertos. The addition of a pedal-board coupled to the manuals, and without separate pipes, would entail little

[1] Hopkins & Rimbault. *History of the Organ.*

trouble, no extra space, and merely nominal expense, and it was universally applied in Germany to the clavichord in this way for the use of organ students.

Handel composed a certain amount of chamber music in his early days: for harpsichord alone, for *viola da gamba* and harpsichord, for two violins and violoncello, with figured bass, and for flute and figured bass. Later came the 'Lessons' for harpsichord, composed for the princesses, his pupils, solos for German flute, oboe or violin with thorough-bass for bass viol or harpsichord, the Sonatas or Trios for two violins, flutes or oboes with similar accompaniment (Opp. 2 and 5), and one or two other works of the kind.

Handel's orchestra was a large one, containing twelve first and twelve second violins, at least four bassoons, and four violoncellos. There were two harpsichords and apparently a considerable number of oboes and flutes. Quantz, in his memoirs, says: 'Handel's band is uncommonly powerful.' Side-drums were used in *Joshua* in the chorus 'See the conquering hero comes,' and occasionally in the march in *Judas Maccabaeus*. The chorus in *Messiah*, 'Lift up your heads,' had two separate wind bands besides the strings, i.e. First band: 2 horns, 2 oboes, bassoons (plural). Second band: 2 horns, 2 oboes, bassoons (plural).

On the occasion of a concert, during the time the trumpets were playing, a thunder-clap happened to burst right over the building; whereupon the king said to Lord Pembroke: 'How sublime! What an accompaniment! How this would have delighted Handel!'

In another place we read:

There was a time when the man-mountain Handel had got the superiority, notwithstanding many attempts had been made to keep him down, and might have maintained it probably, had he been content to have pleased people in their own way; but his evil genius would not suffer it; for imagining, forsooth, that nothing could obstruct him in his career while at the zenith of his greatness, broached another kind of music, more full, more grand (as his admirers are pleased to call it), and, to make the noise the greater, caused it to be performed by at least double the number of voices and instruments than were ever heard in the theatre before. . . . At one time I expected the house to be blown down with his artificial wind; at another time, that the sea would have overflowed its banks and swallowed us up. But beyond everything, his thunder is most intolerable. I shall never get the horrid rumbling of it out of my head. This was, literally, you will say, taking us by storm.

In course of time *Messiah* and other of Handel's oratorios became known on the Continent. As organs were not often found in the concert rooms there, Mozart was commissioned by Baron van Swieten, about 1788, to write additional wind parts for performances of *Messiah* at the house of Count Johann Ester-házy, and of *Alexander's Feast, Acis and Galatea* and the Cecilia Ode, which took place at the Hofbibliothek at Vienna. Other composers followed suit, with less reverence than Mozart had shown: Adam Hiller, for example, who introduced 'extra-ordinary things'[1] into the score of *Messiah*. It does not appear that Mozart ever intended his additional accompaniments for publication: they were merely to be used in the absence of an organ. In 1803, Breitkopf & Härtel published *Messiah* with 'Mozart's' accompaniments; but later investigation has shown that several numbers in this edition were the work of Hiller, in which great liberties were taken with the original score. Per-haps the most salient example is in the aria, 'If God be for us,' which is completely rescored by Hiller, and has been always accepted 'as altered by Mozart.'[2] But Mozart was careful not to touch a note of Handel's music: he altered nothing, but merely added extra wind parts to the original score. The matter was fully investigated by Robert Franz, who published

[1] Robert Franz, Introduction to *Messiah*.
[2] Novello's edition of 1859.

Messiah with Mozart's accompaniments and an important explanatory introduction.

Some admirers of Handel would like to abolish all additional accompaniments and return to the simplicity of the original; but conditions have changed so much that it is doubtful whether this would be an advantage. In the first place, the orchestra of Handel's day usually outnumbered the chorus. Oboes, bassoons and flutes were used in masses like the violins, and not in single instruments to a part as at present; the tone of the ancient wind instruments was much weaker than those of the present day, and audiences have become so accustomed to a richer orchestration that they would, in all probability, find that of Handel's time far too monotonous. It is very doubtful if we shall ever, as a practice, return to this simplicity, though, from an antiquarian point of view, an occasional experiment would be interesting.[1]

A society was established at Boston, Massachusetts, in 1815, called the Handel and Haydn Society for the performance of the works of these composers. It obtained a charter in the following year, and has given many important choral and orchestral works by all the great composers, with a chorus of about six hundred voices.

In 1843 a Handel Society was formed for the publication of a standard edition of the works of Handel by Sir G. A. Macfarren, Sir W. Sterndale Bennett, Sir Henry Bishop, Sir George Smart, Dr. E. J. Hopkins, Dr. Crotch, Moscheles and others. This society published the Coronation Anthems, *L'Allegro, il Pensieroso ed il Moderato, Esther,* Cecilia Ode, *Israel in Egypt* (edited by Mendelssohn), *Acis and Galatea,* the Dettingen *Te Deum, Belshazzar, Messiah,* 13 Chamber Duets and 2 Trios, *Samson, Judas Maccabaeus, Saul* and *Jephtha.* It dissolved

---

[1] Several performances of the work in its original form have been given recently (1935) and proved most satisfactory.—E. B.

in 1848, and the publication of the works was continued by Cramer & Co. until 1855.

In 1856 the Händelgesellschaft was formed at Leipzig for the publication of Handel's works by Dr. Chrysander, Franz, Gervinus, Hauptmann, Jahn, Moscheles, Liszt, Rietz, Meyerbeer and others. The publishers were Breitkopf & Härtel, and the works were edited by Chrysander. The King of Hanover guaranteed the edition against loss, the Prussian Government afterwards taking over the guarantee. After the eighteenth volume the editor had the remainder printed privately under his personal supervision. The edition was completed early in the present century in ninety-seven volumes, plus five supplementary volumes of works from which Handel had borrowed.

CHAPTER XVI

INFLUENCE ON ENGLISH COMPOSERS

HANDEL left no pupils to carry on his work. [Even John Christopher Smith the younger was not taught exclusively by him, for he became a pupil of Pepusch and Roseingrave.] Having assimilated and made his own all the important features in the music of his forerunners, Keiser, Steffani, Purcell, Scarlatti, Lotti and others, he stood absolutely alone; there were no musicians who could approach him in England, and he had no successors. He had imitators, naturally, by the score: composers who could catch the tricks of his style and make a momentary reputation thereby. This, however, is the case with all great composers; none has yet appeared who did not serve as a model to a host of smaller successors.

He wrote in the so-called 'Italian style.' If we compare his Dettingen and Utrecht *Te Deums* with that of Purcell in D major, the difference between the Italian and the English style becomes at once apparent. On reading through the Purcell score one is struck with the boldness of the choral effects, the beauty and tenderness of some of the solos and duets; but on turning to the Handel scores, one sees the same subject treated on a far grander scale. The ritornels are of immense length and importance compared with those of Purcell, the fugal subjects are more fully worked out, the orchestra takes a place that is equal to, and often of greater importance than, the chorus. Both composers wrote their *Te Deums* for festival occasions, and both threw all their energies into the effort to produce the best results known to them. The difference is like the difference between an English and an Italian cathedral: for example, St. Paul's and St. Peter's. St. Paul's stands surrounded by buildings, hardly seen, modest in ornament, but beautiful in its own way and specially dear to the English people. St. Peter's, on the other hand, stands in a clear space of many scores of acres in extent; the beholder is struck by the size, the luxurious ornaments, the brilliant colouring, the enormous spaces both inside and outside the building. In a like manner the musician is struck by the luxuriance and magnificence of the form and accessories of Handel's works as compared with those of his contemporaries, though as regards internal beauty there is little to choose between Purcell and Handel.[1]

But it is just this overpowering grandeur and strength that struck a blow at native English productivity, from which it only began to recover in the latter half of the nineteenth century. English music was practically all Handel or Handelian: our cathedral composers were influenced by him and our audiences would listen to no music made in England except the oratorios of Handel and works modelled on them which could not compete with the Saxon's music that the English nation

[1] The influence of Purcell on Handel is nevertheless very apparent, both in the *Te Deums* and elsewhere. There is no doubt either that what may be called the English popular style greatly influenced Handel, who was extremely susceptible to musical environments, as the thoroughly Italianate character of his music, after a comparatively short sojourn in Italy, proved. Reflections of English song and dance may be found in countless and sometimes unexpected places in Handel's work: in the *Water* and *Fireworks Music,* in *Acis,* in the hornpipe of the B flat major *Concerto grosso* (Op. 6, No. 7), in many of the dance movements at the end of the opera overtures (e.g. *Giustino*) and so on. The chorus 'Love and Hymen' in *Hercules* might have come straight out of Purcell's *King Arthur.* —E. B.

had made its own. Who hears nowadays of performances of any of the oratorios of Arne, Arnold, Boyce, Crotch, Greene or Hayes? Efforts are being made to revive the music of Purcell amongst the cultivated few, but it is scarcely likely that the general public, accustomed to the magnificence of *Messiah,* of *Israel in Egypt,* of *Samson,* will learn to appreciate the equally great though less massive and luxuriant music of Handel's predecessor.[1]

The recovery from the blow dealt at English music began with the appearance of Sterndale Bennett, who for a time stood alone; he was followed by Sullivan and then by a number of younger composers, with Parry and Stanford as leaders of a new movement. After a lapse of nearly a century and a half from the death of Purcell, the English school of composition, begun by him and nipped in the bud by Handel, began to show signs of again coming to life.

But 'Englischer Componist? Kein Componist!' as Schumann said that too many people thought, and there are doubtless many who will say that even if Handel had not appeared, or had remained in Germany, we should have had no great school of English composers during the eighteenth and part of the nineteenth centuries. It is after all doubtful whether the English composers who succeeded Handel, even if they had the advantage of constant production of their works, would have been sufficiently in earnest to carry on Purcell's work. Handel had a remarkable combination of talents: the loftiest enthusiasm, the highest ideals were in him joined with an unusual talent for business, a combination rarely to be found in musicians.

[1] This has proved a false prophecy. The general public nowadays, though it still knows its Purcell less well than *Messiah,* is quite as conversant with him as with *Israel in Egypt* and more than with *Samson,* not to mention the other Handel oratorios which are so inexcusably neglected.—E. B.

Earnestness of purpose is essential in the making of a great composer, and it is just this that is too often lacking among those musicians whose highest aim is to become doctors of music, and who have little conception that music in its highest sense can, if properly used, profoundly affect the well-being of a community. It is not impossible that had Purcell lived he might have founded, through pupils, an English school, and that there would have been no place for Handel in England. But however much Handel may or may not be responsible for the dearth of English composers of the first rank during a century and a half, there is no doubt that the English nation as a whole owes an enormous debt of gratitude to him for the masterly way in which he compelled them to accept and assimilate the grandeur and beauty of his music.

APPENDICES

APPENDIX A

CALENDAR

(Figures in brackets denote the age reached by the person mentioned during the year in question.)

Year Age	Life	Contemporary Musicians
1685	Georg Friedrich Händel born Feb. 23, at Halle, son of Georg Händel (63), district surgeon and barber.	Bach born, March 21; Scarlatti (D.) born, Oct. 26.

Abaco aged 10; Albinoni 11; Ariosti *c.* 25; Blow 37; Böhm 24; Bononcini 13; Buxtehude 48; Caldara *c.* 15; Campra 25; Charpentier *c.* 50; Clarke *c.* 25; Corelli 33; Couperin 17; Croft 7; Desmarets 23; Destouches *c.* 13; Durante 1; Eccles *c.* 22; Fux 25; Geminiani 5; Keiser 11; Kerl 57; Kuhnau 25; Lalande 28; Legrenzi *c.* 60; Lotti 18; Lulli 53; Muffat (sen.) *c.* 40; Pachelbel 32; Pasquini 48; Pepusch 18; Purcell 26; Rameau 2; Reinken 62; Scarlatti (A.) 26; Steffani 31; Telemann 4; Vivaldi *c.* 15.

Year	Age	Life	Contemporary Musicians
1686	1		Marcello born, July 31/ Aug. 1; Porpora born, Aug. 19.
1687	2		Graupner born, Feb.; Lulli (55) dies, March 22; Senaillé born, Nov. 23.
1688	3		Fasch (J. F.) born, April 15; Foggia (84) dies, Jan. 8.
1689	4	Begins to show a distinct musical talent.	
1690	5	His father (68) grows alarmed at his increasing passion for music.	Carey born (approx.); Legrenzi (c. 65) dies, July 26; Muffat (jun.) born, April; Vinci born.
1691	6	His parents vainly endeavour to suppress his love of music.	d'Anglebert (63) dies.
1692	7	Learns to play the clavichord in secret and without help. His father (70), on discovering this, is at last persuaded to allow him to play, though he does not wish him to become a musician.	Tartini born, April 8; Vitali (G. B.) (c. 48) dies, Oct. 12.
1693	8	Visit to relatives at Weissenfels, where he plays the organ so well that the family council and the reigning prince advise his father (71) to let him take up a musical career. The father refuses, but agrees to let him be taught music.	Kerl (65) dies, Feb. 13; Locatelli born; Sammartini (G.) born (approx.).

Year	Age	Life	Contemporary Musicians
1694	9	Begins to study under Zachau (31). He progresses on the clavier and organ, and takes up the violin and oboe.	Daquin born, July 4; Leo born, Aug. 5.
1695	10	Makes great progress and begins to compose. 6 Sonatas for two oboes and bass.	Greene born; Purcell (36) dies, Nov. 21
1696	11	Visit to Berlin, where he plays at court. An offer of a court appointment is refused by his father (74), who wishes him to take up legal studies and orders him back to Halle.	
1697	12	Death of H.'s father (75), Feb. 11. He continues musical studies and writes a number of church cantatas and organ pieces.	Leclair born, May 10; Quantz born, Jan. 30.
1698	13	Goes to the Latin school and composes much in his spare time.	Francœur born, Sept. 28.
1699	14		Hasse born, March 25.
1700	15		Strungk (60) dies, Sept.23.
1701	16	Frequently deputizes for J. C. Leporin at the cathedral and extemporizes on the organ.	Graun born, May 7; Sammartini (G. B.) born.
1702	17	Enters Halle University as a law student, Feb. Leporin, who makes a habit of defaulting, is dismissed from the cathedral and H. is appointed organist, March 13. Large	

Year	Age	Life	Contemporary Musicians
		number of church cantatas composed.	
1703	18	Interrupts his legal studies and resigns his organist's post, summer. He goes to Hamburg, where Mattheson (22) assists him to become known as organist and clavier player, and he becomes second violin at the Opera under the management of Keiser (29). Visit to Lübeck, Aug., to see if the succession to Buxtehude (66) can be secured; but as this means marrying Buxtehude's daughter, Anna Margreta (28), both H. and Mattheson refrain from applying for the succession. Return to Hamburg.	Lampe born.
1704	19	Passion according to St. John performed, Lent. Opera, Almira, begun. Quarrel with Mattheson (23) over the playing of the continuo in the latter's opera, Cleopatra, Dec. 5, and reconciliation, Dec. 30.	Biber (60) dies; Charpentier (c. 69) dies, March; Muffat (sen.) (c. 59) dies, Feb. 23.
1705	20	Almira produced in Hamburg, Jan. 8. It is very successful, and is repeated some twenty times. Second opera, Nero, produced,	

Year	Age	*Life*	*Contemporary Musicians*
		Feb. 25. The Hamburg Opera begins to deteriorate under Keiser (31). H. dissociates himself from it and takes pupils.	
1706	21	Many songs, harpsichord pieces amd cantatas composed, also (approx.) the operas *Florindo* and *Daphne* (originally one work, but divided because of its length). Departure for Florence. Secular cantatas composed there. He is introduced to Prince Ferdinand de' Medici at Pratolino, near Florence, and (?) meets Alessandro Scarlatti (47) there, Sept.	Galuppi born, Oct. 18; Martini born, April 24.
1707	22	Leaves Florence for Rome, Jan. (approx.). Psalms, *Dixit Dominus, Laudate pueri* and others composed there. Return to Florence, July, where his first Italian opera, *Rodrigo,* is produced with great success. Visit to Venice, autumn.	Buxtehude (70) dies, May 9; Clarke (*c.* 47) dies, Dec. 1.
1708	23	Meeting with Lotti (41), Steffani (54) and Gasparini (40) in Venice and friendship with Domenico Scarlatti (23). Return to Rome, early spring, where he is received by the Arcadians, though he is too young to	Blow (60) dies, Oct. 1.

Year	Age	Life	Contemporary Musicians
		be a member. There he meets Corelli (55), Marcello (22) and Pasquini (71). He is also received by Prince Ruspoli and Cardinal Pietro Ottoboni (40). Oratorio, *La Resurrezione,* and cantata, *Il Trionfo del tempo e del disinganno,* composed in Rome, also secular cantatas to words by Cardinal Benedetto Panfili (55), including *Apollo e Dafne* and *Fillide ed Aminta.* Departure for Naples, end of June. French canzonets in the style of Lulli composed there. Pastoral play, *Aci, Galatea e Polifemo,* composed.	
1709	24	Meeting with Cardinal Vincenzo Grimani, who commissions an opera for Venice from H. Third visit to Rome, *c.* autumn. H. hears Calabrian shepherds sing and play their Christmas songs, end of year. Second visit to Venice for the carnival. Opera, *Agrippina,* produced there, Dec. 26.	Benda (F.) born, Nov. 25; Colasse (60) dies, July 17; Duni born, Feb. 9; Richter (F. X.) born, Dec.
1710	25	There he is induced by English and Hanoverian visitors, including Prince	Arne born, March 12; Avison born (approx.); Bach (Wilhelm Friede-

Year	Age	Life	Contemporary Musicians

Ernest of Hanover and Baron Kielmansegge, to go to London. He makes the journey by way of Hanover, where he goes with Steffani (56), who resumes his duties at the electoral court there. He is appointed musical director by the Elector Georg Ludwig (50) and the visit to England is postponed until the autumn, when (?) he visits his mother at Halle and leaves for London. He is presented to Queen Anne (45), and Aaron Hill (25), manager of the King's Theatre, suggests an opera, *Rinaldo*, to him, which he composes, to an Italian libretto by Rossi, in a fortnight, using many earlier pieces.

Contemporary Musicians: mann) born, Nov. 22; Boyce born, Feb. 7; Pasquini (73) dies, Nov. 22; Pergolesi born, Jan. 3.

1711 26 Production of *Rinaldo*, Feb. 24. It is given fifteen times before the opera season closes on June 2. H. appears at Thomas Britton's (*c.* 60) musical club and meets Babell (*c.* 21), who arranges harpsichord lessons on airs from *Rinaldo*. Return to Hanover, early summer, after another visit to

Contemporary Musicians: Holzbauer born; Terradellas born, Feb.

Year	Age	Life	Contemporary Musicians
		Düsseldorf. Visit to Halle, June. Steffani (57) shows him much kindness and influences him musically. Chamber duets composed for Princess Caroline of Anspach. Oboe Concertos and 12 cantatas.	
1712	27	Asks leave of Georg Ludwig (52) for a second visit to England. It is granted on condition that he return within a reasonable time. Arrival in London, late autumn. Production of the opera, *Il Pastor fido,* at the King's Theatre, Nov. 22. Opera, *Teseo,* finished, Dec. 19.	Zachau (49) dies, Aug. 14.
1713	28	Production of *Teseo* at the King's Theatre, Jan. 10. The manager, Owen MacSwiney, fails and decamps, leaving H. and the singers unpaid; but they continue to give the opera at their own risk. *Te Deum* for the Peace of Utrecht finished, Jan. 14. Uncertain whether a work by a foreigner will be sung at the peace celebrations, H. writes a birthday Ode for Queen Anne (48), which is sung, with one by Eccles (c. 50), Feb. 6. The queen is so	Corelli (60) dies, Jan. 10; Dauvergne born, Oct. 4; Krebs born, Feb. 10.

Year	Age	*Life*	*Contemporary Musicians*
		delighted with it that she commands H. to have the *Te Deum* and a *Jubilate* ready for the celebrations. These take place at St. Paul's Cathedral, July 7. Anne is too ill to attend, but hears the works privately later, granting H. a yearly salary of £200. The *Te Deum* is modelled on one by Purcell. The Earl of Burlington (18) invites H. to live at his house in Piccadilly and introduces him to society. Meeting with Pope (25) and Gay (28).	
1714	29	Opera, *Silla,* (?) composed and performed by amateurs at Burlington House. Accession of the Elector Georg Ludwig of Hanover (54) to the English throne as George I. H. is in disgrace at his court for having outstayed his leave from Hanover.	Bach (Carl Philipp Emanuel) born, March 8; Gluck born, July 2; Homilius born, Feb. 2; Jommelli born, Sept. 10.
1715	30	Opera, *Amadigi,* produced at the King's Theatre, May 25. Geminiani (35) endeavours to reinstate H. at court by insisting on being accompanied at the harpsichord by him. Performance of a Suite (*Water*	Alcock born, April 11; Nares born, April; Wagenseil born, Jan. 15.

Year	Age	Life	Contemporary Musicians
		Music) on a boat following the royal barge on the Thames, Aug. 22.	
1716	31	Departure for Hanover in the suite of George I (56), July. Visit to Dresden in search of singers for London. Composition of a Passion Oratorio by Brockes (36). Visits to Hamburg, Anspach and Halle. Return to London, end of year. *Concerto grosso*, F major (Op. 3, No. 4), composed for the benefit of the opera orchestra.	
1717	32	After revivals of *Rinaldo* and *Amadigi*, the opera season closes without any prospect of renewal, end of June. Music by H. played to the court on the Thames, July 17 (? repetition of *Water Music*, see 1715).	Nichelmann born, Aug. 13; Purcell (Daniel) (*c.* 57) dies, Nov.; Stamitz (J. W.) born, June 19.
1718	33	The Earl of Carnarvon (45) invites H. to take up his residence at Canons, near Edgware, in succession to Pepusch (51). He is to conduct the band, play the organ and compose as much as he likes. A series of anthems begun.	Vitali (T. A.) (*c.* 53) dies (approx.).
1719	34	A Royal Academy of Music formed for the	

Year	Age	Life	Contemporary Musicians

production of opera, Feb. The Earl of Carnarvon (47) created Duke of Chandos, April. H. goes to Germany in search of singers. He finds one at Düsseldorf. Summer spent at Hanover. Visit to Dresden, Sept. There he secures several Italian singers for the London season of 1721, meets Lotti (52) again and plays before the Elector Frederick Augustus I (49) of Saxony. Visit to Halle, autumn, where his sister, Dorothea Sophia Michaelsen, has died in 1718. Return to London. Composition of the pastoral cantata, *Acis and Galatea,* on a poem by Gay (34).

1720 35 Italian opera season under the auspices of the Royal Academy of Music opens at the King's Theatre under H.'s direction, April 2. Opera, *Radamisto,* produced there, April 27. The masque, *Haman and Mordecai (Esther,* H.'s first English oratorio), performed on the stage at Canons, Aug. 29. First book of Suites for harpsichord

Agricola (J. F.) born, Jan. 4.

Year	Age	*Life*	*Contemporary Musicians*
		published, Nov. 14. Opening of the second Royal Academy season with *Astarto* by Bononcini (48), who comes to London, Nov. 19. Most of the *Concerti grossi* (Op. 3) composed at Canons.	
1721	36	Production of the opera, *Muzio Scevola,* at the King's Theatre, April 15. The third act is by H., the second by Bononcini (49) and the first either by Ariosti (*c.* 61) or by the cellist Filippo Mattei. The public begins to be divided in its adherence to H. or Bononcini. The latter gains the upper hand after the opening of the third Royal Academy season, Nov. 1, the public, unsettled by the bursting of the South Sea Bubble, favouring lighter entertainments. Production of the opera, *Floridante,* Dec. 9.	Kirnberger born, April.
1722	37	H.'s popularity is more and more overshadowed. Opening of the fourth Royal Academy season, Oct. 27. The opera, *Ottone,* on a libretto by Nicola Haym, is post-	Benda (G.) born, June 30; Kuhnau (62) dies, June 25; Nardini born; Reinken (99) dies, Nov. 24.

Year	Age	Life	Contemporary Musicians
		poned until the arrival of Francesca Cuzzoni (*c.* 22), which has been delayed. She arrives end of Dec., but proves extremely obstinate, refusing to sing the aria 'Falsa immagine' until H. seizes her and threatens to throw her out of the window.	
1723	38	*Ottone* produced at the King's Theatre, Jan. 12. It does much to reinstate H. in the public favour. But *Flavio,* produced May 14, has no great success. Fifth Italian season opens, Nov. 27.	Gassmann born, May 4.
1724	39	Ariosti's (*c.* 64) opera, *Vespasiano,* produced Jan. 14, proves such a failure as to threaten the existence of the Italian Opera. H., to save the situation, hastily finishes *Giulio Cesare,* which is produced Feb. 20. He plays the organ at St. Paul's Cathedral before the Princesses Anne and Caroline, his pupils, Aug. 24. Sixth Royal Academy season opens, Oct. 31. Bononcini (52) has been dismissed. Production of the opera *Tamerlano,* Oct. 31.	Theile (78) dies, June.

Year	Age	Life	Contemporary Musicians
1725	40	Opera, *Rodelinda,* produced at the King's Theatre, Feb. 13. It has an immense success. Seventh Italian season opens, Nov. 30. Ariosti's (*c.* 65) engagement is not renewed. John Christopher Smith (Schmidt) (13), son of H.'s treasurer, becomes his pupil.	Krieger (J. P.) (76) dies, Feb. 6; Scarlatti (A.) (66) dies, Oct. 24.
1726	41	H. becomes a naturalized Englishman, styles himself George Frideric Handel and is created, next to Croft (48), Composer of Musick to the Chapel Royal. Opera, *Scipione,* finished March 2 and produced March 12. Production of the opera, *Alessandro,* in which Faustina Bordoni (33), who has been newly engaged, appears as well as Francesca Cuzzoni (*c.* 26), May 5. A dangerous rivalry between the two singers develops.	Lalande (69) dies, June 18; Philidor born, Sept. 7.
1727	42	Eighth season of Italian opera opens at the King's Theatre, Jan. 7. Opera, *Admeto,* produced, Jan. 31. There is much disturbance, the public having split into two parties supporting either	Croft (49) dies, Aug. 14; Traetta born, March 30.

Year	Age	Life	Contemporary Musicians

Bordoni (34) or Cuzzoni (*c.* 27). Opera, *Riccardo I,* finished, May 16. The two prima donnas engage in a hand-to-hand fight on the stage during a performance of Bononcini's *Astyanax* and there is a disgraceful public demonstration, which brings the season abruptly to a close, June 6. Coronation of George II (44), at which H.'s Coronation Anthems are sung, Oct. 11. Ninth opera season opens, Sept. 30. H. is now sole musical director, but the Royal Academy of Music is so disorganized by intrigues among the singers, and the public so discouraged by the violent demonstrations for and against the artists, that it is impossible to secure enough subscriptions. *Riccardo I* is produced, Nov. 11. Court ball in honour of the king's birthday, Oct. 30. H. has composed several Minuets.

1728 43 Opera, *Siroe,* produced at the King's Theatre, Feb. 17, and *Tolomeo,* April 30. The King's Theatre closes, June 1, and the Royal   Hiller (J. A.) born, Dec. 25; Lœillet (*c.* 53) dies; Marais (72) dies, Aug.; Piccinni born, Jan. 16; Steffani (74) dies, Feb. 12.

Year	Age	Life	Contemporary Musicians
		Academy of Music in its original form is wound up. The public is tired of Italian opera and transfers its affection to Gay's (43) satire on it, *The Beggar's Opera,* which, with music arranged by Pepusch (61), has had an enormously successful run since its production on Jan. 29. A New Royal Academy of Music is formed for the production of Italian opera, summer, with Heidegger as manager and H. as musical director.	
1729	44	H. goes to Italy to hear new operas and engage singers, Jan. He visits Florence, Milan, Venice, Rome and other cities and hears works by Porpora (42), Vinci (38), Hasse (29) and Pergolesi (18). He also becomes acquainted with the librettos of Metastasio (30). At the conclusion of his Italian tour, H. goes to Halle, where he finds his mother blind and infirm, June. Bach (44), who is ill at Leipzig, sends his son Wilhelm Friedemann (19) to Halle to invite H. to go and see	Monsigny born, Oct. 17; Sarti born, Dec. 1.

Year	Age	Life	Contemporary Musicians
		him, but H. is unable to do so. Return to London, end of June. The new Italian season opens at the King's Theatre with the production of the opera, *Lotario,* Dec. 2. It has no great success and the new prima donna, Anna Strada del Pò, does not please.	
1730	45	Opera, *Partenope,* produced at the King's Theatre, Feb. 24. Second New Royal Academy season opens with a revival of *Scipione,* Nov. 3, in which Senesino (*c.* 50) reappears.	Aylward born; Jackson born, May 29; Senaillé (43) dies, Oct. 15.
1731	46	Opera, *Poro,* set to Metastasio's (33) *Alessandro nell' Indie,* produced, Feb. 2. Stage performance without choruses of *Acis and Galatea* at John Rich's (*c.* 49) theatre in Lincoln's Inn Fields, March 26. Third New Royal Academy season opens, Nov. 13.	Cannabich born.
1732	47	Operas, *Ezio* and *Sosarme,* produced at the King's Theatre, Jan. 15 and Feb. 19. Performance of the oratorio, *Esther,* at the house and under the	Haydn born, March 31/ April 1; Linley born.

Year	Age	*Life*	*Contemporary Musicians*

direction of Bernard Gates (*c.* 47) on H.'s birthday, Feb. 23. It is repeated at the 'Crown and Anchor' under the auspices of the Academy of Ancient Music and, May 2, at the King's Theatre under H.'s own direction. Stage performance of *Acis and Galatea* with choruses, May 17. Arne (22) conducts and his sister, Susanna Maria (18), sings the part of Galatea. H. himself gives another performance at the King's Theatre with a mixed cast of English and Italian artists, June 10. Some numbers of the earlier Italian version of 1708 are used. Fourth New Royal Academy season opens, Nov. 4. Opera, *Orlando,* finished, Nov. 20. A series of Sonatas for violin, flute or oboe and harpsichord (Op. 1) begun. Incidental music to Ben Jonson's *The Alchemist,* produced by John Rich (*c.* 50) at Covent Garden. It is mainly an adaptation of the dance tunes from *Rodrigo* of 1707.

Year	Age	Life	Contemporary Musicians
1733	48	*Orlando* produced at the King's Theatre, Jan. 27. Oratorio, *Deborah,* produced there, March 17. H. dismisses Senesino (*c.* 53), who succeeds, with the help of his noble admirers, in opening a rival Italian opera in Lincoln's Inn Fields. Several singers forsake H., and the Prince of Wales's side of the court adheres to Senesino. Porpora (47) is engaged as musical director. Visit to Oxford, where he gives several performances and finishes the oratorio, *Athaliah,* which is produced there, July 10. He declines the title of Mus.Doc. offered him by the university. Visit to Italy to engage singers, including Carestini (*c.* 28). Opera, *Arianna,* finished, Oct. 5. H. opens his season of Italian opera before his opponents are ready, Oct. 30. Walsh brings out a pirated edition of 6 Sonatas for two violins, flutes or oboes with harpsichord (Op. 2), first published by Roger at Amsterdam, and a second series of Suites for	Couperin (65) dies, Sept. 12.

Year	Age	Life	Contemporary Musicians
		harpsichord, consisting of 'lessons' for Princess Anne.	
1734	49	Opera, *Arianna,* produced at the King's Theatre, Jan. 26. H.'s undertaking, being patronized by the unpopular court in opposition to the adherents of the Prince of Wales, is more and more deserted by society, in spite of the momentary success of Carestini (*c.* 29). First performance of a new version of *Il Pastor fido* (*see* 1712), May 18. H. quits the King's Theatre, the lease of which is at once disposed of to the rival company by Heidegger. H. makes an arrangement with Rich (*c.* 52) to produce Italian opera alternately with English drama at Covent Garden at popular prices, summer. The season opens in Lincoln's Inn Fields, Covent Garden not being ready, Oct. 5. Covent Garden opens with *Il Pastor fido,* preceded by a ballet, *Terpsichore,* composed by H. at the request of Rich, who wishes Mlle Sallé to dance on this	Ayrton born; Carter born; Cooke (B.) born; Gossec born, Jan. 17; Sacchini born, July 23.

Year	Age	Life	Contemporary Musicians
		occasion, Nov. 9. Oboe Concertos published. 6 *Concerti grossi* (Op. 3) published, Dec. 7.	
1735	50	Opera, *Ariodante,* produced at Covent Garden, Jan. 8, and *Alcina,* April 16. During Lent H. gives a series of fourteen concerts, at which he performs various oratorios and for which he composes two organ Concertos. Farinelli (30) being now attached to the rival company, H.'s losses become alarming and the season closes on July 2. After a cure at Tunbridge Wells, he retires from public life, autumn, and composes a version of Dryden's *Alexander's Feast* by Newburgh Hamilton. 6 Fugues for harpsichord published by Walsh.	Bach (Johann Christian) born, Sept. 5; Eccles (*c.* 72) dies, Jan. 12; Krieger (J.) (83) dies, July 18.
1736	51	*Alexander's Feast* finished, Jan. 17, and first performed at Covent Garden, Feb. 19. Wedding Anthem performed at the marriage of the Prince of Wales, April 27. Opera season opens at Covent Garden, May 5. Production of the opera, *Atalanta,* in honour of the royal wedding, May 12. Farinelli's (31) success	Anfossi born (approx.); Caldara (*c.* 66) dies, Dec. 28; Fasch (C. F. C.) born, Nov. 18; Pergolesi (26) dies, March 17.

Year	*Age*	*Life*	*Contemporary Musicians*
		at the rival house is rapidly waning, and Fielding's (29) satirical play, *Pasquin,* deals a serious blow to Italian opera. Operas, *Arminio* and *Giustino,* finished, Oct. 14 and 20. Another season opens at Covent Garden, Nov. 6, and the rival company opens, Nov. 23, under the direction of Hasse (37), who has taken the place of Porpora (50).	
1737	52	Production of the operas, *Arminio,* Jan. 12, and *Giustino,* Feb. 16. During Lent H. gives performances of *Esther, Deborah, Alexander's Feast* and a new version of *Il Trionfo del tempo* of 1708, also several new Concertos for organ and other instruments. Worn out by financial cares and excess of work, he has a stroke which paralyses his right arm, April 13. Production of the opera, *Berenice,* May 18. H. undergoes a cure at Aix-la-Chapelle, late summer. He returns to London in excellent health, Nov. Heidegger, collecting the remains of the two failing	Mysliweček born, March 9. Carey (*c. *47) and Lampe (34) produce *The Dragon of Wantley,* a parody of *Giustino,* Oct. 26.

Year	Age	Life	Contemporary Musicians
		Italian opera companies, opens a season at the King's Theatre on his own account, Oct. 29. He invites H. to write two new operas and a pasticcio. Funeral Anthem for Queen Caroline sung in Westminster Abbey, Dec. 17.	
1738	53	Production of the opera, *Faramondo,* at the King's Theatre under Heidegger's management, Jan. 7, of the pasticcio, *Alessandro Severo,* Feb. 25, and of the opera, *Serse,* April 15. Concert at Vauxhall, where Roubiliac's (42) statue of H. is unveiled, May 2. First meeting of the Royal Society for the Support of Decayed Musicians founded by Greene (43) and Festing, of which H. becomes a member, April 19. Arne (28), Boyce (28), Carey (*c.* 48) and Pepusch (71) are present. Oratorios, *Saul* and *Israel in Egypt,* finished, Sept. 27 and Oct. 11. 6 organ Concertos (Op. 4) published by Walsh, Oct. 4. 7 Sonatas for two violins, flutes or oboes and harpsichord (Op. 5) composed.	Battishill born, May; Murschhauser (75) dies, Jan. 6.

Year	Age	*Life*	*Contemporary Musicians*
1739	54	Oratorio, *Saul,* produced at the King's Theatre, Jan. 16, and *Israel in Egypt,* April 4 and 11. Italian opera being now almost completely obliterated, H., who is now at the theatre in Lincoln's Inn Fields, adds oratorios, serenades and odes to his repertory. Composition of Dryden's *Ode for St. Cecilia's Day* finished, Sept. 24. 12 *Concerti grossi* for strings (Op. 6) composed, Sept. 29–Oct. 30. First performance of the *Ode for St. Cecilia's Day* at Lincoln's Inn, Nov. 22. H., like Hogarth (42), takes an active interest in the Foundling Hospital just founded by Captain Coram (71).	Dittersdorf born, Nov. 2; Keiser (65) dies, Sept. 12; Marcello (53) dies, July 24; Rust born, July 6; Wanhal born, May 12.
1740	55	First performance of *L'Allegro, il Pensieroso ed il Moderato* for solo voices, chorus and orchestra, at the theatre in Lincoln's Inn Fields, Feb. 27. Opera, *Imeneo,* finished Oct. 10 and produced Nov. 22, without a suitable Italian company and without success. His last Opera, *Deidamia,* finished,	Arnold born, Aug. 10; Böhm (79) dies (approx.); Lotti (73) dies, Jan. 5; Webbe born.

Year	Age	Life	Contemporary Musicians
		Nov. 20. 12 *Concerti grossi* (Op. 6) and 6 organ Concertos (Op. 7) published by Walsh.	
1741	56	Production of the opera, *Deidamia,* Jan. 10. It is given only three times, Italian opera being now definitely out of fashion. H., utterly discouraged and financially ruined, decides to retire from his public activities and gives a farewell concert, April 8. Oratorio, *Messiah,* begun Aug. 22 and finished Sept. 12. Oratorio, *Samson,* finished, except two numbers, Oct. 29. H. arrives in Dublin, where he has been invited by the Duke of Devonshire, who is Lord Lieutenant of Ireland, Nov. 18. Series of subscription concerts opened in Dublin, Dec. 23. 6 orchestral Concertos by H., Tartini (49) and Veracini (*c.* 56) published by Walsh.	Arne (Michael) born; Désmarets (79) dies, Sept. 7; Fux (81) dies, Feb. 13; Grétry born, Feb. 8; Naumann born, April 17; Paisiello born, May 9.
1742	57	*Hymen,* an English concert version of *Imeneo* (*see* 1740), produced March 24. Production of *Messiah* in Dublin, April 13, and repeated, June 3. Return	Abaco (67) dies, July 12.

Year	Age	Life	Contemporary Musicians
		to London, Aug. 13. Oratorio, *Samson,* completed, Oct. 12.	
1743	58	Production of *Samson,* at Covent Garden, Feb. 18. First London performance of *Messiah,* at Covent Garden, March 23. Secular oratorio, *Semele,* finished, July 4. Oratorio, *Joseph and his Brethren,* finished, Sept. *Te Deum* and Anthem for the victory of Dettingen performed in the Chapel Royal, Nov. 27.	Boccherini born, Feb. 19; Carey (*c.* 53) dies, Oct. 4; Vivaldi (*c.* 73) dies.
1744	59	Production of *Semele* at Covent Garden, Feb. 10, and of *Joseph and his Brethren,* March 2. Secular oratorio, *Hercules,* finished, Aug. 17. Oratorio, *Belshazzar,* finished, autumn (approx.). H. again takes the lease of the King's Theatre, autumn.	Campra (84) dies, June 29; Leo (50) dies, Oct. 31.
1745	60	Production of *Hercules* at the King's Theatre, Jan. 5. Production of *Belshazzar* at one of H.'s subscription concerts at the King's Theatre, March 27. H. is again obliged to give up the performances at the King's Theatre, which his opponents have done their best to damage, April.	Albinoni (71) dies (approx.); Dibdin born, March 4.

Year	Age	Life	Contemporary Musicians
		Meeting with Gluck (31) on his visit to England, autumn.	
1746	61	Production of the *Occasional Oratorio,* specially written for the Covent Garden season, which again proves unprofitable, Feb. 14. H. appears with Gluck (32) at a concert and plays a Concerto of his own, March 25. Oratorio, *Judas Maccabaeus,* finished, Aug. 11.	Hook born, June 3; Stamitz (C.) born, May 7.
1747	62	In Lent H. again takes Covent Garden Theatre for a series of subscription concerts. The season is more successful and *Judas Maccabaeus,* produced April 1, is repeated five times. Oratorios, *Joshua* and *Alexander Balus,* finished, July 4 & Aug. 19.	
1748	63	*Alexander Balus* and *Joshua* produced at Covent Garden, which Handel has again taken for a series of Lenten concerts, March 9 and 23. Oratorios, *Solomon* and *Susanna,* finished, June 13 and Aug. 24.	Shield born, March 5.
1749	64	*Susanna* and *Solomon* produced during Lent at Covent Garden, Feb. 10 and March 17. Music	Cimarosa born, Dec. 17; Destouches (*c.* 77) dies (approx.); Vogler born, Jan. 15.

Year	Age	Life	Contemporary Musicians

written for the fireworks to be held in Green Park in celebration of the Peace of Aix-la-Chapelle, April 27. H. offers the governors of the Foundling Hospital the proceeds of a concert and is elected one of the governors and guardians, May 4. The concert held in the chapel of the hospital, May 27, and an Anthem composed for the occasion performed. Oratorio, *Theodora,* finished, July 31.

1750 65 H. finishes music to a dramatic piece by Smollett (29) based on the *Alcestis* of Euripides, to be staged by Rich (*c.* 68) at Covent Garden, Jan. 8. It is withdrawn, and he uses nearly all the music for the interlude, *The Choice of Hercules,* which is finished July 5. *Theodora* produced at Covent Garden without success, March 16. H. for the first time plays the organ presented by him to the Foundling Hospital, and conducts *Messiah* there, May 1. He pays his last visit to Germany, summer.

Bach (65) dies, July 28; Bononcini (78) dies (approx.); Salieri born, Aug. 19; Sammartini (G.) (*c.* 57) dies (approx.); Veracini (*c.* 65) dies.

Year	Age	Life	Contemporary Musicians
1751	66	*The Choice of Hercules* produced at Covent Garden, March 1. H. visits Cheltenham to take the waters, the symptoms of his illness of 1737, recurrent ever since, making themselves strongly felt, spring to June 13. His eyesight begins to fail. Oratorio, *Jephtha*, finished, Aug. 30. On seeking medical advice, H. finds that blindness is imminent, winter.	Lampe (48) dies, July 25.
1752	67	Production of *Jephtha* at Covent Garden, Feb. 26. His Lenten seasons there now enjoy universal recognition and he is able to recover something of his lost fortune. Unsuccessful operation to his eyes, May 3.	Clementi born, (?) Jan.; Pepusch (82) dies, July 20; Reichardt born, Nov. 25; Zingarelli born, April 4.
1753	68	Is now almost totally blind. His former pupil, John Christopher Smith (41), acts as his amanuensis.	Dalayrac born, June 13; Viotti born, May 23.
1754	69	Unable to write new works, he is able, with the help of Smith (42), to revise and add to old ones. He also appears at concerts occasionally, playing harpsichord and organ from memory or extemporizing.	Kozeluch born.
1755	70		Durante (71) dies, Aug. 13; Winter born.

Year	Age	Life	Contemporary Musicians
1756	71	Suffers from great depression.	Mozart born, Jan. 27; Umlauf born.
1757	72	Production of *The Triumph of Time and Truth*, a new version of *Il Trionfo del tempo* of 1708 and 1737, produced at Covent Garden, with additional numbers dictated to J. C. Smith (45).	Pleyel born, June 1; Scarlatti (Domenico) (72) dies; Stamitz (J.) (40) dies, March 30.
1758	73	His depression increases as his health deteriorates. Towards the end of the year his appetite leaves him and he has premonitions of his approaching end. But he still appears at some concerts.	Dagincourt (74) dies; Zelter born, Dec. 11.
1759	74	In spite of his blindness and failing health, H. conducts a performance of *Messiah* at Covent Garden, March 30. He is seized with faintness afterwards and has to take to his bed. Handel dies in London, April 14.	Graun (58) dies, Aug. 8. Agricola (J. F.) aged 39; Alcock 44; Anfossi *c.* 23; Arne (T. A.) 49; Arne (M.) 18; Arnold 19; Avison *c.* 49; Aylward 29; Ayrton 25; Bach (W. F.) 49; Bach (C. P. E.) 45; Bach (J. C.) 24; Battishill 21; Benda (F.) 50; Benda (G.) 37; Boccherini 16; Boyce 49; Cannabich 28; Carter 25; Cimarosa 10; Clementi 7; Cook (B.) 25; Dalayrac 6; Daquin 65; Dauvergne 46; Dibdin 14; Dittersdorf 20; Duni 50; Fasch (J. F.) 71; Fasch (C. F. C.) 23;

Year Age   Life   *Contemporary Musicians*

Francœur 61; Galuppi 53; Gassmann 36; Gazzaniga 16; Geminiani 79; Gluck 45; Gossec 25; Graun 58; Graupner 72; Grétry 18; Hasse 60; Haydn 27; Hiller (J. A.) 31; Holzbauer 48; Hook 13; Jackson 29; Jommelli 45; Kirnberger 38; Kozeluch 5; Krebs 46; Leclair 62; Linley 27; Locatelli 66; Martini 53; Monsigny 30; Mozart 3; Muffat (jun.) 69; Mysliweček 22; Nardini 37; Nares 44; Naumann 18; Nichelmann 42; Paisiello 18; Philidor 33; Piccinni 31; Pleyel 2; Porpora 73; Quantz 62; Rameau 76; Reichardt 7; Richter (F. X.) 50; Rust 20; Sacchini 25; Salieri 9; Sammartini (G. B.) *c.* 58; Sarti 30; Shield 11; Stamitz (C.) 13; Tartini 67; Telemann 78; Traetta 32; Umlauf 3; Viotti 6; Vogler 10; Wagenseil 44; Wanhal 20; Webbe 19; Winter 4; Zelter 1; Zingarelli 7.

APPENDIX B

OPERAS

Admeto (1727) (73).

Agrippina (1709), Vincenzo Grimani [2] (57).

Alcina (1735), A. Marchi (86).

Alessandro (1726), Antonio Rolli (72).

Almira, Königin von Castilien (1704), Friedrich Feustking (55).

Amadigi (1715) (62).

Arianna (1734), Francis Colman (83).

Arminio (1737) (89).

Ariodante (1735), Antonio Salvi (85).

Atalanta (1736) (87).

Berenice (1737), A. Salvi (90).

Deidamia (1741), Rolli (94).

Ezio (1732), Metastasio (80).

Faramondo (1738), Apostolo Zeno (91).

Flavio (1723), Nicola Haym (67).

Floridante (1721), Rolli (65).

Giulio Cesare (1724), Haym (68).

Giustino (1737), Count Beregani (88).

Imeneo (1740) (93).

Lotario (1729), A. Salvi (77).

Muzio Scevola (1721), Rolli (third act only by Handel) (64).

---

[1] Based on the complete Händelgesellschaft edition, the number of whose volumes are given in brackets.

[2] Names given after the dates are those of the librettists.

Orlando (1733), Braccioli (82).

Ottone (1723), Haym (66).

Partenope (1730), Silvio Stampiglia (78).

Pastor fido, Il (first version, 1712), Giacomo Rossi (59).

Pastor fido, Il (second version, 1734) (84).

Poro (1731), Metastasio's *Alessandro nell' Indie* (79).

Radamisto (1720), Haym (63).

Riccardo primo, Rè d'Inghilterra (1727), Rolli (74).

Rinaldo (two versions, 1711 and 1731), Rossi (58).

Rodelinda (1725), Haym (70).

Rodrigo (1707) (56).

Scipione (1726), Rolli (71).

Serse (1738), N. Minato (92).

Silla (1714) (61).

Siroe (1728), Haym, after Metastasio (75).

Sosarme (1732), Noris (81).

Tamerlano (1724), Haym (69).

Teseo (1713), Haym (60).

Tolomeo, Rè d'Egitto (1728), Haym (76).

Lost Hamburg Operas:
  Daphne (c. 1706), Hinsch.
  Florindo (c. 1706), Hinsch.
  Nero (1705), Feustking.

Advertised in 1739, but probably never performed:
  Jupiter in Argos (MS. in the Fitzwilliam Museum, Cambridge).

Unperformed and unpublished:
  Alfonso primo.
  Flavio Olibrio.
  Honorius.
  Tito.
  Unnamed Opera (MS. in the Fitzwilliam Museum).

Recitatives to 11 Pasticcios compiled by Handel from works by various composers (1730–47).

Handel

BALLET

Terpsichore (1734) (84).

INCIDENTAL MUSIC

Alcestis (1750), Tobias Smollett (46).
Alchemist, The (1732), Ben Jonson.

SERENATAS, MASQUES, PASTORALS, ODES AND INTERLUDES

Aci, Galatea e Polifemo (two versions, 1708 and 1732) (53).
Acis and Galatea (1719), John Gay (3).
Alexander's Feast (1736), Dryden (12).
Allegro, il Pensieroso ed il Moderato, L' (1740), Charles Jennens, after Milton (6).
Choice of Hercules, The (1751) (18).
Haman and Mordecai (first version of *Esther*) (1720), Pope, after Racine (40).
Hercules (1745), Rev. T. Broughton (4).
Hymen. English concert version of the opera *Imeneo* (1742).
Ode for the Birthday of Queen Anne (1713) (46).
Ode for St. Cecilia's Day (1739), Dryden (23).
Parnasso in festa, Il (1734) (54).
Praise of Harmony (*c.* 1739), Newburgh Hamilton.
Semele (1744), after Congreve (7).

ORATORIOS

Alexander Balus (1748), Rev. Thomas Morell (33).
Athaliah (1733), Samuel Humphreys (5).
Belshazzar (1745), Charles Jennens (19).
Deborah (1733), Humphreys (29).
Esther (second version of *Haman and Mordecai*, 1732), Humphreys (41).

Appendix B.—Catalogue of Works

Israel in Egypt (1739), words from the Bible (16).

Jephtha (1752), Morell (44).

Joseph and his Brethren (1744), Rev. James Miller (42).

Joshua (1748), Morell (17).

Judas Maccabaeus (1747), Morell (22).

Messiah (1742), words from the Bible (45).

Occasional Oratorio (1746), ? Morell (43).

Resurrezione, La (1708) (39).

Samson (1743), Newburgh Hamilton, after Milton (10).

Saul (1739), Jennens (13).

Solomon (1749), ? Morell (26).

Susanna (1749) (1).

Theodora (1750), Morell (8).

Trionfo del tempo e del disinganno, Il (1708 and 1737), Benedetto Panfili (24).

Triumph of Time and Truth, The (1757) (20).

PASSION MUSIC

Der für die Sünden der Welt gemarterte und sterbende Jesus (1716), Barthold Heinrich Brockes (15).

Johannespassion (1704), Gospel of St. John and arias by Wilhelm Postel (9).

CHURCH MUSIC

Chandos Anthems (1716–18) (34–5):

1. *O be joyful in the Lord.*
2. *In the Lord I put my trust.*
3. *Have mercy upon me.*
4. *O sing unto the Lord a new song.*
5. *I will magnify Thee.*
6. *As pants the hart.*

7. *My song shall be alway.*
8. *O come, let us sing.*
9. *O praise the Lord with one consent.*
10. *The Lord is my light.*
11. *Let God arise.*
12.   *praise the Lord, ye angels of His.*

Coronation Anthems (1727) (14):
1. *Zadok the Priest.*
2. *The King shall rejoice.*
3. *My heart is inditing.*
4. *Let Thy hand be strengthened.*

Dettingen Anthem (1743) (36).
Dettingen *Te Deum* (1743) (25).
Dixit Dominus (1707) (38).
Foundling Hospital Anthem (1749) (36).
Funeral Anthem for Queen Caroline (1737) (11).
Hymns.   Rev. C. Wesley (MS. in the Fitzwilliam Museum):
  O Love divine, how sweet thou art.
  Rejoice, the Lord is King.
  Sinners, obey the Gospel Word.

Laudate pueri, F major (1702) (38).
Laudate pueri, D major (1707) (38).
Nisi Dominus (1702–7) (38).
O praise the Lord, anthem (36).
Salve Regina, G minor (38).
Silete venti, motet (1708) (38).
Te Deum, A major (*c.* 1727) (37).
Te Deum, B flat major (1716–18) (37).
Te Deum, D major (*c.* 1714) (37).
Utrecht *Te Deum* and *Jubilate* (1713) (31).
Wedding Anthem for Princess Anne (1734) (36).
Wedding Anthem for the Prince of Wales (1736) (36).

Appendix B.—Catalogue of Works

VOCAL CHAMBER MUSIC

6 *Alleluias* for voice and harpsichord (various dates) (38).

72 Italian Cantatas for one or two voices and instruments (50–3).

7 Italian Cantatas (MSS. in the Fitzwilliam Museum).

20 Italian Duets with continuo (1707–8, 1741–5) (32):

1. *Caro autor di mia doglia.*
2. *Giù nei Tartarei regni.*
3. *Sono liete, fortunate.*
4. *Troppo cruda, troppo fiera.*
5. *Che vai pensando.*
6. *Amor gioje mi porge.*
7. *Va, speme infida.*
8. *A mirarvi io sono intento.*
9. *Quando in calma.*
10. *Tacete, ohimè, tacete.*
11. *Conservate, raddoppiate.*
12. *Tanti strali al sen.*
13. *Langue, geme, sospira.*
14. *Se tu non lasci amore.*
15. *Quel fior che all' alba ride.*
16. *No, di voi non vo' fidarmi.*
17. *No, di voi non vo' fidarmi.*
18. *Beato in ver.*
19. *Fronda leggiera.*
20. *Ahi, nelle sorti umane.*

2 Italian Trios with continuo (32):

1. *Se tu non lasci amore.*
2. *Quel fior che all' alba ride.*

INSTRUMENTAL CHAMBER MUSIC

Hornpipe for the Concert at Vauxhall (1740) (48).

8 *Sinfonie diverse* (48).

15 Solos for a German flute, oboe or violin and continuo, Op. 1 (*c.* 1732) (27).

I   245

Sonata for 2 violins, bass and organ, G minor (48).

Sonata for *viola da gamba* and cembalo, C major (*c.* 1705) (48).

3 Sonatas for flute and cembalo (*c.* 1710) (48).

9 Sonatas for 2 violins, oboes or flutes and continuo, Op. 2 (1733) (27).

7 Sonatas for 2 violins or German flutes and continuo, Op. 5 (1738) (27).

6 Sonatas or Trios for two oboes and continuo (1696) (27).

ORCHESTRA

6 *Concerti grossi,* for flutes, oboes, bassoons and strings, Op. 3 (1729) (21):

1. B flat major-G minor. 2. B flat major. 3. G major. 4. F major. 5. D minor. 6. D major-minor.

12 *Concerti grossi,* for strings, Op. 6 (1739) (30):

1. G major. 2. F major. 3. E minor. 4. A minor. 5. D major. 6. G minor. 7. B flat major. 8. C minor. 9. F major. 10. D minor. 11. A major. 12. B minor.

Concerto, C major, for 2 oboes, bassoon, 4 horns, strings and continuo (47).[1]

Concerto, D major, for 2 oboes, bassoon, 4 horns, 2 trumpets, drums, strings and continuo (47).[1]

Concerto, F major, for 2 oboes, bassoon, 2 horns, strings and continuo (47).

Concerto grosso, C major, for 2 oboes and strings (21).

Concertos:

1. B flat major, for oboe and strings (21).
2A. B flat major, for oboe and strings (21).
2B. F major, for 2 horns and strings (21).
3. G minor, for oboe and strings (21).
4. (Sonata) B flat major, for solo violin, oboes and strings (21).

---

[1] These two works are identical, and both are used in the *Fireworks Music.*

Appendix B.—Catalogue of Works

Double Concerto (*a due cori*), E flat major (? 1740–50) (47).
Double Concerto, F major (? 1740–50) (47).
Fireworks Music (1749) (47).
Overture for the pasticcio, *Alessandro Severo* (1738) (48).
Overture for the pasticcio, *Oreste* (1734) (48).
Overture in B flat major (48).
Water Music (*c.* 1715) (47).

ORGAN AND ORCHESTRA

6 Concertos, Op. 4 (1738) (28):

    1. G minor. 2. B flat major. 3. G minor. 4. F major. 5. F major. 6. B flat major.

6 Concertos, Op. 7 (1740) (28):

    1. B flat major. 2. A major. 3. B flat major. 4. D minor. 5. G minor. 6. B flat major.

5 Concertos (48):

    1. F major. 2. A major. 3. D minor. 4. D minor. 5. F major.

HARPSICHORD MUSIC

Capriccio, F major (2).
Capriccio, G minor (2).
Chaconne, F major (2).
Courante e due Minuetti, F major (2).
Fantasia, C major (2).
6 Fugues (*c.* 1720) (2).
Lesson, A minor (2).
Preludio ed Allegro, G minor (2).
6 Short Fugues (48).
Sonata, C major (2).
Sonata, C major (2).

Handel

Sonatina, B flat major (2).

Suite, D minor (2).

Suite, G minor (2).

Suites (or Lessons) (1720) (2):

   1. A major. 2. F major. 3. D minor. 4. E minor. 5. E major.[1] 6. F sharp minor. 7. G minor. 8. F minor.

Suites (or Lessons) (1733) (2):

   1. B flat major.[2] 2. G major. 3. D minor. 4. D minor. 5. E minor. 6. G minor. 7. B flat major. 8. G major. 9. G major (*Chaconne*).

Various Suites (48).

---

[1] Containing the *Harmonious Blacksmith* variations.

[2] Containing the air with variations on which Brahms wrote variations of his own for piano.

APPENDIX C

Albinoni, Tomasso (1674–1745), Venetian violinist and composer.

Antinori, Luigi (born *c.* 1697), Italian tenor singer, who first appeared in London in 1725.

Ariosti, Attilio (born *c.* 1660), Italian operatic composer, who pro-duced his first opera, *Dafne*, at Venice in 1686.

Arne, Susanna Maria (1714–66), English contralto singer, sister of Thomas Augustine Arne (1710–78), married Theophilus Cibber in 1734.

Arrigoni, Carlo, Italian lutenist and composer, published *Cantate da Camera* in London in 1732.

Avolio (or *Avoglio*), *Signora,* Italian soprano singer of whose career nothing is known apart from its coincidence with that of Handel.

Babell, William (*c.* 1690–1723), English harpsichord player, violinist and composer, member of the royal band and for some years organist at All Hallows Church, Bread Street, in London.

Baldassari, Benedetto, Italian tenor singer, in London 1720–2.

Baldi, Italian counter-tenor singer, in London 1725–8.

Banister, John (died 1735), English violinist and teacher of his instrument, composer for the theatre, son of John Banister (1630–79).

Bates, Joah (1741–99), English organist and scholar, conductor of the Concert of Ancient Music in London from its foundation in 1776.

Beard, John (*c.* 1717–91), English tenor singer, chorister at the Chapel Royal under Gates (q.v.) in his boyhood, appeared first as a mature singer in works by Handel in 1736.

Berenstadt, Gaetan, Italian bass singer of German descent, the first record of whose appearance in London dates from 1717.

Bernacchi, Antonio (1685–1756), Italian male soprano singer and teacher, first heard in London in 1716.

Berselli, Matteo, Italian tenor singer, who came to London with Senesino (q.v.) in 1720.

Bertolli, Francesca, Italian contralto singer, first heard in London in 1729.

Böhm, Georg (1661–1733), German composer, organist at Hamburg before 1698, then at St. John's Church, Lüneburg.

Bononcini (or *Buononcini*), *Giovanni Battista* (born 1672), Italian opera composer, son of Giovanni Maria Bononcini (*c.* 1640–78), whose pupil he was and whom he succeeded as chapel-master of the church of San Giovanni in Monte at Modena, his birthplace. Attached to the court of Vienna in 1692 and of Berlin in 1696; produced his first operas in Rome in 1694. Vienna and Italy, 1706–20; London, 1720–32.

Bononcini, Marc Antonio (1675–1726), Italian composer, brother of the preceding.

Bordoni, Faustina (1693–1783), Italian mezzo-soprano singer, made her first appearance in Venice in 1716 and came to London ten years later. Married Hasse (q.v.) in 1730.

Boschi, Giuseppe, Italian bass singer, member of St. Mark's, Venice; (?) sang Polyphemus in Handel's *Aci* in Naples, 1709. First appeared in London in 1711.

Boyce, William (1710–79), English composer and organist, boy chorister at St. Paul's Cathedral in London and later pupil of Greene (q.v.), whom he succeeded in 1755 as Master of the King's Band. Organist of the Chapel Royal from 1758. Published a collection of English *Cathedral Music*, 1760–78.

Brockes, Barthold Heinrich (1608–1747), poet and important official in Hamburg.

Buxtehude, Dietrich (1637–1707), Swedish [1] composer and organist, settled in Denmark and from 1668 organist of St. Mary's Church at Lübeck.

---

[1] Always regarded as a Dane, but proved by Pirro to have been born at Helsingborg in Sweden.

Caccini, Giulio (1558 or 1560–c. 1615), Italian singer, lutenist and composer, one of the group of Florentine artists who initiated opera.

Caffarelli (*Gaetano Majorano*) (1703–83), Italian male contralto singer, made his first stage appearance in Rome in 1724 and first sang in London in 1738.

Campioli (*Antonio Gualandi*), Italian male contralto singer born in Germany, made his first appearance in Berlin in 1708. First came to London in 1731.

Caporale, Andrea (died c. 1756), Italian violoncello player who came to London in 1734 and joined Handel's opera orchestra in 1740.

Carestini, Giovanni (c. 1705–c. 1759), Italian male soprano singer, afterwards a contralto. Came out in Rome in 1721 and made his first London appearance in 1733.

Carey, Henry (c. 1690–1743), English poet, composer and dramatist, pupil of Roseingrave (q.v.) and Geminiani (q.v.).

Carissimi, Giacomo (? 1604–74), Italian composer who cultivated the forms of oratorio and cantata in their early stages.

Castrucci, Pietro (1679–1752) and *Prospero* (died 1760), Italian violinists, who came to London in 1715, Pietro becoming leader of Handel's opera orchestra and Prospero a member of it.

Cibber, Susanna Maria. See Arne.

Clari, Giovanni Carlo Maria (c. 1669–c. 1745), Italian composer, chapel-master successively at Pistoia, Bologna and Pisa.

Clayton, Thomas (c. 1670–c. 1730), English composer and adapter, who set Addison's opera, *Rosamond,* which proved a complete failure, in 1707.

Clegg, John (1714–c. 1750), English violinist of outstanding gifts, who became insane in 1744.

Clive, Catherine (*Kitty, née Raftor*) (1711–85), English stage singer attached to Drury Lane Theatre in London, 1728–41.

Corsi, Jacopo (died c. 1604), Florentine nobleman and amateur composer, who took a share in the initiation of opera.

Croft, William (1678–1727), English organist and composer, pupil of John Blow at the Chapel Royal, organist at St. Anne's, Soho, from 1700 and organist with Jeremiah Clarke at the Chapel Royal from 1704; Master of the Children there from 1715.

Cuzzoni, Francesca (*c.* 1700–70), Italian soprano singer, first appeared in Venice in 1719 and in London in 1722.

Dieupart, Charles (died *c.* 1740), French violinist, harpsichord player and composer settled in London.

Dubourg, Matthew (1703–67), English violinist, pupil of Geminiani (q.v.), for many years in Dublin and towards the end of his life in London, his birthplace.

Durastanti, Margherita (born *c.* 1695), Italian soprano singer, who came to London in 1720 and again in 1733.

Eccles, John (*c.* 1663–1735), English composer, at first for the stage, member of the King's Band from 1694 and Master from 1700.

l'Épine, Francesca Margherita de (died 1746), Italian or French singer, who first came to England in 1692, remaining there until her death and marrying Pepusch (q.v.) in 1718.

Erba, Dionigi, Italian composer, chapel-master at the church of San Francesco, Milan, in 1692.

Fabri, Annibale Pio (1697–1760), Italian tenor singer also known under the name of 'Balino,' who first came to England in 1729. He was also a composer.

Farinelli (*Carlo Broschi*) (1705–82), Italian male soprano singer, made his first appearance in Rome in 1722, when he had already acquired some fame in southern Italy, and went to Vienna in 1724. His first appearance in London was in 1734.

Festing, Michael Christian (died 1752), English violinist and composer for his instrument in London, pupil of Geminiani (q.v.). Made his first appearance about 1724 and became a member of the king's private band in 1735. Musical director of Ranelagh Gardens from 1742.

Frasi, Giulia, Italian singer, who first appeared in London in 1743.

Galilei, Vincenzo (*c.* 1533–91), Florentine amateur composer and theorist, who took a share in the first attempts at opera. Father of the astronomer Galileo Galilei.

Galli, Signora (died 1804), Italian mezzo-soprano singer settled in

London, where she first appeared in 1743 and remained until her death.

Galuppi, Baldassare (1706–85), Venetian composer, who produced his first opera at Vicenza in 1722. He was in London in 1741–3, became vice chapel-master at St. Mark's in Venice in 1748 and chapel-master in 1762.

Gasparini, Francesco (1668–1727), Italian composer, pupil of Corelli and Pasquini (q.v.), chorus master at the Ospedale di Pietà in Venice and appointed chapel master of St. John Lateran in Rome in 1725.

Gates, Bernard (1685–1773), English theorist, singer and composer, Gentleman of the Chapel Royal from 1708 and Master of the Children some time before 1732.

Geminiani, Francesco (1667–1762), Italian violinist and composer, pupil of Corelli in Rome, came to England in 1714 and lived in London, Dublin, Paris and again in Ireland until his death.

Gizziello (*Gioacchino Conti*) (1714–61), Italian male soprano singer, who first appeared in Rome in 1729 and made his first London appearance in 1736.

Greber, Jakob, German composer, who came to London in 1692 with Margherita de l'Épine (q.v.) and settled there.

Greene, Maurice (1695–1755), English organist and composer in London, chorister at St. Paul's Cathedral as a boy, where he became organist in 1718. In 1727 he succeeded Croft (q.v.) as organist and composer to the Chapel Royal.

Grimaldi. See Nicolini.

Habermann, Franz Johann (1706–83), Bohemian composer, who published six masses in 1747.

Hasse, Johann Adolph (1699–1783), German composer of Italian operas, born near Hamburg, where he came out as tenor at Keiser's (q.v.) Opera. Afterwards sang at Brunswick, where he produced his first opera in 1721. Then went to Italy to study dramatic music under Porpora (q.v.) and Alessandro Scarlatti. Appointed musical director and manager of the royal opera at Dresden in 1731. Married Faustina Bordoni (q.v.) in 1730.

Keiser, Reinhard (1674–1739), German composer, studied under Schelle at St. Thomas's School in Leipzig. Went to the court of Brunswick in 1692 and to Hamburg two years later, where he made the Opera the most distinguished in Germany for a time and composed 116 works for it. He also wrote church music, including oratorios and a Passion according to St. Mark.

Kerl (or Kerll), Johann Caspar (1627–93), German organist and composer, born in Saxony, but settled early in Vienna as a pupil of Valentini. Then studied in Rome under Carissimi (q.v.) and probably the organ under Frescobaldi.[1] In the service of the Elector of Bavaria in Munich, 1656–74. Went to Vienna as private teacher and was appointed court organist there in 1677.

Kuhnau, Johann (1660–1722), German organist, clavier player, composer and writer on music, cantor at Zittau, went to Leipzig in 1682, became organist at St. Thomas's Church in 1684 and cantor in 1701, in which post he preceded Bach.

Lampe, John Frederick (Johann Friedrich) (1703–51), German bassoon player and composer at Brunswick; came to England about 1725 and settled in London, but went to Dublin in 1748 and to Edinburgh in 1750.

Legrenzi, Giovanni (c. 1625–90), Italian composer, organist at Clusone near Bergamo, his birthplace, then chapel-master at Ferrara. Between 1664 and 1672 he became director of the Conservatorio dei Mendicanti at Venice and in 1685 chapel master at St. Mark's there.

Leo, Leonardo (1694–1744), Neapolitan composer, first appeared with the production of a sacred drama in 1712 and brought out his first opera in 1714. He wrote a vast number of operas, also oratorios and much church music.

Leveridge, Richard (c. 1670–1758), English bass singer and song writer in London, who made his first appearance before Purcell's death in 1695 and sang until a few years before that of Handel, his last recorded appearance being in 1751. He was also a composer of songs and theatre music.

---

[1] But Kerl was only sixteen when Frescobaldi died.

Lotti, Antonio (c. 1667–1740), Venetian composer, singer in the Doge's chapel as a boy, produced his first opera at the age of sixteen. Became second organist at St. Mark's, Venice, in 1692 and first in 1704. He was at Dresden in 1717–19.

Mancini, Francesco (1679–1739), Italian composer, pupil of the Conservatorio di San Loreto at Naples, afterwards a teacher there and from 1728 its principal master. Produced the opera *L'Idaspe fedele* (*Hydaspes*) in London in 1710.

Marcello, Benedetto (1686–1739), Italian composer, pupil of Lotti (q.v.) and Gasparini (q.v.) in Venice. Of noble birth, he held no musical posts, but important government appointments.

Mattei, Filippo, Italian violoncellist and composer at the Opera in London.

Mattheson, Johann (1681–1764), German writer on music, organist and composer, first sang female parts at the Hamburg Opera, then composed two operas (1699 and 1704), became cantor at Hamburg Cathedral in 1715, wrote several books on music, the most important being *Das neu eröffnete Orchester* (1713), *Der vollkommene Capellmeister* (1739) and *Grundlage einer Ehrenpforte* (1740).

Merighi, Antonia, Italian contralto singer, who first appeared in London in 1729.

Mersenne, Marin (1588–1648), French musical theorist, author of various treatises, the most important being *Harmonie universelle*.

Metastasio (*Pietro Trapassi*) (1698–1782), Italian poet, librettist and translator. He lived in Vienna for some years.

Mizler, Lorenz Christoph (1711–78), German musical writer and editor, pupil of Bach in Leipzig, founded the Association for Musical Science there in 1738 and edited a periodical, *Die neu eröffnete Musik-Bibliothek,* 1739–54.

Montagnana, Antonio, Italian bass singer, who first appeared in London in 1731.

Muffat, Gottlieb (1690–1770), German composer, pupil of Fux in Vienna, where he became court organist and music master to the imperial children.

Nicolini (*Nicola Grimaldi*) (born c. 1673), Italian male soprano singer, later a contralto, made his first appearance, in Rome, about 1694. First came to England in 1708.

Pachelbel, Johann (1653–1706), German organist and composer, went to Vienna as a pupil of Kerl (q.v.) and was his deputy organist in the imperial chapel. Subsequently organist at Eisenach, Erfurt, Stuttgart and Gotha. Appointed organist of St. Sebaldus's Church at Nuremberg, his native city.

Pasquini, Bernardo (1637–1710), Italian composer, who as a young man became organist of Santa Maria Maggiore in Rome.

Pepusch, John Christopher (*Johann Christoph*) (1667–1752), German composer and theorist born in Berlin, appointed to the Prussian court at the age of fourteen, emigrated first to Holland and came to England about 1700, where he settled in London for the rest of his life. Married Margherita de l'Épine (q.v.) in 1718.

Peri, Jacopo (1561–1633), Florentine composer, who took an important share in originating opera.

Porpora, Niccola Antonio (1686–1767), Italian composer, theorist and singing teacher, came to London as Handel's rival in 1729.

Praetorius, Michael (1571–1621), German writer on music and musical instruments, author of the *Syntagma musicum*.

Randall, John (1715–99), English organist and composer, pupil of Gates (q.v.) at the Chapel Royal, organist of King's College, Cambridge, from 1743 and professor there in succession to Greene (q.v.) from 1755.

Reinken (or *Reincken*), *Johann Adam* (1623–1722), German organist and composer for his instrument, appointed organist at St. Catherine's Church in Hamburg, where he remained until his death.

Robinson, Anastasia (c. 1698–1755), English singer, made her first stage appearance in 1714 and retired ten years later, having married the Earl of Peterborough in 1722.

Roseingrave, Thomas (1690–1766), English or Irish composer and organist, son of Daniel Roseingrave (c. 1650–1727). Organist of St. George's, Hanover Square, London, 1725–38.

Senesino (*Francesco Bernardi*) (c. 1680–c. 1750), Italian male soprano singer, attached to the court opera at Dresden in 1719 and there invited by Handel to London, where he first appeared in 1720.

Smith, John Christopher (1712–95), English organist and composer of German descent, son of Johann Christoph Schmidt of Anspach, who came to England as Handel's treasurer and copyist.

Snow, Valentine (died 1770), English trumpeter, appointed Trumpeter to the King in 1753 in succession to John Shore (died 1752).

Stanley, Charles John (1713–86), English organist, blind from the age of two, pupil of Greene (q.v.), later organist of several London churches.

Steffani, Agostino (1654–1728), Italian composer and diplomat, who spent much of his time in diplomatic missions at German courts, but was a remarkable composer as well as a scholar and priest.

Strada del Pò, Anna, Italian soprano singer, who first appeared in London in 1729.

Stradella, Alessandro (c. 1645–82), Italian composer of noble birth who appears to have held no regular musical appointments, and what is known of his career seems to be based more on legend than on fact.

Swieten, Gottfried van, Baron (1734–1803), Austrian diplomat and musical amateur in Vienna.

Telemann, Georg Philipp (1681–1767), German composer, studied at the university of Leipzig 1700–4, was appointed organist to the New Church there and founded a *Collegium musicum.* After holding various posts at Sorau, Eisenach and Frankfort, he was appointed cantor of the Johanneum and musical director to the five principal churches at Hamburg, posts which he held until his death.

Tesi-Tramontini, Vittoria (1700–75), Italian contralto singer, who made her first stage appearance at a very early age. In 1719 she was at Dresden, where Handel met her, but did not engage her.

Tunder, Franz (1614–67), German organist and composer, pupil of Frescobaldi in Rome, became organist of St. Mary's Church at Lübeck, his native city. Predecessor there of Buxtehude (q.v.).

Urio, Francesco Antonio, Italian composer at Milan, whose first published work, a set of Motets, appeared in 1690.

Valentini (Valentino Urbani), Italian male contralto singer, afterwards a counter-tenor, who first came to London in 1707.

Vinci, Leonardo (1690–1730), Italian composer, who studied in Naples and produced his first known comic opera there in 1719.

Wagenseil, Georg Christoph (1715–77), composer in Vienna.

Waltz, Gustavus, German bass singer, who was for a time Handel's cook.

Weideman, Charles (Carl Friedrich Weidemann), German flute player, settled in London about 1726.

Weldon, John (1676–1736), English composer and organist, pupil of Purcell, became organist of New College, Oxford, in 1694. Succeeded Blow as organist of the Chapel Royal in 1708.

Young, Cecilia (1711–89), English singer, married Arne (1710–78) in 1736.

Zachau, Friedrich Wilhelm (1663–1712), German composer, theorist and organist at Halle, first teacher of Handel.

APPENDIX D

BIBLIOGRAPHY

Bairstow, E. C., 'Handel's Oratorio "The Messiah."' (Oxford and London, 1928.)

Bingley, W., 'Musical Biography.' (London, 1714.)

Bishop, John, 'Brief Memoirs of George Frederick Handel.' (London, 1856.)

Bouchor, M., 'Israël en Égypte: Étude.' (Paris, 1888.)

Bowley, Thomas, 'The Grand Handel Festival at the Palace. (London, 1857.)

Bredenförder, Elisabeth, 'Die Texte der Händel-Oratorien: eine religionsgeschichtliche und literar-soziologische Studie.' (Leipzig, 1934.)

Brownlow, 'Memoranda or Chronicles of the Foundling Hospital.' (London, 1847.)

Burney, Charles, 'A General History of Music.' (London, 1776–89.)

—— 'An Account of the Musical Performances in Westminster Abbey and the Pantheon in Commemoration of Handel.' (London, 1785.)

Callcott, W. H., 'A Few Facts in the Life of Handel.' (London, 1850.)

Chrysander, F., 'G. F. Händel.' 3 vols. (unfinished). (Leipzig, 1858–67.)

Clark, Richard, 'Reminiscences of Handel, the Duke of Chandos, etc.' (London, 1836.)

Coxe, J. C., 'Anecdotes of G. F. Handel and J. C. Smith.' (London, 1799.)

Delany, Mary, 'Autobiography and Correspondence of Mary Granville, Mrs. Delany.' Edited by Lady Llanover. (London, 1861–2.)

Dent, Edward J., 'Handel' ('Great Lives' Series). (London, 1934.)

Flower, Newman, 'George Frideric Handel: his Personality and his Times.' (London, 1922.)

Förstemann, Karl Eduard, 'G. F. Haendel's Stammbaum, nach Originalquellen und authentischen Nachrichten.' (Leipzig, 1844.)

Franz, Robert, 'Ueber Bearbeitungen älterer Tonwerke, namentlich Bachscher und Händelscher Vokalmusik.' (Leipzig, 1871.)

—— 'Der Messias, unter Zugrundelegung der Mozartschen Partitur.' (Leipzig, 1884.)

Handel, G. F. Letters and Writings. Edited by Erich H. Müller. (London, 1935.)

Händel-Jahrbuch. Herausgegeben von Rudolf Steglich. (Leipzig, 1929, etc.)

Hawkins, John, 'A General History of the Science and Practice of Music.' (London, 1776 and 1853.)

—— 'An Account of the Institution and Progress of the Academy of Ancient Music.' (London, 1770.)

Heinrich, E., 'G. F. Händel, ein deutscher Tonmeister.' (1884.)

Herder, V., 'Händel, dessen Lebensumstände.' (Leipzig, 1802.)

Kidson, Frank, 'The Beggar's Opera: its Predecessors and Successors.' (Cambridge.)

King, John, 'Commemoration of Handel.' (London, 1819.)

Leichtentritt, Hugo, 'Händel.' (Stuttgart, 1924.)

Mainwaring, J., 'Memoirs of the Life of the late G. F. Handel.' (London, 1760.)

Malcolm, James Peller, 'Manners and Customs in London during the Eighteenth Century.' (London, 1811.)

Mattheson, Johann, 'Grundlage einer Ehrenpforte.' (Hamburg, 1740; Berlin, 1910.)

—— 'G. F. Händel's Lebensbeschreibung.' (Hamburg, 1761.)

Milnes, Keith, 'Memoir relating to the Portrait of Handel by Francis Kyte.' (London, 1829.)

Müller-Blattau, J., 'Georg Friedrich Händel.' (Potsdam, 1933.)

Appendix D.—Bibliography

Opel, J. O., 'Mitteilungen zur Geschichte der Familie des Tonkünstlers Händel.' (1885.)

Parry, C. H. H., 'Studies of Great Composers.' (London, 1900.)

Prout, Ebenezer, 'The Orchestra of Handel.' (Proceedings of the Musical Association, Leeds, 1885–6.)

Robinson, Percy, 'Handel and his Orbit.' (London, 1908.)

Rockstro, W. S., 'Life of Handel.' (London, 1883.)

Rolland, Romain, 'Haendel.' (Paris, 1910.)

—— 'Handel.' Translated by A. Eaglefield Hull. (New York, 1923.)

Schoelcher, Victor, 'The Life of Handel.' (London, 1857.)

Squire, W. Barclay, 'Catalogue of the King's Music Library: Vol. I, Handel's MSS.' (London, British Museum, 1927.)

Stothard, Anna Eliza, 'Handel, his Life, Personal and Professional. (London, 1857.)

Streatfeild, R. A., 'Handel.' (London, 1909.)

—— 'The Case of the Handel Festival.' (London, 1897.)

Taut, Kurt, 'Verzeichnis des Schrifttums über Georg Fr. Händel. (Leipzig, 1934.)

Taylor, Sedley, 'The Indebtedness of Handel to Works by Other Composers.' (Cambridge, 1906.)

Townsend, Horatio, 'An Account of Handel's Visit to Dublin.' (1852.)

Webster, Clarinda A., 'Handel: an Outline of his Life and Epitome of his Works.' (London, 1881.)

Weissebeck, J. M., 'Der grosse Musikus Händel im Universalruhme.' (Nuremberg, 1809.)

INDEX

INDEX

Index